A Decade of Cooking
THE COSTCO WAY™

A Decade of Cooking
THE COSTCO WAY™

Celebrating recipes using Costco products

Tim Talevich
Editorial Director

With a foreword by
Tim Rose and Jeff Lyons

Issaquah, Washington

Senior Vice President E-commerce and Publishing:	Ginnie Roeglin
Publisher:	David W. Fuller
Editorial Director:	Tim Talevich
Art Director:	Doris Winters
Associate Editorial Director:	Anita Thompson
Associate Art Director:	Lory Williams
Associate Editor:	Judy Gouldthorpe
Senior Designer:	Brenda Shecter Tradii
Photographers:	Darren Emmens Chris McArthur Devin Seferos
Food Stylists:	Amy Muzyka-McGuire Christine Jackson
Cover Stylist:	Kim Holderman
Kitchen Manager:	Linda Carey
Studio Assistant:	Melissa Fraser
Business Manager:	Jane Klein-Shucklin
Advertising Manager:	Melanie Woods
Assistant Advertising Manager:	Kathi Tipper
Advertising Assistants:	Steve Trump Toni Pinto Clementine Trujillo
Production Manager:	Pam Sather
Prepress Supervisor/Color Specialist:	MaryAnne Robbers
Assistant Production Manager:	Antolin Matsuda
Online Editor:	David Wight
Print Management:	James Letzel and Ayako Chang, GSSI
Distribution:	Rossie Cruz

27

61

Cover photo: *the Kirkland Signature™ All American Chocolate Cake, available at your local Costco warehouse. See related recipe on page 121.*

Photographs of members for Member Favorites section:
Jennifer Blakely: Steve Fujimoto, page 17
Julie Coolidge: Len Wood, page 16
Melissa Culp: Ryan Lavine, page 12
Dian Duyck & Karen Stevenson: Vern Uyetake, pages 10 & 15
Jesse Fitzgerald & Vivienne Tart: Rob Sumner, pages 15 & 11
Pam Hauck: Jesse Valley, www.jessevalley.com, page 16
Ellen Hennecke & Denise Snakard:
   Joe Cyganowski, pages 14 & 17
Cheryl Shaw: Deb Hellman, page 13
Peggy Temple: Chad Harder, page 12
Gin Wadkins: Tim Berger, page 11

FIRST EDITION
Printed by Toppan Leefung Printing (Shanghai) Co., Ltd, Shanghai, China
ISBN-13: 978-0-9819003-3-9
ISBN-10: 0-9819003-3-x
Library of Congress Control Number: 2011912914

70

32

138

151

206

Contents

The world's best chefs have the ability to infuse dishes with their unique personalities. We asked several top chefs to do their magic with products from these great companies:

All food photographs by Iridio Photography, Seattle, Washington, with the following exceptions:

California Pear Advisory Board: page 208 (right)
David Loftus for Jamie Oliver: pages 94-95
Ferrero: page 25 (right)
Foster Farms: page 110
Getty Images: pages 2, 14, 229
Ingram Publishing: page 16
Media Bakery: pages 10, 11, 13, 17
Shutterstock: page 12

To Our Valued Members

We are delighted to offer this gift in time for the holidays—the tenth annual book in *The Costco Way* cookbook series—to thank you for your business and loyal membership. This book has been made possible through the support of Costco's many food suppliers.

To help mark this 10-year milestone we've featured a special cake—in this case Costco's famous Kirkland Signature All American Chocolate Cake—on our cover. Although you won't find the recipe included here (it's a trade secret), you can purchase this cake in the bakery section of our warehouses. And you can use this delicious cake in a recipe for Chocolate Almond Bonbons on page 121.

The first thing you'll see as you start leafing through this year's book is a selection of members' favorite recipes from the past nine cookbooks in *The Costco Way* series. What better way to celebrate a tenth anniversary than to take a look back at highlights from years past? I hope you enjoy seeing these member favorites as much as I did. The best recipes truly are timeless.

Returning again in this anniversary edition is our special "Chef's Choice" section in the middle of the book. It features recipes from many of our favorite celebrity chefs such as Jamie Oliver, Aaron McCargo, Jr., and Lidia Matticchio Bastianich. These top chefs have worked their magic to develop recipes using their favorite ingredients from Costco.

Old or new, the secret to all the great dishes featured in this book is top-quality ingredients. When you purchase your ingredients from Costco, you know that you are getting the best—and at a great price.

We hope you enjoy *A Decade of Cooking The Costco Way* and that you try out our recipes with your family and friends. You can also find our past years' cookbooks online at Costco.com. Just type "Costco Cookbooks" in the search window on our home page.

Bon appétit from all of us at Costco. And here's to the next 10 years!

Ginnie Roeglin,
Senior Vice President,
E-commerce and Publishing

Foreword

A decade ago we had an idea: How about a cookbook that highlights all the great food products available at Costco? The result was our first cookbook, *Entertaining The Costco Way*, published in 2002. Ten years later, here we are celebrating our tenth edition, *A Decade of Cooking The Costco Way*. In that time, *The Costco Way* series has featured some 2,500 recipes, along with countless serving tips, menu suggestions and other helpful information—all focusing on Costco's wonderful food.

Looking back, it's amazing to see how quickly a decade can pass. But it's equally interesting to take note of all the changes in the world of food that have taken place since we published our first cookbook. For starters, food is a hot topic in our daily lives. The Food Network is popular, celebrity chefs are all over TV and book covers, and people are much more sophisticated about everything related to food.

Tim Rose

The food industry itself has undergone significant changes. We're able to bring in foods to Costco warehouses from all corners of the world—and quickly. Organic foods have become mainstream. More attention is paid to safety—and we continue working on more improvements. People today want to know what they're eating and where it's from. And they're willing to try new recipes and foods.

We think these are all good developments. At Costco, our goal is to offer our members the very best in quality at the best possible price in all our products. In our food departments, this means the best cuts, highest grades, freshest products and variety—at a great value.

Jeff Lyons

And the next decade? We'll work to continue improving food quality, develop healthy new products and make feeding your family as affordable as possible. This will be a huge challenge: We expect our business to double over the next decade. Meeting our goals will require us to find new, sustainable sources of top-quality foods around the world and to support effective new growing and harvesting techniques.

It should be an exciting 10 years. Stay tuned!

Tim Rose,
Senior Vice President,
Foods and Sundries

Jeff Lyons,
Senior Vice President,
Fresh Foods

About This Book

Time flies … even when we're in the kitchen! Welcome to the tenth annual book in our *The Costco Way* cookbook series. In keeping with our tradition, this book is to be handed out to members on a first-come, first-served basis the weekend after Thanksgiving as a token of our appreciation.

We have several special features in *A Decade of Cooking The Costco Way*:

• We have been asking readers of our monthly magazine, *The Costco Connection*, to let us know which were their favorite recipes from past editions. These are showcased in a section beginning on page 10.

• We also asked our fabulous food suppliers to choose their favorite recipes from among the many they have provided through the years. These have been noted with a special "Supplier Favorite" logo throughout the book.

• And we have specially designated in our Supplier Listing at the back of the book those suppliers who have been participating in the cookbooks from the first book in the series, *Entertaining The Costco Way*, published in 2002.

Once again you will find our popular "Chef's Choice" chapter with recipes developed by some of the country's most accomplished chefs. All of these chefs have achieved national renown with cookbooks of their own, television shows and/or exceptional restaurants. Thanks to all of them for helping with this year's benchmark edition.

Please note that every recipe has been identified with the supplier's name and logo. We want to thank each of these suppliers for their support of this book. (Note additionally that some branded products may not be sold in your part of the country. In such cases you should substitute a similar product.)

As of this November, we will have distributed just under 15 million *The Costco Way* cookbooks, containing more than 2,500 recipes. I hope you enjoy this year's celebration of recipes past, even as you find new joys here for your upcoming repasts!

David W. Fuller,
Publisher

Note on brands *Many of the recipes in this book were submitted by companies that hold copyrights on the recipes and/or trademark applications/registrations on the brands listed in the recipes. Each of the companies represented in this book asserts its ownership of the trademarks, applications/registrations and copyrights it holds on its company name, brands or recipes. Trademark, application/registration and copyright symbols have been eliminated from the titles and text of the recipes by the publishers for design and readability purposes only.*

A Decade of Cooking
THE COSTCO WAY ™

Celebrating a decade of your favorite recipes

IT'S NOT EASY choosing a favorite recipe, but here's a trick offered by Costco member Julie Coolidge: Just look in your cookbook for the page with the most food smears.

As we prepared our 10th annual cookbook, we asked members to send us their favorite recipes from the first nine books in "The Costco Way" series. Judging by the enthusiastic response, it's clear there are a lot of smeared pages in beloved cookbooks across the country.

We are featuring a few of those favorite recipes here. Enjoy!

You can find all recipes from this book and past years online at Costco.com. Just type "Costco Cookbooks" in the search window on our home page.

DIAN DUYCK
Cornelius, Oregon

Our family loves this salad! It is so versatile. We can vary the nuts, use dried or fresh fruit (fresh pineapple is awesome), add different cheeses and different meats. It is also a great way to use leftovers."

Cranberry Almond Spinach Salad

1 tablespoon butter
¾ cup blanched, slivered almonds
1 pound Boskovich Farms Fresh 'N' Quick Spinach
1 cup sweetened dried cranberries
4 ounces feta cheese, crumbled
2 tablespoons toasted sesame seeds
1 tablespoon poppy seeds
½ cup sugar
2 teaspoons minced onion
¼ teaspoon paprika
¼ cup white wine vinegar
¼ cup cider vinegar
½ cup vegetable oil

Melt butter in a small pan over medium heat. Add almonds and cook until lightly toasted. Remove from heat and set aside to cool.

Chop or tear spinach into bite-size pieces and place in a large salad bowl.

Add toasted almonds, cranberries and feta.

To make dressing, whisk together sesame seeds, poppy seeds, sugar, onion, paprika, vinegars and vegetable oil.

Add dressing to taste and gently toss the salad.

Makes 8 servings.

Recipe from 2005, *Creative Cooking The Costco Way*, page 38.

German Apple Pancake

Recipe from 2008, *In The Kitchen The Costco Way*, page 34.

APPLE TOPPING

¼ cup butter
  or margarine

2 cups peeled,
  thinly sliced apples

¼ cup sugar

½ teaspoon ground
  cinnamon

PANCAKE BATTER

1 cup Krusteaz
  Buttermilk Complete
  Pancake Mix

¾ cup water

½ teaspoon
  vanilla extract

½ teaspoon
  ground cinnamon

GIN WADKINS
Santa Clarita, California

To prepare the topping, place butter in a 9-inch microwave-safe pie pan. Microwave on high for 45-60 seconds, or until butter is melted. Stir in apples, sugar and cinnamon. Cover and microwave on high for 3-4 minutes, or until apples are tender.

To prepare the batter, place pancake mix, water, vanilla and cinnamon in a medium bowl and blend with a wire whisk. Pour evenly over the cooked apples.

Microwave, uncovered, on high for 3-5 minutes, or until a toothpick inserted in the center comes out clean. Let stand for 3-5 minutes, then invert onto a serving plate. Optional serving suggestion: Sprinkle with additional cinnamon and confectioners' sugar. Makes 6-8 servings.

Tip: To use a conventional oven, preheat to 350°F. Prepare apple topping as directed. Bake, uncovered, for 10 minutes, or until apples are tender. Prepare pancake batter and pour evenly over the cooked apples. Bake, uncovered, for 13-15 minutes, or until a toothpick inserted in the center comes out clean.

> "If I feel like making a special breakfast for my family or have house guests, I can whip this up in no time. My son says it's like having apple pie for breakfast!"

Good Morning Apple Cake

1 18.25-ounce package
  yellow cake mix

3 large eggs

1⅓ cups milk

½ teaspoon ground
  cinnamon

2 medium-sized Borton
  apples, the variety of
  your choice

STREUSEL TOPPING

¾ cup old-fashioned oats

¾ cup chopped pecans
  or walnuts

½ cup packed dark
  brown sugar

½ teaspoon ground
  cinnamon

½ cup melted butter

Preheat oven to 350°F. Grease and flour a 13-by-9-inch baking pan.

To prepare the streusel topping, combine all ingredients in a medium bowl and mix well. Set aside.

Beat cake mix, eggs, milk and cinnamon in a large mixer bowl until just moistened. Beat for 2 minutes at medium speed.

Core and slice apples; fold into the batter. Pour half of the batter into the prepared pan. Sprinkle with half of the streusel topping. Top with the remaining batter. Sprinkle with the remaining topping.

Bake for 40-45 minutes, or until a toothpick inserted in the center comes out clean. Makes 8-10 servings.

Recipe from 2010, *Smart Cooking The Costco Way*, page 17.

> "I just love it and serve it up with whip cream. It is so moist and the little crunch or texture of the apple makes the difference."

VIVIENNE TART
Seattle, Washington

Cranberry-Orange Mix

3 cups Corn Chex cereal
3 cups Rice Chex cereal
3 cups Wheat Chex cereal
1 cup sliced almonds
¼ cup butter or
  margarine, melted
¼ cup packed brown sugar
¼ cup frozen orange juice
  concentrate, thawed
½ cup sweetened dried
  cranberries

Preheat oven to 300°F. In an ungreased large roasting pan, mix cereals and almonds; set aside.

Place butter, brown sugar and juice concentrate in a microwavable measuring cup. Microwave, uncovered, on high for 30 seconds; stir. Pour over cereal mixture, stirring until evenly coated.

Bake for 30 minutes, stirring after 15 minutes.

Stir in cranberries.

Spread on waxed paper or foil to cool. Store in an airtight container. Makes 20 servings.

Recipe from 2006, *Cooking in Style The Costco Way*, page 39.

"This is a wonderful party treat that surprises many people with the orange, tangy, sweet flavor. I also add pistachios and pecans from Costco!"

PEGGY TEMPLE
Superior, Montana

Sausage-Stuffed Mushrooms

12 ounces breakfast sausage
18 Cardile Brothers large
  white mushrooms
2 8-ounce packages cream
  cheese, softened
¾ cup dry bread crumbs
¾ cup red wine, divided
Bacon bits (optional)

Preheat oven to 325°F. Cook sausage in a large deep skillet over medium-high heat, stirring and breaking up with a fork, until evenly browned. Drain and set aside.

Clean mushrooms with a damp cloth. Remove, chop and reserve stems.

In a medium bowl, gently mix the chopped mushroom stems, cream cheese and bread crumbs. Stir in the sausage and ¼ cup wine. For a different taste, add bacon bits.

Spoon the sausage mixture into the mushroom caps. Transfer to a large baking dish and cover with remaining red wine. Bake for 25-30 minutes, or until lightly browned. Makes 6 servings.

Recipe from 2007, *Favorite Recipes The Costco Way*, page 35.

MELISSA CULP
North Wales, Pennsylvania

"This is my signature appetizer that I take to cocktail parties and serve at my own."

Italian Sausage with Roasted Tomatoes and Polenta

2 pounds Premio sweet Italian sausages
2 tablespoons olive oil
18 ripe plum (Roma) tomatoes, split lengthwise
12 garlic cloves, crushed
1 cup chicken broth

4 tablespoons balsamic vinegar
1 teaspoon dried oregano
1 18-ounce tube precooked polenta
½ cup grated Romano cheese

Preheat oven to 350°F. Split sausages in half lengthwise, place in a lightly oiled roasting pan or casserole, and roast for 15-20 minutes. Remove sausages from the pan and reserve.

Raise oven temperature to 400°F. Add tomatoes to the pan and roast until they start to soften, 10-15 minutes. Stir in garlic.

Remove pan from the oven and place on a stovetop burner over medium heat. Add broth and vinegar. Simmer, scraping the bottom, until it starts to thicken. Add oregano, sausages and juices from the sausages.

Meanwhile, cut polenta into ½-inch slices and heat according to package directions. Arrange polenta on an ovenproof platter. Sprinkle with half of the cheese.

Check seasoning of sausage mixture and then spoon over polenta. Top with remaining cheese and bake for 5-10 minutes, or until cheese has melted. Makes 12-16 servings.

Recipe from 2006, *Cooking in Style The Costco Way*, page 33.

"Talk about waking up your tastebuds! The balsamic really adds rich flavor. It is listed as an appetizer, but I also make it as a main dish. When I serve it as an appetizer, I cut the sausage and polenta in smaller pieces. Rave compliments every time!"

CHERYL SHAW
San Diego, California

> The specialty of my house and my nomination for one of the best recipes ever. This makes a wonderful summer dish with halibut and fresh vegetables being plentiful then. The dish looks and presents beautifully and pairs nicely with white wine for a special meal."

ELLEN HENNECKE
Mokena, Illinois

Parmesan Potato-Crusted Halibut with Heirloom Tomato and Zucchini

2 tablespoons grated Parmesan cheese
4 tablespoons instant mashed potatoes
1 teaspoon dried thyme
Salt and pepper
4 tablespoons extra-virgin olive oil, divided
4 6-ounce portions halibut fillet

8 large heirloom tomatoes, chopped, or 2 pints organic cherry tomatoes, halved
¼ cup chopped green onion
2 cups diced zucchini
1 bunch fresh basil, chopped
2 teaspoons sherry vinegar

Preheat oven to 350°F.

In a shallow bowl, combine Parmesan, potatoes, thyme, and salt and pepper to taste.

Heat a nonstick ovenproof sauté pan over medium heat. Add 2 tablespoons olive oil.

Coat 1 side of halibut with the potato mixture, pressing to adhere. Place fillets potato side down in the heated sauté pan.

Meanwhile, combine the remaining ingredients in a bowl. Season with salt and pepper to taste. Set aside.

When the potato is golden brown (about 5 minutes), carefully turn the fillets over and place the pan in the oven. Cook until almost done, about 5 minutes.

Add the tomato-zucchini mixture to the pan, being careful not to cover the halibut. Continue cooking for 2 minutes, or until the halibut is just cooked. Makes 4 servings.

Recipe from 2007, *Favorite Recipes The Costco Way*, page 168.

Recipe from 2009, *Home Cooking The Costco Way*, page 172.

Spinach Ravioli Lasagna with Pesto Panko Bread Crumbs

Nonstick cooking spray
1 23-ounce package Cibo
  Naturals Alfredo Sauce, divided
1 38-ounce package Monterey
  Pasta Co. Spinach & Cheese
  Ravioli, cooked according to
  package directions
¼ cup Kirkland Signature by
  Cibo Naturals Basil Pesto
1 cup roasted red peppers
  (jarred or canned), sliced
  into ½-inch strips

PESTO PANKO BREAD CRUMBS
1 cup panko bread crumbs
½ cup Kirkland Signature by
  Cibo Naturals Basil Pesto
1 cup shredded
  mozzarella cheese
¼ cup grated Parmesan cheese

Preheat oven to 350°F. Coat a 13-by-9-inch baking pan with cooking spray. To prepare the bread crumbs, mix all ingredients in a small bowl until thoroughly combined. Set aside.

Smooth 1½ cups of Alfredo sauce over the bottom of the prepared pan. Layer 18 of the ravioli in slightly overlapping rows—3 across and 6 lengthwise. Smooth ½ cup Alfredo sauce over the ravioli. Dot with pesto.

Layer the remaining ravioli in slightly overlapping rows—3 across and 6 lengthwise. Tuck any extra ravioli into this layer. Smooth ½ cup Alfredo sauce over the ravioli. Place the red pepper strips evenly across the top. Sprinkle with Pesto Panko Bread Crumbs.

Cover with foil and bake until the sauce is bubbling, about 35 minutes. Remove the foil and broil until the bread crumbs are lightly browned.

Let the lasagna rest for about 5 minutes. Serve with a large spoon. Makes 12 servings.

KAREN STEVENSON
Lake Oswego, Oregon

This is a wonderful variation on traditional lasagna, easy to prepare, and everyone loves the pesto panko bread-crumb topping."

With Costco's quality food products and my desire to cook healthy food that actually tastes good, this recipe was a real winner..."

JESSE FITZGERALD
Maple Valley, Washington

Turkey Meatloaf with Prune Glaze

2 tablespoons olive oil
1 yellow onion,
  finely chopped
2 celery stalks,
  finely chopped
2 carrots, finely chopped
3 garlic cloves, minced
3 slices white bread,
  crusts removed
½ cup low-fat milk
2 eggs

1-2 tablespoons salt
½ teaspoon *each* ground
  black pepper, dried
  thyme and garlic powder
¼ cup fresh parsley,
  chopped
1 cup chopped Kirkland
  Signature/Sunsweet
  pitted dried plums
¼ cup fresh bread crumbs
3 pounds ground turkey

GLAZE
½ cup Kirkland
  Signature/Sunsweet
  pitted dried plums
¾ cup Sunsweet
  prune juice
2 tablespoons
  Dijon mustard
2 tablespoons packed
  light brown sugar
¼ cup chicken broth

Preheat oven to 350°F. Heat oil in a skillet over medium-high heat. Add onions, celery, carrots and garlic; cook for 5 minutes, or until softened. Remove from the heat and let cool. Soak bread slices in milk until both sides are moist, about 15 seconds.

In a large bowl, whisk eggs with salt, pepper, thyme, garlic powder and parsley. Add soaked bread, cooled vegetables, dried plums, bread crumbs and ground turkey. Fold all the ingredients together until well combined. Put the meatloaf in a 9-by-5-inch loaf pan. To prepare the glaze, combine all ingredients in a saucepan and cook over medium heat for 10 minutes. Let cool and then puree. Set aside.

Bake the meatloaf for 45 minutes. Baste with glaze and bake for another 45 minutes, or until the internal temperature is 170°F, basting with glaze every 10 minutes. Makes 6-8 servings.

Recipe from 2010, *Smart Cooking The Costco Way*, page 149.

Caramel Apple Pork Chops

4 boneless pork loin chops,
  ¾ inch thick
Vegetable oil
¼ cup packed light brown sugar
¼ teaspoon ground cinnamon
¼ teaspoon grated nutmeg

Salt and pepper
2 tart Borton apples
  (Granny Smith, Pink Lady
  or Braeburn)
4 tablespoons butter
4 tablespoons chopped pecans

Heat a skillet over medium-high heat. Brush pork chops lightly with oil and cook for 5-6 minutes on each side, or until evenly browned. Remove from the pan and keep warm.

In a small mixing bowl, combine brown sugar, cinnamon, nutmeg, and salt and pepper to taste. Core apples and slice into ½-inch wedges. Add butter to the skillet and stir in the apples and brown-sugar mixture. Cover and cook over medium-high heat for 3-4 minutes, just until the apples are tender.

Remove the apples with a slotted spoon and arrange on top of the chops; keep warm. Continue cooking the mixture in the skillet, uncovered, until the sauce thickens slightly. Spoon the sauce over the apples and chops. Sprinkle with pecans. Makes 4 servings.

Recipe from 2009, *Home Cooking The Costco Way*, page 111.

"It is delicious as well as quick and easy to make. This is a regular at our table and my husband often asks for it."

PAM HAUCK
Ramsey, Minnesota

Recipe from 2009, *Home Cooking The Costco Way*, page 198.

Strawberries and Cream Trifle

1 14-ounce can Eagle Brand sweetened
  condensed milk
1½ cups cold water
1 4-serving size package instant vanilla-
  flavor pudding and pie filling mix
1 8-ounce container frozen whipped
  topping, thawed
4 cups sliced fresh strawberries,
  plus more for garnish
1 cup Smucker's Special Recipe
  Strawberry Preserves
1 large (9-inch) prepared angel food cake,
  cut into ¾-inch cubes (about 8 cups)
2 tablespoons sliced almonds,
  for garnish (optional)

Whisk sweetened condensed milk and water in a large bowl. Add pudding mix and whisk for 2 minutes, until well blended. Refrigerate for 5 minutes. Fold in whipped topping. Stir together sliced strawberries and strawberry preserves.

Spoon 2 cups of the pudding mixture into the bottom of a 4-quart clear glass trifle bowl or round glass serving bowl. Top with half the cake cubes, half the strawberries and half the remaining pudding mix. Repeat the layers, ending with pudding.

Refrigerate for 3-4 hours, or until set. Garnish with sliced strawberries and almonds just before serving. Makes 10-12 servings.

"My 14-year-old daughter asked me how I could narrow down my selection of "favorite recipes" from the Costco cookbooks I have. I told her it was easy—find the page with the most food smears!"

JULIE COOLIDGE
Orcutt, California

Chocolate Croissant Shell

½ cup chocolate chips
1 Vie de France butter croissant
¾ cup raspberry ice cream

OPTIONAL GARNISH
¼ cup whipped cream
Raspberries

Melt chocolate chips in the microwave or over low heat in a saucepan. Meanwhile, place a cooling rack on top of a cookie sheet. Slice croissant in half and place the halves side by side on the rack. Pour the melted chocolate over the croissant halves, coating the entire surface. Let sit for about 15 minutes, or until the chocolate is firm. Fill the bottom half of the croissant with ice cream and place the other half on top. If desired, serve with whipped cream and raspberries. Makes 1 serving.

DENISE SNAKARD
Winnetka, Illinois

"My guests love this dessert at Christmas time! The presentation is so pure and simple looking and everyone forgets the calories. I use peppermint ice cream for the filling and top with crushed candy canes."

Recipe from 2009, *Home Cooking The Costco Way*, page 209.

"I love this recipe!!! It has a perfect balance of flavors between the tangy lemon and the sweet glaze poured on top. The glaze oozes down into the bread, making it so moist and delicious."

Lemon Bread

1½ cups all-purpose flour
½ teaspoon salt
1 teaspoon baking powder
6 tablespoons butter, softened
1 cup sugar
2 eggs
½ cup milk

Grated peel and juice of 1 lemon
¼ cup poppy seeds (or chopped walnuts)
½ cup confectioners' sugar

JENNIFER BLAKELY
Visalia, California

Preheat oven to 350°F. Grease and flour a 9-by-5-inch loaf pan.

Whisk together flour, salt and baking powder.

In a large bowl, cream butter, sugar and eggs together until light and fluffy. Add milk alternately with the flour mixture in 2 parts; mix well. Stir in grated lemon peel and poppy seeds.

Pour the batter into the prepared loaf pan. Bake for 60 minutes, or until a toothpick inserted in the center comes out clean. Let the bread cool in the pan for 5 minutes.

Mix together lemon juice and confectioners' sugar to make a glaze. Remove the bread from the pan. Pour the glaze over the warm bread (poking holes in the bread first will make it absorb more of the glaze). Makes 10 servings.

Recipe from 2009, *Home Cooking The Costco Way*, page 177.

Breakfasts

Potato and Onion Frittata
Basin Gold Cooperative

4 tablespoons extra-virgin olive oil

1 Basin Gold* baker russet potato, diced into ¼-inch cubes

½ Basin Gold* jumbo yellow onion, chopped

2 garlic cloves, minced

1 cup fresh spinach leaves, washed and patted dry

Salt and freshly ground pepper

8 large eggs (or 12 large egg whites)

¼ teaspoon crushed red pepper

½ cup grated Parmesan cheese, divided

Salsa, for garnish (optional)

Heat oil in an 11½-inch ovenproof skillet over medium-low heat. Add potatoes and sauté until golden and tender in the center, about 8 minutes. Add onion and garlic; cook for another 2-3 minutes. Add spinach and cook for another minute, or until wilted. Season to taste with salt and pepper.

Preheat the broiler. In a bowl, whisk together eggs, red pepper and ¼ cup Parmesan. Add to the skillet. Cook, stirring, until the mixture begins to set but the eggs still have some give, about 3-4 minutes.

Sprinkle with the remaining Parmesan and place under the broiler. Broil until the top is set and the cheese and egg mixture are golden brown, about 3-4 minutes. Remove from the broiler, let cool for a few minutes, and slice into wedges.

Garnish with salsa and serve. Makes 6-8 servings.

* Brands may vary by region; substitute a similar product.

Sausage and Zucchini Frittata
Jimmy Dean

8 large eggs

1 teaspoon dried basil

2 packages (12 links) Jimmy Dean Fully Cooked Turkey Sausage, coarsely chopped

1 cup chopped zucchini

½ cup sliced mushrooms

½ cup chopped fresh tomato

½ cup (2 ounces) shredded reduced-fat Italian cheese blend

Preheat oven to 350°F.

In a medium bowl, beat eggs and basil with a wire whisk until well blended.

In a large ovenproof skillet, cook and stir sausage, zucchini and mushrooms over medium heat for 5-6 minutes, or until the vegetables are tender. Add the eggs, but do not stir.

Bake for 22-27 minutes, or until a knife inserted near the center comes out clean.

Remove from the oven. Top with tomato and cheese. Let stand for 5 minutes, or until the cheese has melted. Cut into wedges to serve. Makes 6 servings.

Croque Madame
La Brea Bakery

Butter, softened

8 ¼-inch-thick slices La Brea Bakery*
  Sourdough Loaf

8 ounces Gruyère cheese, sliced

12 ounces smoked ham,
  such as Black Forest, sliced

4 extra-large eggs

3 tablespoons unsalted butter

Fleur de sel or kosher salt

Freshly cracked black pepper

Butter 1 side of each slice of bread. Set 4 of the bread slices buttered side down and cover with cheese slices, folding the cheese back in toward the middle if it extends past the edges of the bread. Place 3-4 slices of ham on each sandwich in an even layer over the cheese. Place the top slice of bread over the ham, buttered side up.

Grill the sandwiches in a moderately hot skillet until the bread is golden brown and the cheese has melted, about 3-3½ minutes per side.

Crack 2 eggs into 2 separate bowls to check that the yolks aren't broken. In two 6-inch nonstick skillets, melt half of the butter over medium-high heat, until it starts to bubble. Pour 1 egg into each pan, being careful not to break the yolk. Add a teaspoon of water to each pan, sprinkle the eggs with salt to taste, and cover the pans. Cook the eggs for about 3 minutes for a soft-cooked egg or 5-6 minutes if you like your eggs firm. Wipe out the skillets, and fry the other 2 eggs in the remaining butter.

Center a fried egg over each of the grilled sandwiches and sprinkle with pepper to taste. Makes 4 servings.

* Brands may vary by region; substitute a similar product.

La Brea Bakery

Potato-Cheddar Gnocchi with Bacon and Eggs
Alsum Farms & Produce, Inc./RPE, Inc.

3 pounds Wisconsin* russet potatoes, peeled and quartered
2 eggs, beaten
¼ cup half-and-half
4 ounces grated Cheddar
2 teaspoons salt
12 ounces (about 2½ cups) all-purpose flour
2 pounds plum tomatoes
2 tablespoons olive oil
2 teaspoons salt
½ teaspoon black pepper
1 cup chopped basil
12 eggs, poached
24 bacon strips, cooked

Steam potatoes over boiling water, covered, for 15 minutes, or until tender. Transfer to a bowl and mash. Cool slightly, then gently mix in eggs, half-and-half, cheese and salt. Add flour gradually, mixing gently. If dough is sticky, add flour. Divide into 8 pieces. Roll each piece into a 1-inch-diameter rope; flatten slightly and cut into 24 gnocchi. Transfer to a pan lined with a lightly floured towel; cover with another towel. Refrigerate.

Preheat oven to 475°F. Quarter tomatoes and halve each quarter. Toss with oil, salt and pepper. Spread on a sheet pan. Roast for 20 minutes, or until soft and slightly browned.

Bring a large pot of lightly salted water to a boil. Add 16 gnocchi; boil 5 minutes, or until cooked through.

Transfer to a bowl; add 8 tomato pieces and 4 teaspoons basil. Toss gently. Top with 1 warm poached egg and 2 bacon strips. Makes 12 servings.

* Brands may vary by region; substitute a similar product.

Bulgur Wheat with Pineapple, Pecans and Basil
Dole

2 cups water
1 cup bulgur
1 20-ounce can Dole Tropical Gold* pineapple chunks or Dole* pineapple chunks, drained
½ cup chopped pecans
2 tablespoons chopped fresh basil
2 tablespoons chopped Italian parsley
1½ teaspoons olive oil

Combine water and bulgur in a large saucepan. Heat to boiling, then reduce the heat, cover, and simmer for 35-40 minutes, or until the bulgur is tender but not mushy.

Transfer the bulgur to a large bowl; let cool to room temperature.

Stir pineapple chunks, pecans, basil, parsley and oil into the bulgur. Serve at room temperature. Makes 4 servings.

Nutritional information: Each serving has 309 calories, 6 g protein, 46 g carbohydrates, 13 g fat, 1 g saturated fat, 0 mg cholesterol, 9 g fiber, 21 mg sodium, 16 g sugar.

* Brands may vary by region; substitute a similar product.

Ham and Scalloped Potato Wellingtons
Reser's Fine Foods

Parchment paper

1 egg, slightly beaten

1 tablespoon water

2 sheets frozen puff pastry, thawed

40-ounce tray Reser's* Top Baked Scalloped Potatoes, unheated, divided into 8 even portions

8 ounces Swiss cheese slices, cut into 2-inch squares

8 teaspoons Dijon mustard

8 1-ounce ham slices, cut into 2-inch squares

Preheat oven to 400°F. Line a sheet pan with parchment paper.

Mix egg and water in a small cup. Set aside.

On a lightly floured cutting board, roll out each sheet of pastry into a 14-by-14-inch square; cut into four 7-inch squares.

In the middle of each pastry square, place a portion of scalloped potatoes with the browned cheese side down. Top with cheese, mustard and then ham.

Pull the edges of each square toward the center and press together to seal (you can use a little bit of water to seal).

Carefully flip the packets over and place seam-side down on the prepared pan. Lightly brush the tops with the egg and water mixture.

Bake for 30 minutes, or until golden brown. Makes 8 servings.

* Brands may vary by region; substitute a similar product.

Wild Alaskan Salmon Benedict with Citrus Cheese Sauce
Morey's

2 portions Morey's* Seasoned Grill Salmon

4 large eggs

2 English muffins

1 tablespoon sliced green onions

CITRUS CHEESE SAUCE

1 cup heavy cream

2 tablespoons butter

¾ cup shredded Cheddar/Jack cheese

2 teaspoons lime juice

⅛ teaspoon smoked paprika

⅛ teaspoon sea salt

⅛ teaspoon ground black pepper

Prepare salmon according to package directions.

While the salmon is cooking, prepare the cheese sauce. In a saucepan, combine cream and butter. Cook over medium heat, stirring frequently, until the butter has melted and the mixture is near boiling. Add cheese and whisk until it has melted and the mixture is thoroughly blended. Stir in lime juice, paprika, salt and pepper. Reduce the heat to low and keep warm. Whisk before serving.

Remove and discard the skin from the cooked salmon and cut the fillets in half.

Poach the eggs.

Split and toast the English muffins.

Place a muffin half on each serving plate. Layer each muffin half with salmon and poached egg, top with a generous ladleful of cheese sauce, and sprinkle with green onions. Serve immediately. Makes 4 servings.

* Brands may vary by region; substitute a similar product.

Cheesy Veggie Sausage Breakfast Casserole
MorningStar Farms

Cooking spray

8 large eggs, lightly beaten (see note)

1 cup cottage cheese

¼ cup milk

1 teaspoon dried oregano leaves

¼ teaspoon garlic powder

¼ teaspoon salt

¼ teaspoon ground pepper

1 10-ounce package frozen chopped spinach, thawed and well drained

1½ cups (6 ounces) shredded Cheddar or mozzarella cheese

6 MorningStar Farms* Veggie Sausage Breakfast Patties, thawed and crumbled

½ cup sliced green onions

8 cherry tomatoes, for garnish (optional)

8 fresh parsley sprigs, for garnish (optional)

Preheat oven to 325°F. Coat a 13-by-9-by-2-inch baking dish with cooking spray. In a large bowl, beat together eggs, cottage cheese, milk, oregano, garlic powder, salt and pepper.

Squeeze excess moisture out of spinach. Add spinach, cheese, breakfast patties and green onions to the egg mixture and stir to blend. Pour into the prepared pan. Bake for 35-40 minutes, or until set. Let stand for 10 minutes before serving. Cut into squares to serve. Garnish with tomatoes and parsley. Makes 8 servings.

Note: For a low-cholesterol version, replace the 8 eggs with 2 cups of refrigerated egg substitute.

MorningStar FARMS®

Mediterranean Quiche with Hash-Brown Crust

Cal-Maine Foods/Hickman's Family Farms/Hillandale Farms/Norco/NuCal Foods/Oakdell Egg Farms/Wilcox Farms

3½ cups frozen shredded
   hash brown potatoes

Cooking spray

1 tablespoon butter

1 cup chopped onion

1 large garlic clove, minced

1 small zucchini, quartered,
   thinly sliced (2 cups)

1 cup diced red bell pepper

1 cup chopped drained oil-packed
   artichoke hearts

4 eggs

½ cup milk

½ cup shredded part-skim
   mozzarella cheese (2 ounces)

½ teaspoon dried basil leaves

½ teaspoon dried oregano leaves

2 cups marinara sauce, warmed

Preheat oven to 425°F.

Press potatoes evenly onto the bottom and sides of a greased 10-inch quiche dish or pie plate. Coat lightly with cooking spray. Bake until the potatoes are lightly browned and crisp, about 30 minutes.

Reduce oven setting to 375°F.

Heat butter in a large nonstick skillet over medium heat. Add onions and garlic; sauté until tender, 3-4 minutes. Add zucchini, bell pepper and artichokes; sauté until crisp-tender.

In a large bowl, beat eggs, milk, cheese, basil and oregano until blended. Add the zucchini mixture and mix well. Pour into the potato crust.

Bake in the center of the oven until a knife inserted near the center comes out clean, about 45 minutes. Let stand for 5 minutes.

Cut into wedges. Serve with marinara sauce. Makes 4 servings.

Nutritional information: Each serving has 452 calories, 19 g protein, 57 g carbohydrates, 17 g fat, 206 mg cholesterol, 8 g fiber, 845 mg sodium.

Grilled Egg and Cheese Sandwiches
Kirkland Signature/Michael Foods

2 ounces sliced pancetta

Nonstick cooking spray

1 cup (8 ounces) Kirkland Signature Real Egg

2 tablespoons butter

8 slices sourdough bread

8 slices deli-style provolone cheese

4 slices tomato

1 cup loosely packed arugula

Heat a large nonstick skillet over medium-high heat. Cook pancetta until crisp. Drain pancetta on paper towels; discard grease.

Coat four 6-ounce custard cups with cooking spray. Add ¼ cup Real Egg to each cup. Cook in the microwave on high for 1-2 minutes, or until the eggs are set but still moist.

Melt butter in a large skillet over medium-low heat. Add 4 bread slices. Top each slice with 1 slice cheese, 1 slice tomato, a quarter of the pancetta, 1 cooked egg, a quarter of the arugula, 1 slice cheese and the remaining bread slice.

Cook the sandwiches for 2 minutes. Carefully flip the sandwiches and continue to cook until the bread is browned. Makes 4 servings.

Hazelnut Spread Swirl Ring
Nutella

¼ cup warm water

½ package active dry yeast

2 tablespoons sugar, divided

⅛ teaspoon salt

1½ cups all-purpose flour, divided

⅓ cup unsalted butter, softened

Cooking spray

½ cup Nutella hazelnut spread

1 tablespoon water, for brushing

Using an electric mixer, stir together warm water, yeast, 1 tablespoon sugar and salt. Add ½ cup flour and butter; mix until blended. Add remaining flour and mix for 2 minutes. Grease a large bowl with cooking spray and place the dough in it, turning once. Cover with plastic and let stand for 1 hour in a warm place, until doubled in volume.

Preheat oven to 375°F. Line a baking sheet with foil or parchment paper.

When the dough has fully risen, punch it down. On a floured surface, roll out to a 12-by-16-inch rectangle. Spread evenly with Nutella, leaving a 1-inch band around the edges. Tightly roll into a 16-inch-long log. Brush the ends with a little water, then bring together to form a ring. Transfer to the baking sheet. Slice into 12 buns, cutting only partially through so the buns are still connected. Gently separate the buns. Brush with 1 tablespoon water and sprinkle with 1 tablespoon sugar. Bake for 35 45 minutes, or until golden brown. Serve with fruit. Makes 12 servings.

Pound Cake French Toast
Dawn Food Products

Butter or cooking spray
2 large eggs
1 cup milk
½ teaspoon ground cinnamon
½ teaspoon vanilla extract
1 Kirkland Signature pound cake,
**   cut into 12 slices**

Parchment paper
¾-1 cup chocolate-hazelnut spread
**   such as Nutella**
2 bananas, sliced
Maple syrup

Heat a griddle to medium-high. Lightly coat with butter or cooking spray. In a shallow bowl, beat eggs. Add milk, cinnamon and vanilla; stir until well blended. Dip pound cake slices in the egg mixture. Cook on the hot griddle until golden brown.

Form a cone out of parchment paper and cut a ⅛-inch opening in the tip. Put Nutella in the cone and squeeze over the French toast. Alternatively, warm the Nutella and drizzle over the French toast with a spoon.

Top the French toast with banana slices and drizzle with maple syrup. Serve hot. Makes 6 servings.

Tip: Sliced banana nut muffins can be substituted for the pound cake.

Dawn
FOOD PRODUCTS, INC.

Cheddar Bacon Waffles
Tillamook

2 large eggs

1 cup milk

3 tablespoons
vegetable oil

1½ cups all-purpose flour

1 tablespoon
baking powder

2 teaspoons sugar

½ teaspoon salt

1 cup (4 ounces) shredded
Tillamook Medium
Cheddar Cheese

8 pieces cooked bacon

Tillamook salted butter
and real maple syrup,
for serving

While the waffle iron is heating, make the batter. Place eggs in a bowl and beat well. Whisk in milk and oil.

In a separate bowl, blend flour, baking powder, sugar and salt. Add to the egg mixture and stir until the batter is smooth. Stir in cheese.

When the waffle iron is hot, pour in enough batter to fill, then lay a piece of cooked bacon across the batter before closing the iron. Cook according to the manufacturer's instructions.

Serve with butter and maple syrup. Makes 8 servings.

Recipe provided by Heidi Gibson of The American Grilled Cheese Kitchen.

Tillamook®
Tastes better because it's made better.

Mediterranean Bread Pudding
Houweling Nurseries

Butter

½ (8 ounces) multi-grain
bread loaf, cut into
¾-inch cubes

3 tablespoons olive oil

2 shallots, thinly sliced

2 garlic cloves, minced

16 ounces Houweling's*
grape tomatoes, halved

1 cup sliced green olives

Salt and pepper

1 packed cup chopped
fresh basil leaves

1½ cups shredded
Parmesan

7 large eggs,
at room temperature

1¼ cups whole milk

1 teaspoon salt

½ teaspoon pepper

Preheat oven to 375°F. Butter a 13-by-9-inch glass baking dish. Add bread cubes and set aside.

In a skillet, heat oil over medium-high heat. Add shallots and garlic; cook, stirring constantly, until fragrant, about 1 minute. Add tomatoes, olives, and salt and pepper to taste. Cook until slightly soft, about 2 minutes. Remove from the heat and stir in basil.

Pour the tomato mixture and Parmesan over the bread cubes and stir to combine.

In a bowl, beat eggs, milk, salt and pepper until smooth. Pour over the bread mixture and toss to coat.

Bake until puffed and golden, about 25 minutes. Remove and let cool for 5 minutes. Cut into squares and serve. Makes 6-8 servings.

* Brands may vary by region; substitute a similar product.

Savory Bread Pudding
Vie de France

2 tablespoons plus 2 teaspoons unsalted butter, divided

1 cup diced onions

¼ cup diced green bell pepper

¼ cup diced red bell pepper

¾ teaspoon salt, divided

¼ teaspoon ground black pepper, divided

2 teaspoons minced garlic

1 tablespoon chopped fresh parsley

6 ounces diced Canadian bacon or ham

8 large eggs

3 cups milk

½ cup heavy cream

1½ teaspoons Creole seasoning, divided

8 day-old Vie de France butter croissants, cubed

8 ounces Gouda or Fontina cheese, grated

½ cup fine dry bread crumbs

½ cup freshly grated Parmesan cheese

2 tablespoons unsalted butter, melted

Preheat oven to 350°F. Grease a 13-by-9-inch baking dish with 1 tablespoon butter.

In a medium skillet, melt 2 teaspoons butter over medium-high heat. Add onions, bell peppers, ¼ teaspoon salt and ⅛ teaspoon pepper and cook until soft, about 3 minutes. Add garlic and cook for 30 seconds. Stir in parsley and remove from the heat.

In another medium skillet, melt 1 tablespoon butter over medium-high heat. Add meat and cook for 3 minutes. Drain on paper towels.

In a large bowl, beat eggs. Whisk in milk, cream, 1 teaspoon Creole seasoning, ½ teaspoon salt and ⅛ teaspoon pepper. Add croissants and let stand for 5 minutes. Stir in meat, onion mixture and Gouda or Fontina. Pour into the baking dish, cover with foil, and bake for 50-55 minutes.

Combine bread crumbs, Parmesan, melted butter and ½ teaspoon Creole seasoning. Sprinkle over the pudding. Return to the oven, increase heat to 375°F, and bake until set in the center and golden brown on top, about 20 minutes. Let stand for 15 minutes before serving. Makes 8-10 servings.

Bagel Pudding
Einstein Brothers Bagels/Noah's Bagels

3 Kirkland Signature plain bagels
3 large eggs
1¼ cups 2% or whole milk
½ cup half-and-half
¼ cup sugar

1½ teaspoons ground cinnamon
1 tablespoon vanilla extract
½ cup pecan halves (optional)
Butter

Cut bagels into ½- to 1-inch cubes. Spread out on a cookie sheet and let dry overnight.

Place eggs, milk, half-and-half, sugar, cinnamon, vanilla and pecans in a large bowl and blend thoroughly. Add bagel cubes and mix gently by hand.

Liberally butter the bottom and sides of an 8-inch round cake pan. Pour the contents of the bowl into the pan and spread evenly. Cover with plastic wrap and refrigerate for at least 3 hours and up to overnight.

Preheat oven to 350°F. Remove the plastic wrap and bake the pudding for 20-25 minutes, or until golden brown and firm to the touch. Makes 6 servings.

Tips: To serve 12, double the amount of all ingredients, place in a 13-by-9-inch pan, and bake for 25-30 minutes. Garnish with berries if desired.

NOAH'S BAGELS

Appetizers & Beverages

Peach Bruschetta
I.M. Ripe

4 tablespoons white or dark balsamic vinegar

2 I.M. Ripe* peaches, pitted and diced

2 tablespoons olive oil

2 large shallots, thinly sliced

8 sage leaves

4-6 ounces goat cheese

8 ½-inch-thick diagonal slices of baguette, lightly toasted

In a small saucepan, cook vinegar over low heat until reduced to 2 tablespoons.

Place diced peaches in a medium bowl.

Heat oil in a skillet over medium-high heat. Add shallots and sauté until crisp. Add the shallots to the peaches and toss gently.

Place whole sage leaves in the skillet and cook over medium-high heat until crisp. Remove gently to a plate.

To assemble the bruschetta, spread goat cheese on toasted baguette slices. Spoon the peach mixture on top of the goat cheese. Drizzle with balsamic reduction and place a whole crisp sage leaf on top. Makes 8 servings.

Tips: A combination of peaches and nectarines can be used. There's no need to skin the fruit.

Recipe created by Peggy Thurlow.

* Brands may vary by region; substitute a similar product.

Date Citrus Flatbreads
*Bard Valley Medjool Date Growers/
Rio Blanco/Sunkist Growers*

1 tablespoon olive oil

1 large onion, sliced into thin rings

⅛ teaspoon salt

2 cups shredded mozzarella cheese

2 medium-large premade pizza crusts, cut into 4 flatbreads (or use flatbread dough)

2 Sunkist* Minneola tangelos, navels or clementines, peeled, segmented and cut into bite-size pieces

¾ cup pitted and chopped Bard Valley* Medjool dates

1 teaspoon dried rosemary

2 tablespoons crumbled feta cheese

Heat oil in a nonstick sauté pan over medium heat. Add onions and sauté for 10 minutes. Reduce the heat, sprinkle salt over the onions, and cook for 20 minutes, stirring occasionally, until the onions are a rich brown color.

Preheat the oven broiler.

Sprinkle mozzarella over flatbreads. Place under the broiler until the cheese starts to melt, about 2 minutes.

Remove from the oven and top with the caramelized onions, citrus pieces, dates and rosemary. Sprinkle with feta.

Place back under the broiler for another minute, or until the toppings are hot and the bread browns slightly. Cut lengthwise into 8 pieces.

Makes 8 servings.

* Brands may vary by region; substitute a similar product.

Walnut-Crusted Brie on Toasts with Apple-Cherry Chutney

Stemilt Growers

1 5-ounce wedge of Brie (skin on)

1 cup walnuts, roughly chopped (in food processor)

1 egg

1 teaspoon 2% milk (or heavy cream)

Sliced baguette

APPLE-CHERRY CHUTNEY

3 tablespoons unsalted butter

1½ tablespoons minced shallot

⅓ cup firmly packed light brown sugar

2 tablespoons fresh lemon juice (Meyer lemon, if available)

1 teaspoon freshly grated orange zest

1 Stemilt* Fuji apple, peeled and finely diced

1 cup halved Stemilt* fresh cherries

2 tablespoons minced dried apricots

3 tablespoons golden raisins

⅛ teaspoon ground allspice

1 teaspoon apple cider vinegar

Pinch of white pepper

Preheat oven to 350°F. Place Brie wedge in the freezer for 15 minutes.

To prepare the chutney, melt butter in a large saucepan over medium heat. Add shallots and cook until softened, about 2 minutes. Add brown sugar, lemon juice and orange zest. Continue cooking until the sugar has completely dissolved, about 2 minutes.

Add other chutney ingredients. Bring the mixture to a low boil and simmer, stirring intermittently, until the liquid is reduced by about half and the sauce has thickened, about 15 minutes. Remove from the heat, cover, and set aside.

Place chopped nuts in a shallow dish. Crack egg into a separate shallow dish. Add milk and whisk until well combined.

Remove Brie from the freezer and dip in the egg wash, coating on all surfaces. Transfer to the walnut dish and turn to coat with nuts, gently pressing to ensure coverage.

Place the cheese on a baking sheet. Bake for about 15 minutes. Transfer to a serving tray. Toast baguette slices and arrange on a tray with the cheese. Transfer the chutney to a serving bowl and set beside the cheese and toasts. Serve immediately. Makes 4-6 servings.

* Brands may vary by region; substitute a similar product.

Seared Fresh Brown Turkey Figs

Stellar Distributing

4 fresh California Brown Turkey figs, cut in half lengthwise

Fine granulated sugar

Olive oil

8 toasted baguette slices or crackers

4 ounces Brie, sliced

4 slices crisp fried bacon, cut in half

Sprinkle fig halves very lightly with sugar.

Lightly coat a cast iron skillet with oil; heat to very hot. Arrange the fig halves, cut side down, in the pan and sear for about 2 minutes. Remove from the pan and let cool.

Top toasted baguette slices with cheese and bacon. Arrange the figs, cut side up, on top. Makes 4 servings.

Nutritional information: Each serving has 350 calories, 11 g protein, 35 g carbohydrates, 19 g fat, 35 mg cholesterol, 4 g fiber, 470 mg sodium, 11 g sugar.

Grapes with Goat Cheese and Walnuts

Divine Flavor

8 ounces cream cheese

8 ounces goat cheese

Salt (optional)

1 pound Divine Flavor red or green seedless grapes

8 ounces walnuts, finely chopped

Combine cream cheese and goat cheese; mix until well blended. If desired, add a pinch of salt.

Thoroughly wash grapes and dry them well.

Coat each grape with the cheese mixture. Roll in chopped walnuts to coat. Makes 4 servings.

Tip: These can be prepared one day ahead and stored, covered, in the refrigerator. They are very easy to make and delicious.

DIVINE FLAVOR

Persimmon Wedges with Toasted Hazelnuts

Regatta Tropicals

2 large Regatta Tropicals* Fuyu persimmons

Hazelnut oil

1½ cups warm toasted hazelnuts

Cut persimmons into ½-inch-thick wedges. Arrange on a plate. Drizzle with hazelnut oil.

Place warm hazelnuts in a bowl. Serve persimmons with hazelnuts. Makes 8 servings.

Recipe courtesy of Tori Ritchie, www.tuesdayrecipe.com.

* Brands may vary by region; substitute a similar product.

Spinach Potato Patties

River Ranch Fresh Foods

1 pound boiling potatoes, peeled and diced

¼ cup hot milk

4 ounces butter, divided

2 cups olive oil, divided

1 pound River Ranch* fresh spinach

1 garlic clove, chopped

6 green onions, white parts finely diced and green parts chopped, divided

1 teaspoon lemon juice

Grated zest of 2 lemons, divided

Salt and pepper, to taste

3 large eggs, divided

½ cup soda water

2 cups panko bread crumbs, divided

3 cups white rice flour

Boil potatoes, drain, and press through a ricer. Whisk in milk and 1 tablespoon butter until fluffy. Cool.

Heat 1 teaspoon butter and 2 tablespoons oil in a skillet over medium heat. Add spinach, garlic and white onion tops; cook until limp. Remove spinach mixture and drain, reserving juice. Finely chop the spinach.

Return the spinach juice to the skillet and continue cooking until reduced by half. Stir in lemon juice, half of zest, salt and pepper. Cool.

Combine potatoes, spinach mixture and spinach juice. Stir in 1 beaten egg, soda water, then 1½ cups bread crumbs. Shape into patties.

In 3 separate bowls, place 2 beaten eggs, ½ cup bread crumbs and flour. In that order, dip each patty into each bowl. Working in batches, fry in oil and butter over green onion tops and lemon zest until golden brown. Makes 24 servings.

* Brands may vary by region; substitute a similar product.

Loaded Baked Potato Dip

Sensible Portions

3-4 slices turkey bacon
½ cup low-fat Greek yogurt
½ cup fat-free sour cream
½ teaspoon garlic salt
1-2 teaspoons hot sauce

¾ cup shredded Cheddar cheese
1 tablespoon sliced fresh chives, plus more for garnish
Freshly cracked pepper
1 20-ounce bag Sensible Portions Veggie Straws, Lightly Salted

Bake or pan-fry bacon until crisp. Set aside on a paper towel to cool.

In a medium bowl, combine yogurt, sour cream and garlic salt. Add 1 teaspoon of hot sauce for enhanced flavor or 2 teaspoons for an added kick. Stir in shredded cheese and chives. Crumble the cooled bacon and add a portion to the mixture. Transfer to a serving bowl.

Garnish with extra bacon, chives and cracked pepper to taste.

Cover and chill for 1 hour or to desired temperature. Serve with Veggie Straws. Makes 4 servings.

Granny Smith Apple Salsa

Domex Superfresh Growers

1 large tomato, cored and finely chopped

¾ cup finely chopped sweet onion

3 tablespoons freshly squeezed lime juice

1 large jalapeño chile, cored, seeded and finely chopped

2 Superfresh Growers* Granny Smith apples

2 tablespoons minced fresh cilantro

1 tablespoon honey

Salt and freshly ground black pepper

Corn chips, for serving

In a medium bowl, stir together tomato, onion, lime juice and jalapeño.

Quarter and core apples and cut into fine dice. Stir apples into the tomato mixture with cilantro, honey, and salt and pepper to taste.

Refrigerate for up to 6 hours before serving.

To serve, spoon the salsa into a serving bowl and place a bowl of corn chips alongside. Makes 6-8 servings.

* Brands may vary by region; substitute a similar product.

DOMEX
superfresh
growers®

Garlic Shrimp-Stuffed Sweet Mini Peppers au Gratin

Royal Flavor

½ cup butter

5 garlic cloves, finely diced

¼ white onion, diced

2 fresh serrano peppers, finely diced

½ pound raw shrimp, peeled and diced

Salt and pepper

½ cup olive oil, as needed

15-20 Royal Flavor* mini bell peppers

½ pound Monterey Jack cheese, grated

Preheat oven to 350°F.

Melt butter over medium heat in a large skillet. Add garlic, onions and serrano peppers; sauté until the onions are translucent.

Add diced shrimp to the skillet and cook until the shrimp is opaque. Season to taste with salt and pepper. Remove from the heat.

Heat oil slowly in a frying pan to 300°F (keep the temperature below 350°F to prevent bitterness). Add salt and pepper to taste. Fry the peppers until tender and then place on paper towels to absorb the excess oil.

Make a small cut along the side of each pepper and remove the seeds. Stuff with the shrimp mixture. Place the stuffed peppers in a lightly oiled pan. Top with grated cheese.

Bake for 10 minutes, or until the cheese is lightly browned. Let stand for a few minutes and serve warm. Makes 10-12 servings.

* Brands may vary by region; substitute a similar product.

Lavash Party Bites

Kirkland Signature/Lavash Flatbread Chips

½ cup fine- or medium-grain bulgur wheat

2-3 cups fresh parsley leaves (about 2 bunches), minced

4 medium green onions, thinly sliced

2 medium tomatoes (about 12 ounces), cored, seeded and cut in medium dice

1 teaspoon olive oil

⅓ cup fresh lemon juice (2-3 lemons)

Salt

Prepared hummus, for serving

Kirkland Signature lavash chips, for serving

Soak bulgur in 2 cups warm water for 1-1½ hours. If you do not have much time, heat it in the microwave for 2 minutes.

Squeeze out excess water from the bulgur, rinse in cold water to chill, and transfer to a medium bowl. Add parsley, green onions and tomatoes.

Sprinkle with oil and lemon juice. Add salt to taste and mix all the ingredients together with a spoon to make tabbouleh.

Spread a small amount of hummus on each lavash chip, then top with a small amount of tabbouleh. Makes 6-8 servings.

Mediterranean Nachos

Sabra

4 cups pita chips

2 tablespoons Sabra* Roasted Garlic Hummus

2 tablespoons Sabra* Roasted Red Pepper Hummus

8-10 grape tomatoes, cut in half lengthwise

¼ cup chopped zucchini (about ¼-inch chunks)

2 tablespoons chopped Greek olives

2 tablespoons chopped pepperoncini

1½ cups shredded mozzarella

Preheat oven to 375°F.

Lay pita chips in a 9- to 10-inch ovenproof skillet or other pan or baking dish of a similar size. Top each with small spoonfuls of hummus, evenly distributed.

Sprinkle tomatoes, zucchini, olives and pepperoncini over the chips. Top with shredded mozzarella.

Bake for 15-20 minutes, or until the cheese has melted and the edges are beginning to brown. Serve warm. Makes 4 servings.

* Brands may vary by region; substitute a similar product.

Spicy Roasted Red Pepper Hummus with Baked Pita Chips

Kirkland Signature/Olde Thompson

1 15-ounce can garbanzo beans, drained and rinsed

1 12-ounce jar roasted red peppers, drained

2 tablespoons olive oil

⅛ teaspoon Kirkland Signature granulated garlic

½ teaspoon Kirkland Signature sea salt, plus more to taste

½ teaspoon Kirkland Signature crushed red pepper, plus more to taste

PITA CHIPS

6 pita breads

¼ cup olive oil

1 teaspoon Kirkland Signature sea salt

½ teaspoon Kirkland Signature Malabar ground pepper

Combine garbanzo beans, peppers, oil, garlic, salt and crushed red pepper in a food processor. Blend until smooth, about 1 minute. Season to taste with additional salt and crushed red pepper and blend to combine. Transfer the hummus to a bowl, cover and refrigerate for at least 30 minutes. Meanwhile, preheat oven to 350°F.

To prepare the pita chips, brush both sides of the pitas with oil and sprinkle with salt and pepper. Cut each pita into 8 wedges and place the wedges on a large baking sheet in a single layer. Bake until the chips begin to brown, about 6 minutes. Flip the chips and return to the oven until they begin to brown on the second side, about 6 minutes. Remove from the oven and let cool.

Serve the pita chips with chilled hummus. Makes 8 servings.

Grilled Portabella Mushrooms with Montreal-Style Steak Seasoning

Cardile Brothers/Giorgio Fresh/Monterey Mushrooms

4 large Portabella caps,
4-6 inches in diameter (see tips)

MARINADE
¾ cup canola oil
½ cup red (or white) wine vinegar

¼ cup soy sauce
¼ cup packed light brown sugar
4 tablespoons Montreal-style
steak seasoning blend

In a bowl, combine marinade ingredients and blend well with a whisk.

Place mushrooms in a shallow nonmetallic dish or pan and pour the marinade over the mushrooms. Marinate in the refrigerator for 2 hours, turning occasionally to ensure uniform coating. Preheat the grill to medium-high.

Remove the mushrooms from the marinade and place on the hot grill. Grill on each side for 5 minutes, or until tender. Remove the mushrooms from the grill, slice, and serve immediately. Makes 4 servings.

Tips: You can also use baby Portabellas for this recipe. Use a grill pan and adjust cooking times accordingly. Also, you can bake the large mushrooms in a 350°F oven for 5-7 minutes; less time for the smaller mushrooms.

Disappearing Buffalo Chicken Dip

Unilever

2 cups diced or shredded
  cooked chicken

¼ cup cayenne
  pepper sauce

1 cup Hellmann's* or
  Best Foods* Real or
  Light Mayonnaise

1 cup shredded Cheddar
  cheese (about 4 ounces)

2 tablespoons finely
  chopped green onions
  (optional)

1 teaspoon lemon juice

¼ cup crumbled
  blue cheese

Celery sticks or other
  dippers, for serving

Preheat oven to 375°F.

In a bowl, toss chicken with pepper sauce. Stir in
mayonnaise, Cheddar, green onions and lemon
juice. Turn into a shallow 1½-quart casserole.
Sprinkle with blue cheese.

Bake, uncovered, for 20 minutes, or until bubbling.
Serve hot with celery and/or your favorite dippers.
Makes 3 cups.

* Brands may vary by region; substitute a similar product.

Unilever

Sticky Raspberry Chipotle Ham Rolls

Farmland Foods

¾ cup butter

½ cup minced sweet
  yellow onion

1 6-ounce package
  Kirkland Signature
  spiral-ham glaze mix

½ cup raspberry jam

1 teaspoon plus 1 table-
  spoon prepared yellow
  mustard, divided

½-1 teaspoon chipotle
  chile powder

1 8-ounce container
  honey-nut cream cheese

24 small Hawaiian
  dinner rolls

24 2-by-2-inch slices
  Kirkland Signature
  spiral-sliced ham

24 slices Havarti or
  Muenster cheese

Melt butter in a saucepan over medium-high heat.
Add onion and cook until tender. Add glaze mix,
jam, 1 teaspoon mustard and chipotle powder.
Bring to a boil; remove from the heat and let cool.

In a small bowl, combine cream cheese and
1 tablespoon mustard; mix until smooth. Set aside.

Slice dinner rolls in half. Spread cream cheese
mixture on each bottom half. Top with 1 slice of
ham and 1 slice of cheese (folded into quarters).
Add top half of bun.

Place the sandwiches in 2 buttered 13-by-9-by-2-
inch pans. Pour the raspberry sauce mixture evenly
over the ham rolls. Cover tightly with aluminum
foil; refrigerate overnight.

Preheat oven to 350°F. Bake the ham rolls, covered,
for 25 minutes. Remove the foil and bake for an
additional 10 minutes, or until heated through.
Serve warm. Makes 24 appetizer servings.

Farmland.
Good Food from the Heartland®
Since 1959

Zesty Guacamole

Don Miguel Mexican Foods

3-4 avocados

2 tablespoons lemon juice (or to taste)

½ cup diced red bell pepper

1½ small jalapeños, finely chopped
  or minced

1 cup chopped green onions

1 cup chopped cilantro

Salt, pepper, garlic powder and
  cayenne pepper

1 small tomato, diced

Cut avocados in half, remove the pit, and scoop out the flesh into a bowl. Gently mash with a fork until semi-smooth in texture. Add lemon juice to prevent browning and for added flavor.

Stir in bell pepper and jalapeño. Stir in green onions and cilantro. Season to taste with salt, pepper, garlic powder and cayenne pepper, stirring until well blended.

Cover tightly and refrigerate for 30 minutes. (Placing the pits on top will help to preserve the color of the guacamole. Remove before serving.)

When ready to serve, add diced tomato and stir. This dip is delicious with any of your favorite Don Miguel products, especially empanadas. Makes 6-8 servings.

Tip: Set aside a small amount of red bell pepper and cilantro and sprinkle on top of the guacamole as a garnish.

Ham and Brie Quesadillas with Cranberry Salsa

Farmland Foods

9 ounces Brie cheese, diced

6 burrito-size flour tortillas

3 Kirkland Signature spiral-sliced ham slices, cut in half

3 tablespoons butter

CRANBERRY SALSA

1 cup whole berry cranberry sauce

1 cup diced apple

3 tablespoons pecan pieces

1 tablespoon horseradish

1 teaspoon grated orange zest

To prepare the salsa, combine cranberry sauce, apple, pecans, horseradish and orange zest. Set aside.

Sprinkle diced Brie (about ⅓ cup) on one half of each tortilla. Top with a ham slice. Fold the tortilla in half, forming a half-moon shape.

Melt 1 tablespoon butter in a large skillet over medium heat. Place 2 filled tortillas in the skillet and cook for about 1 minute on each side, or until browned and crisp. Repeat with the remaining butter and filled tortillas.

Cut each quesadilla into 4 wedges. Serve topped with cranberry salsa. Makes 24 appetizer servings.

Bacon-Wrapped SPAM Bites

Hormel Foods/Kirkland Signature

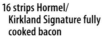

16 strips Hormel/ Kirkland Signature fully cooked bacon

1 12-ounce can SPAM Less Sodium, cut into 32 cubes

32 wooden toothpicks

½ cup honey mustard

¼ cup firmly packed brown sugar

2 tablespoons apple juice

Preheat oven to 400°F.

Cut each bacon slice in half. Wrap bacon around each cube of SPAM; secure with a toothpick. Place in a 13-by-9-inch baking dish.

In a bowl, combine mustard, brown sugar and apple juice; mix well. Drizzle over the bacon-wrapped SPAM.

Bake for 15-20 minutes, or until the bacon is crisp. Makes 16 servings.

Coconut and Lime Grilled Shrimp
Market Source

Grated zest and juice of
  1 Market Source* lime

2 garlic cloves

¼ cup chopped
  yellow onion

⅓ cup fresh
  cilantro, chopped

⅓ cup shredded
  sweetened coconut

¼ cup olive oil

¼ cup soy sauce

1 pound raw medium
  shrimp, peeled
  and deveined

Metal or wood skewers

In a blender, combine lime zest, lime juice, garlic, onion, cilantro, coconut, oil and soy sauce. Blend until smooth.

Combine the sauce with shrimp in a resealable bag and toss to coat. Marinate in the refrigerator for at least 2 hours but not more than 4 hours.

Preheat an outdoor grill to medium-high. Make sure there are no flames, just glowing charcoal.

If you are using wood skewers, soak them in water for at least 20 minutes so they don't catch fire. Thread the shrimp onto skewers.

Grill the shrimp for 2-3 minutes, until nicely browned, and then turn over to brown the other side for 2-3 minutes. Makes 6 servings.

Brands may vary by region; substitute a similar product.

Spicy Southwestern Mussels
Penn Cove Shellfish

4 pounds Penn Cove*
  mussels or
  Mediterranean mussels

¼ cup extra-virgin olive oil

½ cup chopped
  Roma tomatoes

½ cup chopped
  green onions

2 tablespoons
  chopped garlic

1 tablespoon crushed
  red pepper flakes

2 tablespoons chopped
  fresh cilantro

Juice of ½ lemon

1 12-ounce bottle of beer
  (your choice)

Crusty bread, for serving

Rinse mussels under cold running water. Discard any mussels that do not try to stay closed after the shell is squeezed shut, have broken shells, or have an "off" odor.

Heat oil in a large skillet over medium heat. Add tomatoes, green onions, garlic and red pepper; sauté briefly. Add mussels, cilantro, lemon juice and beer. Cover and turn the heat to high. Steam for 5-7 minutes, or until the mussels are all open and the meats are no longer translucent. Discard any that do not open.

Spoon the mussels into serving bowls and ladle the sauce over the top. Serve immediately. Accompany with bread and cold ale. Makes 8-16 appetizer servings or 4-6 entrée servings.

Tip: Store uncooked mussels in the refrigerator, covered with ice or a damp cloth. Drain any liquid from the container daily.

Brands may vary by region; substitute a similar product.

Mussels with Diced Fresh Tomatoes and Chardonnay
North Coast Seafoods

½ cup diced fresh tomatoes

2 tablespoons minced garlic

2 pounds North Coast Seafoods* PEI mussels

1 cup Chardonnay

Juice of 1 lemon

1 tablespoon chopped fresh parsley

1 tablespoon sliced green onion

Salt and pepper

¼ pound butter

Crusty bread, for serving

In a large sauté pan, cook tomatoes and garlic over medium heat for about 3 minutes.

Increase the heat to high. Add mussels and wine. Cover the pan and cook for 3-4 minutes, or until the mussels have opened.

Add lemon juice, parsley, green onion, and salt and pepper to taste. Add butter and toss everything in the pan. Pour into a serving bowl.

Serve with crusty bread. Makes 4 servings.

Tip: This dish will serve 2 as an entrée.

* Brands may vary by region; substitute a similar product.

Sweet and Spicy Mixed Nuts

Ann's House of Nuts/Harvest Manor Farms

Silicon baking mat (Silpat) and/or parchment paper

4 tablespoons corn syrup

4 tablespoons sugar

¼ teaspoon Worcestershire sauce

¼ teaspoon cayenne pepper

¼ teaspoon Chinese five-spice powder

⅛ teaspoon ground cumin

Up to 1 tablespoon freshly squeezed orange juice

2 cups Kirkland Signature Extra Fancy Mixed Nuts

Preheat oven to 350°F. Line a cookie sheet with Silpat or greased parchment paper.

In a bowl, combine corn syrup, sugar, Worcestershire sauce, cayenne, five-spice powder, cumin and enough orange juice to blend; the mixture will be thick. Add nuts, mixing gently to coat.

Spread the nuts on the prepared cookie sheet.

Bake for 5 minutes, then stir to coat. Bake 10 minutes longer, or until bubbly.

Immediately turn the nuts onto a sheet of parchment paper, as the coating hardens quickly. Keep turning and separating until the nuts no longer stick to the parchment or each other. The nuts should be cooled individually, not clumped together. Makes 6-8 servings.

Crunchy Cranberry-Cinnamon Snack

Quick & Easy

General Mills

¼ cup sugar

1 teaspoon ground cinnamon

¼ cup butter or margarine

1½ cups Corn Chex* cereal

1½ cups Rice Chex* cereal

1½ cups Wheat Chex* cereal

½ cup dried cranberries, dried cherries or raisins

In a small bowl, mix sugar and cinnamon.

In a large microwavable bowl, microwave butter, uncovered, on high for about 40 seconds, or until melted. Stir in cereals until evenly coated. Microwave for 2 minutes, stirring after 1 minute.

Sprinkle half of the sugar mixture evenly over the cereal and stir. Sprinkle with the remaining sugar mixture and stir. Microwave for 1 minute. Stir in cranberries.

Spread on paper towels to cool. Store in an airtight container. Makes 8 servings.

Nutritional information: Each ½-cup serving has 190 calories, 2 g protein, 31 g carbohydrates, 6 g fat, 15 mg cholesterol, 2 g fiber, 240 mg sodium, 14 g sugar.

* Brands may vary by region; substitute a similar product.

Make Chex Party Mix!

Making the Best Coffee … with a French Press

Kirkland Signature

Fresh cold tap or bottled water, about 6 ounces per cup

San Francisco Bay or Kirkland Signature premium whole bean coffee

Coffee grinder

French press

Cream, sugar or other preferred condiments

Put water on to boil.

Grind coffee coarser than for drip—it should look like coarse sand.

Remove the French press plunger and add the ground coffee, about 1 rounded tablespoon per cup; adjust to taste.

Remove the boiling water from the heat and let cool slightly, 10 seconds or so. Add enough of the water to wet all the grounds. Wait a few seconds.

Add the remaining water, and briskly stir. Wait 2 minutes, then stir briskly again.

Wait 2 more minutes, then very slowly insert the plunger and press down as far as it will go. You will "feel" the right speed. DO NOT remove the plunger; leave it pushed down.

Pour and add your favorite condiments.

Notes: There will be more "solids" in French press coffee. If you have difficulty getting the plunger down, the coffee was ground too fine. If the coffee tastes too strong, try grinding coarser, using less, or brewing for a shorter time. If it's too weak, try grinding finer, using more, or brewing longer.

Cucumber Mojito with Vodka

Mastronardi Produce/SUNSET

4-5 slices SUNSET* cucumber
4-5 sprigs fresh mint, leaves removed
Ice
2 ounces Kirkland Signature vodka

1½ tablespoons fresh lime juice
1½ tablespoons simple syrup (see note)
1½ ounces soda water
Cucumber wheel and fresh mint sprig,
    for garnish

Drop cucumber slices and mint leaves into a cocktail shaker. With a muddler, press the cucumber and mint to release their flavors. Fill the shaker with ice. Add vodka, lime juice and simple syrup. Cap and shake vigorously. Add soda water.

Pour into a large glass. Garnish with a cucumber wheel on the rim of the glass and a mint sprig. Makes 1 serving.

Note: Simple syrup is available at bar supply stores. You can make it by combining 2 cups sugar with 2 cups water. Bring to a quick boil. Cool. Store, covered, in the refrigerator for up to 1 month.

Brands may vary by region; substitute a similar product.

Cranberry Limeade
Kirkland Signature/Cott

Quick & Easy

3 cups Kirkland Signature cranberry juice cocktail

2 6-ounce cans frozen limeade concentrate, thawed

2 20-ounce bottles sparkling water, chilled

Lime wedges and cranberries, for garnish

Mix cranberry juice cocktail and limeade concentrate in a large plastic or glass pitcher. Refrigerate for about 1 hour, or until chilled.

Just before serving, stir in sparkling water. Serve over ice. Garnish with lime wedges and cranberries. Makes 4-6 servings.

Sunkist Sangria Blanca
Sunkist Growers

½ cup freshly squeezed Sunkist* orange juice

½ cup freshly squeezed Sunkist* lemon juice

½ cup sugar

1 bottle (750 ml) Chablis or other dry white wine, chilled

1 bottle (10 ounces) club soda, chilled

Ice cubes

¼ cup Curaçao or other orange-flavored liqueur

1 Sunkist* lemon and orange, cut into cartwheel slices

In a large pitcher, combine orange juice, lemon juice and sugar; stir to dissolve the sugar.

Add the remaining ingredients and stir well. Makes 6 servings.

Nutritional information: Each serving has 210 calories, 0.3 g protein, 28 g carbohydrates, 0 g fat, 0 mg cholesterol, 0.1 g fiber, 13 mg sodium.

* Brands may vary by region; substitute a similar product.

Sunkist

Tropical Citrus Spritzer
Apple & Eve

3 (6.75-ounce) Apple & Eve*
Fruitables Tropical Orange
juice boxes, chilled

3 cups Apple & Eve* Ruby
Red Grapefruit Juice
Cocktail, chilled

3 cups lemon/lime
carbonated beverage
(or seltzer), chilled

Ice cubes

2 cups assorted cut fresh
fruit (such as orange and
kiwi slices, pineapple
wedges and halved
strawberries)

Fresh mint sprigs,
for garnish

In a large bowl or pitcher, stir together the juices.
Add lemon/lime beverage or seltzer and stir gently.

Fill 8 decorative tall glasses about two-thirds full
of ice. Divide fruit among the glasses.

Pour the juice mixture into the glasses. Garnish with
mint sprigs. Makes 8 servings.

* Brands may vary by region; substitute a similar product.

Ultimate Lemon and Lime Soda
Paramount Citrus

2 tablespoons fresh-
squeezed Paramount
Citrus* lime juice

1 tablespoon fresh-
squeezed Paramount
Citrus* lemon juice

3 ounces chilled
soda water

Long fresh lemon and lime
zest twists, for garnish

ZESTY LIME SYRUP

3 tablespoons finely
minced lime zest
(with no white pith)

2 cups sugar

2 cups water

To prepare the syrup, combine zest, sugar and
water in a small saucepan. Bring to a boil over
high heat. Boil for 1 minute, then remove from the
heat and let cool. (You can store the syrup in the
refrigerator for up to 3 weeks.) Makes 2¼ cups.

Fill a large tall glass with ice. Add lime juice,
lemon juice and ¼ cup of the syrup. Add soda
water and stir.

Garnish with lemon and lime zests twisted together.
Makes 1 serving.

* Brands may vary by region; substitute a similar product.

PARAMOUNT
Citrus

Strawberry Banana Smoothie

Campbell's

1 cup V8 V-Fusion Strawberry Banana Juice*
1 cup vanilla low-fat yogurt

½ cup frozen strawberries
½ cup sliced banana

Place juice, yogurt, strawberries and banana in a blender. Cover and blend until the mixture is smooth. Serve immediately. Makes 2 servings.

* *Brands may vary by region; substitute a similar product.*

Soups & Sides

Cheddar Soup with Granny Smith Apples

Domex Superfresh Growers

3 tablespoons
  unsalted butter

1 large onion, diced

⅓ cup all-purpose flour

2 teaspoons dry mustard

4 cups chicken broth

2 Superfresh Growers*
  Granny Smith apples

1 cup apple cider
  or apple juice

10 ounces sharp Cheddar
  cheese, grated (about
  3 cups)

Hot pepper sauce

Salt and freshly ground
  black pepper

Melt butter in a large saucepan over medium heat. Add onions and sauté until tender and aromatic, 5-7 minutes.

Sprinkle flour and dry mustard over the onions and stir to evenly coat.

Continue cooking, stirring often, for 1-2 minutes.

Add broth, stirring until well blended.

Peel, quarter and core 1 of the apples and finely chop it. Add apple to the soup, cover, reduce the heat to low, and simmer until the soup is thickened and the apple is tender, about 10 minutes.

Stir in cider and grated cheese and cook a few minutes longer, stirring constantly, until the cheese is fully melted.

Puree the soup in a blender. Stir in a few drops of hot pepper sauce and salt and pepper to taste.

Quarter and core the remaining apple and cut in ½-inch dice.

Ladle the soup into warmed bowls, sprinkle with diced apple and serve immediately. Makes 4-6 servings.

* Brands may vary by region; substitute a similar product.

Smoky Apple and Butternut Squash Soup

Pennsylvania Apple/New York Apple

1 tablespoon butter

1 tablespoon olive oil

3 large onions, finely
  chopped (about 4½ cups)

1 teaspoon chipotle
  chile powder

2 pounds butternut squash,
  peeled and cut into
  chunks (about 6 cups)

1 pound sweet Eastern*
  apples, peeled and
  cut into chunks (about
  3½ cups)

1 cup apple juice
  (more if necessary)

1 cup chicken broth

½ teaspoon salt

½ teaspoon ground
  black pepper

Toasted pecans, sour
  cream and thin apple
  slices, for garnish
  (optional)

Heat butter and oil in a large saucepan over medium heat. Add onions and chipotle powder; cook, stirring, until the onions are tender, about 10 minutes.

Add squash, apples, apple juice, chicken broth, salt and pepper; bring to a boil. Cover and cook over low heat until the apples and squash are very soft, about 30 minutes. Cool.

Puree with an immersion blender or a food processor. Return to the saucepan and bring to a simmer, adding more apple juice or broth if needed.

Garnish with toasted pecans, sour cream swirls and apple slices, if desired. Makes 7 servings.

Nutritional information: Each serving (1 cup) has 130 calories, 2 g protein, 23 g carbohydrates, 4 g fat, 1.5 g saturated fat, 5 mg cholesterol, 3 g fiber and 290 mg sodium.

* Brands may vary by region; substitute a similar product.

Fall Harvest Soup Puree

Kirkland Signature/Bolthouse Farms

¼ cup butter

2 sweet potatoes, peeled and chopped

1 apple, peeled, cored and chopped

1 onion, chopped

½ cup lentils

½ teaspoon ground ginger

½ teaspoon ground black pepper

1 teaspoon salt

½ teaspoon ground cumin

½ teaspoon chili powder

½ teaspoon paprika

1½ cups Kirkland Signature* 100% Organic Carrot Juice Organic

2½ cups vegetable broth

Feta cheese crumbles

Shredded carrots

Melt butter in a large pot over medium-high heat. Add sweet potatoes, apple and onion to the pot and cook, stirring, for 10 minutes.

Stir in lentils, ginger, pepper, salt, cumin, chili powder, paprika, carrot juice and vegetable broth. Bring to a boil, then reduce the heat to medium-low, cover, and simmer for 30 minutes, or until tender.

Use an immersion blender to puree the soup in the cooking pot. (Or puree in small batches in a blender.)

Bring the pureed soup to a simmer over medium-high heat, about 10 minutes. Add water as needed to thin the soup to your preferred consistency.

To serve, sprinkle with feta and carrots. Makes 6 servings.

* Brands may vary by region; substitute a similar product.

Thai Tom Yum Soup

Westhaven

Dry white wine (optional)

5 pounds Westhaven* whole live littleneck clams

4 cups water or seafood stock (unsalted)

1 15-ounce can whole peeled plum tomatoes, chopped

3 ounces button mushrooms or shiitake mushrooms, halved or sliced

Lime or lemon juice, soy sauce and fish sauce, for seasoning

Fresh cilantro leaves, for garnish

TOM YUM PASTE

1 tablespoon fish sauce

1 tablespoon palm sugar

1 tablespoon chili paste

1 teaspoon lime juice

To prepare the tom yum paste, combine all ingredients in a bowl. Set aside.

Cover the bottom of a large pot with 1 inch of water or a slosh of white wine. Bring to a rapid boil over high heat. Add clams to the pan, cover, and cook for 4-5 minutes, shaking the pan to evenly distribute the heat. Remove the clams as they open, so they don't overcook. Shuck the clams.

In a saucepan, bring water or seafood stock to a boil. Stir in tom yum paste and tomatoes. Add clams and mushrooms. Bring back to a boil.

Just before serving, season to taste with lime or lemon juice, soy sauce and fish sauce. Garnish with cilantro and serve hot. Makes 6 servings.

* Brands may vary by region; substitute a similar product.

WESTHAVEN.

QUALITY OCEAN INTERNATIONAL

Sunset Chilled Gazpacho Soup with Crab

Mastronardi Produce/SUNSET

1½ teaspoons minced fresh garlic

¼ cup diced white onion

1 cup peeled, seeded and diced
  SUNSET* cucumber

½ cup diced SUNSET* red, yellow
  or orange pepper

¼ cup coarsely chopped fresh cilantro

¼ cup coarsely chopped Italian parsley

1½ cups diced rustic bread
  (crusts removed)

1 pound SUNSET* Campari tomatoes,
  diced (about 2 cups)

⅓ cup thinly sliced celery

½ cup extra-virgin olive oil

2 tablespoons sherry vinegar

1½ teaspoons sugar

1 teaspoon salt

¼ teaspoon ground black pepper

¼ teaspoon crushed red pepper

1 cup water

GARNISHES

¾ cup fresh crabmeat

Cilantro leaves

In a large bowl, combine all ingredients. In 2 or 3 batches, process the ingredients in a food processor or large blender until almost pureed. The gazpacho should still have some texture.

Mix all the processed batches together and refrigerate, covered, in a nonreactive (plastic, glass or stainless steel) container for at least 4 hours or overnight.

Serve cold in chilled bowls. Garnish each bowl with a small mound of crab in the center and cilantro if desired. Makes 4-6 appetizer servings.

* Brands may vary by region; substitute a similar product.

Steelhead, Roasted Pepper and Corn Chowder

AquaGold Seafood/Michael Cutler

3 red bell peppers
Olive oil
1 steelhead fillet (2-2½ pounds)
Salt and pepper
¼ pound pancetta, cut in ¼-inch dice
1 jumbo yellow onion, finely diced

¼ cup dry sherry
1 15-ounce can cream-style corn
16 ounces frozen corn kernels
32 ounces fat-free half-and-half
½ teaspoon cayenne pepper
2 medium red potatoes, cut in medium dice

Preheat oven to 450°F.

Coat bell peppers with oil; place on a baking sheet. Place steelhead, skin side down, on a separate baking sheet; season with salt and pepper. Bake steelhead for 15 minutes. Roast peppers for 30 minutes, or until the skins are blackened and split. Set both aside to cool.

Add pancetta to a 5-quart pot and brown over medium heat; set aside. Add onion, lightly salt and cook until tender, about 3 minutes. Add sherry and cook until completely evaporated.

Add corn, half-and-half, cayenne and potatoes. Remove skin, core and seeds from the peppers; cut in ½-inch dice and add to the pot. Simmer until the potatoes are tender, about 30 minutes. Do not boil.

Remove skin and dark meat from the steelhead. Break fish into bite-size pieces. Add steelhead and pancetta to the pot and heat through. Season with salt and pepper. Serve immediately. Makes 6 servings.

White Bean Chicken Chili
Kirkland Signature/Kerry

3 tablespoons vegetable oil

2 cups diced yellow onion

3 cups boneless, skinless chicken breast cut in bite-size pieces (about 4 breasts)

1 tablespoon finely minced fresh garlic

1 quart Kirkland Signature Organic or Natural Chicken Stock

2 15-ounce cans white beans, drained and rinsed

1 cup frozen corn

2 4-ounce cans diced green chiles

2 teaspoons dried oregano leaves

1 teaspoon ground cumin

1 teaspoon ground coriander

2 tablespoons freshly squeezed lime juice

Chopped fresh cilantro, shredded Monterey Jack, sour cream and crushed tortilla chips, for serving

Heat oil in a 4-quart pot over medium heat. Add onions and sauté just until soft and translucent.

Add chicken and sauté until no longer pink. Stir in garlic and sauté until fragrant, about 30 seconds.

Add chicken stock, beans, corn, chiles, oregano, cumin and coriander. Turn the heat to low and simmer for 20 minutes.

Stir in lime juice. Remove from the heat.

Serve in bowls, garnished with cilantro, shredded cheese, sour cream and/or crushed tortilla chips. Makes 8 servings.

Tip: Shredded or diced Kirkland Signature rotisserie chicken can be substituted for the chicken breast.

Creamy Chicken Tortilla Soup
ConAgra Foods

2 10-ounce cans Ro*Tel* Original Diced Tomatoes & Green Chilies, undrained

2 14-ounce cans reduced-sodium chicken broth

1 16-ounce can Rosarita No Fat Traditional Refried Beans

½ cup frozen whole kernel corn

2 cups shredded cooked chicken

Fried corn tortilla strips or chips (optional)

Shredded Monterey Jack cheese (optional)

Combine undrained tomatoes and chicken broth in a medium saucepan. Stir in beans and corn. Bring to a boil, then reduce the heat to low and simmer for 5 minutes, stirring frequently.

Add chicken and heat through.

Serve topped with tortilla strips and cheese, if desired. Makes 4 servings.

* Brands may vary by region; substitute a similar product.

Frozen Plum Soufflés with Chilled Plum Basil Soup

Farms Co S.A.

SOUFFLÉS

2¼ cups chopped pitted Fruit Stand
   by Farms Co* Angeleno plums

¾ cup sugar, divided

4 large egg yolks

⅓ cup light corn syrup

3 tablespoons unsalted butter, softened

1 cup chilled whipping cream

1 teaspoon vanilla extract

SOUP

2¼ cups chopped pitted Fruit Stand
   by Farms Co* Angeleno plums
   (about 1 pound)

⅓ cup sugar

6 tablespoons water

2 plums, halved, pitted and sliced

2 tablespoons thinly sliced basil leaves

To prepare the soufflés, combine chopped plums and ¼ cup sugar in a heavy medium saucepan. Simmer over medium heat until the mixture is reduced to 1½ cups, stirring often, about 8 minutes. Using a hand blender, puree until smooth. Chill until cold.

In a medium metal bowl, whisk yolks, corn syrup, butter and ¼ cup sugar. Set the bowl over a saucepan of simmering water. Whisk constantly for about 5 minutes, or until the mixture thickens. Remove from the heat and beat until cool and thick, about 5 minutes.

Beat cream, vanilla and ¼ cup sugar in a large bowl until stiff peaks form. Fold in the plum puree and then the egg mixture. Spoon the mixture into 6 to 8 individual (6-ounce) soufflé dishes. Cover with plastic and freeze overnight or up to 1 week.

To prepare the soup, combine chopped plums, sugar and water in a heavy medium saucepan. Simmer over medium heat for about 3 minutes, or until the sugar has dissolved. Transfer to a food processor and puree. Cover and chill until cold.

To serve, place the soufflés in warm water for 30 seconds one at a time. Unmold each in a bowl. Pour soup around the soufflé, add plum slices, and garnish with basil. Serve immediately. Makes 6-8 servings.

* Brands may vary by region; substitute a similar product.

FruitStand
Farmsco S.A.

Aromatic Fresh Pea Soup with a Hint of Spice
New World Farms

2-3 ounces pancetta
or bacon

1½ pounds New World
Farms* fresh shelled
English peas

5-6 ounces fresh trimmed
French beans

4 cups chicken stock
(regular or low sodium)

1 bay leaf

Salt and pepper

SPICE BLEND

2 teaspoons sugar

4 teaspoons curry powder

1 teaspoon garam masala

1 teaspoon ground cumin

1 teaspoon ground
black pepper

1 teaspoon ground turmeric

¼ teaspoon garlic powder

To prepare the spice blend, combine all ingredients and mix well. Set aside.

Heat a medium-size pot over medium heat. Add pancetta or bacon and cook, stirring, for 5 minutes.

Add peas, beans and 2 tablespoons spice blend. Cook over medium heat, stirring, for 2-3 minutes.

Add chicken stock and bay leaf. Cook, covered, until the peas and beans are tender, about 7-8 minutes. Remove the pot from the stove and let cool for about 1 hour.

Discard the bay leaf. Transfer the mixture to a blender and puree.

Pour the soup back into the pot and heat until warm. Season to taste with salt and pepper. Add more spice blend if desired. If you prefer a thinner soup, add more chicken stock. Makes 6 servings.

Brands may vary by region; substitute a similar product.

NEW WORLD FARMS®

Jalapeño Cornbread
Rupari Foods

This dish is a delicious complement to Tony Roma's ribs.

4 tablespoons honey

2 sticks (8 ounces) butter

1 cup all-purpose flour

1 cup corn flour

1 cup cornmeal

2 tablespoons
baking powder

1 teaspoon sugar

3 large eggs

1 cup canned creamed corn

1 cup milk

½ cup sour cream

4 jalapeños, seeded
and chopped

1 cup shredded pepper
jack cheese

Pinch of salt

8- to 10-inch cast iron
frying pan

Warm honey and butter in a small saucepan over medium heat until the butter is melted.

In a bowl, combine flour, corn flour, cornmeal, baking powder and sugar.

In another bowl, whisk together half of the honey butter mixture with eggs, corn, milk and sour cream. Slowly add to the dry ingredients, stirring continuously. Stir in jalapeños, cheese and salt.

Lightly spray the frying pan, then place it on the middle shelf of the oven. Preheat oven to 425°F.

Pour the batter into the hot pan and bake for 25-30 minutes, or until the top is lightly browned and a toothpick inserted in the center comes out clean. Remove from the oven and let cool for 10-15 minutes. Brush with the remaining honey butter.

Serve with Tony Roma's ribs. Makes 4-6 servings.

TONY ROMA'S
WORLD · FAMOUS · RIBS

Mediterranean Pipérade

BC Hot House Foods, Inc./The Oppenheimer Group

1 tablespoon extra-virgin olive oil or butter

1 medium onion, chopped

2 plump garlic cloves, minced

3 greenhouse-grown sweet bell peppers (a combination of red, yellow and orange peppers), coarsely chopped

4 large hothouse tomatoes, coarsely chopped

1 teaspoon fresh thyme leaves or ½ teaspoon dried thyme

Hot sauce

Salt and freshly ground pepper

Heat oil or butter in a large nonstick skillet or heavy casserole over medium heat.

Add onion and cook until tender. Add garlic and peppers and cook for 10 minutes, stirring often.

Add tomatoes and thyme. Season to taste with hot sauce, salt and pepper. Simmer for about 10 minutes.

Cover, reduce the heat, and simmer for another 15 minutes.

Serve as the perfect accompaniment for eggs or as a topping for pizza, pasta, bruschetta or toast. Makes 5-6 servings.

expect the world from us

Stuffed and Roasted Sweet Bell Peppers
Village Farms

1 cup quinoa

7 red, yellow and orange Village Farms* sweet bell peppers

1 tablespoon olive oil

1 red onion, chopped

½ pound sliced mushrooms

1 cup chopped carrots

½ cup chopped fresh parsley

¼ pound baby spinach

1½ teaspoons ground cinnamon

¾ teaspoon ground cumin

Salt and pepper to taste

½ cup roasted salted cashews

Cook quinoa according to package directions.

Core, seed and chop 1 bell pepper. Slice the tops off the other 6 peppers and remove cores and seeds.

Heat oil in a large skillet over medium heat. Cook onion, stirring occasionally, until transparent, 8-10 minutes. Add mushrooms and cook until soft, 4-5 minutes. Add carrots and chopped pepper; cook until soft. Stir in parsley and spinach. As the spinach wilts, stir in cinnamon, cumin and cooked quinoa, tossing gently to combine. Add salt, pepper and cashews; cook for 1-2 minutes. Set aside until just warm.

Preheat oven to 350°F. Oil a 13-by-9-inch baking pan.

Pack the filling evenly into the 6 bell peppers. Replace the top of each pepper and arrange upright in the prepared pan. Cover snugly with foil and bake until the peppers are tender and juicy and the filling is hot throughout, about 1 hour. Makes 6 servings.

Brands may vary by region; substitute a similar product.

All-Season Green Bean and Corn Casserole
Bybee Foods

4 tablespoons butter, divided

5 tablespoons extra-virgin olive oil

4 cups sliced fresh mushrooms

1 medium white or yellow onion, chopped

1 tablespoon unbleached flour

1 cup half-and-half

1 cup grated Jarlsberg cheese (or white Cheddar cheese)

½ teaspoon dried thyme or 2 tablespoons chopped fresh thyme

4 tablespoons chopped fresh chives, divided

2 cups Bybee Foods* Organic Petite Green Beans, thawed ⬥Organic

1 cup Bybee Foods* Organic Supersweet Corn, thawed ⬥Organic

Sea salt and freshly ground pepper

1 cup dry bread crumbs

2 tablespoons freshly grated Parmesan cheese

Preheat oven to 375°F.

In a large skillet over medium heat, combine 2 tablespoons butter, oil, mushrooms and onions. Cook, stirring occasionally, for 8-10 minutes, or until they begin to sweat.

Stir in flour. Stir in half-and-half, Jarlsberg, thyme and 2 tablespoons chives; cook for an additional 5 minutes.

Add green beans, corn, and salt and pepper to taste. Stir well and transfer to a greased 13-by-9-inch baking dish.

Melt remaining butter and combine with bread crumbs, Parmesan and remaining chives. Sprinkle over the casserole.

Bake, uncovered, for 30 minutes, or until the casserole is hot and bubbling. Let rest for 10 minutes before serving. Makes 5-6 servings.

Brands may vary by region; substitute a similar product.

Sweet and Spicy Coleslaw

Trinity Fruit

6 cups shredded green cabbage

2 cups shredded red or purple cabbage

2 cups shredded carrots

½ cup thinly sliced green onions

3 fresh California white-flesh nectarines,
   diced into ¼-inch cubes

3 jalapeños, diced, with seeds removed

1 cup mayonnaise

2 tablespoons vinegar

1 tablespoon white sugar

1 teaspoon dried celery seeds

½ teaspoon salt

½ teaspoon pepper

In a large bowl, combine cabbages, carrots, green onions, nectarines and jalapeños. In a small bowl, stir together mayonnaise, vinegar, sugar, celery seeds, salt and pepper. Pour over the cabbage mixture. Toss lightly to coat. Cover and chill for 2-4 hours. Makes 10-12 servings.

Recipe created by Travis Jones.

Natural Herb-Roasted Potatoes
MountainKing Potatoes

1¾ pounds MountainKing*
Butter Gold potatoes,
cut into 1-inch pieces

3 garlic cloves, minced

3-4 tablespoons olive oil

Coarse salt and freshly
ground pepper

1 sprig fresh rosemary,
leaves removed

Preheat oven to 350°F.

Place potatoes and garlic on a rimmed baking sheet. Drizzle with oil and season to taste with salt and pepper. Toss to coat.

Roast until dark golden brown and tender, 30-45 minutes. During the last 5 minutes of roasting, increase the temperature to 500°F and sprinkle with rosemary leaves.

Remove from the oven and serve.
Makes 4-6 servings.

* Brands may vary by region; substitute a similar product.

Healthy, Simple Au Gratin Potatoes
Top Brass/Farm Fresh Direct

2 pounds of your
favorite potatoes

3 tablespoons sea salt

1 tablespoon
granulated garlic

Pepper, to taste

Dried minced onions or
minced fresh onions,
to taste

3-4 cups shredded cheese
(Cheddar or marble)

1 quart low-fat milk

Preheat oven to 350°F. Grease a 12-by-9-inch baking dish.

Peel (or scrub) potatoes and slice thin.

Layer ⅓ of the potatoes in the prepared pan. Sprinkle with ⅓ of salt, garlic, pepper, onions, cheese and milk. Repeat with 2 more layers.

Bake until the potatoes are tender, 60-90 minutes. Makes 6-8 servings.

Tip: For a creamier dish, add a can of low-fat cream of mushroom soup to the milk.

Salads

Mediterranean Chicken Salad
Ready Pac

4 6-ounce boneless, skinless chicken breasts

¼ cup fresh lemon juice

2 garlic cloves, crushed

1 teaspoon salt

¾ teaspoon freshly ground black pepper

1 16-ounce bag Ready Pac* Grand Parisian Complete Salad

½ cup thinly sliced red onion, cut in half

½ cup pitted Kalamata olives, drained and cut in half

2 teaspoons capers, drained

1 tablespoon Italian herb seasoning

2 tablespoons olive oil

Arrange chicken in a shallow glass baking dish. In a small bowl, whisk together lemon juice, garlic, salt and pepper. Pour over the chicken. Let stand for 1 hour at room temperature, turning once.

Meanwhile, remove the feta cheese, cranberries, frosted almonds and dressing from the salad bag and set aside. Place the salad greens in a salad bowl and add onion slices, olives and capers. Toss lightly with salad forks. Chill.

Remove the chicken from the marinade; drain well. Generously coat the chicken with Italian herbs.

Heat oil in a skillet over medium heat. Add the chicken and sauté for 3-4 minutes on each side, or until cooked through. Transfer to a platter and let rest for 1-2 minutes.

Remove the chilled salad greens mixture from the refrigerator. Add feta cheese, cranberries, frosted almonds and dressing. Toss. Serve the salad topped with diagonally sliced chicken breast strips. Makes 4 servings.

* Brands may vary by region; substitute a similar product.

California Grilled Chicken Salad
Taylor Fresh

4 medium boneless, skinless chicken breasts

2 tablespoons canola oil

Salt, pepper and garlic powder

6 cups Taylor Fresh* baby spring mix ♥Organic

3 Roma tomatoes, cut into wedges

2 ripe avocados, cut into bite-size pieces

½ red onion, thinly sliced

½ cup shaved Parmesan cheese

4 tablespoons extra-virgin olive oil

3 tablespoons balsamic vinegar

Preheat the grill to medium-high.

Rub chicken with canola oil and sprinkle with salt, pepper and garlic powder to taste. Grill until thoroughly cooked, 5-7 minutes per side.

Divide spring mix, tomatoes, avocados, onion and Parmesan among serving dishes.

In a small bowl, whisk together olive oil, vinegar, ½ teaspoon salt and ¼ teaspoon pepper.

Slice the chicken and place on top of the salads. Drizzle the dressing over the salads. Makes 4 servings.

* Brands may vary by region; substitute a similar product.

Cherry Walnut Chicken Salad
GoodHeart Brand Specialty/Ventura Foods

Quick & Easy

2 cups Kirkland Signature rotisserie chicken salad

¾ cup dried cherries

¾ cup roasted chopped walnuts

¼ cup blue cheese crumbles

In a large bowl, combine all ingredients and toss to blend. Makes 2 servings.

Curried Chicken and Grape Salad
Kirschenman

SUPPLIER FAVORITE 2007

1 roasted chicken

1 cup Kirschenman* red or green seedless grapes

½ cup diced dried apricots

¼ cup thinly sliced red onion

½ cup golden raisins

¼ cup toasted pine nuts

½ cup diced celery

½ cup thinly sliced green onions

Butter lettuce leaves, for serving

DRESSING

½ cup mayonnaise

2 teaspoons curry powder

2 teaspoons honey

2 teaspoons lemon juice

2 teaspoons lime juice

Remove skin, then the meat from the roasted chicken and cut the meat into cubes.

Place the chicken in a large bowl and add grapes, apricots, red onion, raisins, pine nuts, celery and green onions. Toss gently.

To prepare the dressing, combine all ingredients and mix well.

Pour the dressing over the chicken salad and toss until the mixture is coated.

Serve in butter lettuce cups. Makes 4 entrée or 6 luncheon servings.

Recipe created by Linda Carey, culinary specialist.

* Brands may vary by region; substitute a similar product.

Sweet Apple Pear Pecan Salad
Kingsburg Orchards

8 cups mixed loose-leaf
  garden lettuce
1 large Kingsburg Orchards*
  apple pear, cored and thinly sliced
½ cup dried cranberries
¼ cup thinly sliced red onion
¾ cup candied pecans

DRESSING
¾ cup vegetable oil
½ cup packed light brown sugar
¼ cup white vinegar
Pinch of salt, pepper and garlic powder
1 seasoning packet from chicken-flavor
  Top Ramen
½ teaspoon honey

To prepare the dressing, combine all ingredients in a salad dressing bottle and shake until evenly mixed.

In a large serving bowl, combine lettuce, apple pear, dried cranberries, onion and pecans. Toss the salad until evenly mixed. Add dressing to taste. Makes 4 servings.

Tip: Refrigerate any remaining dressing.

Brands may vary by region; substitute a similar product.

Cuties Salad with Fennel, Feta and Honey Citrus Dressing

Sun Pacific

1 large or 2 small fennel
  bulbs, trimmed

6 Cuties* clementines

6 cups mixed spring greens
  (about 5 ounces)

¾ cup crumbled feta cheese

HONEY CITRUS DRESSING

2 Cuties* clementines,
  peeled and segmented

½ cup cider vinegar

2 tablespoons
  minced shallots

1½ teaspoons
  Dijon mustard

1½ teaspoons kosher salt

2 tablespoons honey

Freshly ground
  black pepper

1 cup olive oil

To prepare the dressing, combine all ingredients in a blender and process until smooth. Keep refrigerated for up to 1 week.

Finely shave fennel with a sharp knife or mandoline. Crisp in ice water for 10 minutes. Spin dry before using.

Remove peel from the clementines and cut the fruit into ¼-inch-thick slices. Set aside.

In a large bowl, toss greens and fennel with ½ cup of dressing to coat nicely. Serve on a large platter or divide among individual plates.

Top the salad with the sliced clementines and sprinkle with feta. Drizzle with a little extra dressing if desired. Makes 8 servings.

* Brands may vary by region; substitute a similar product.

Winter Fruit Salad with Mustard-Lime Vinaigrette

Cecelia Packing/Earth Source Trading/Sun World

8 cups torn salad greens

2 Cara Cara navel oranges,
  peeled and sectioned

1 cup Scarlotta
  Seedless grapes

1 pear, cored and
  thinly sliced

¼ cup chopped walnuts

**MUSTARD-LIME
VINAIGRETTE**

4 teaspoons fresh lime juice

2 teaspoons Dijon mustard

2 teaspoons white
  wine vinegar

1 teaspoon honey

¼ cup water

½ teaspoon sea salt

¼ teaspoon freshly ground
  black pepper

4 tablespoons olive oil

To prepare the vinaigrette, combine lime juice, mustard, vinegar, honey, water, salt and pepper in a small bowl. Slowly pour in oil, whisking constantly until blended.

In a large salad bowl, toss salad greens, fruit and walnuts.

Drizzle the vinaigrette over the salad and gently toss to coat. Serve immediately. Makes 8 servings.

Orange Sesame Chicken Salad

Sunkist Growers

20 square wonton wrappers

2¾ cups vegetable oil, divided

1 head romaine lettuce, cut into bite-size pieces (about 8 cups)

¼ cup soy sauce

¼ cup Sunkist* freshly squeezed lemon juice

2 tablespoons sugar

1 tablespoon distilled white vinegar

1 teaspoon salt

½ teaspoon ground black pepper

1 tablespoon toasted sesame oil

3-4 cups coarsely shredded cooked chicken (from a Costco rotisserie chicken)

½ cup chopped green onions

2 Sunkist* navel, Cara Cara or Valencia oranges, peeled and segmented

½ cup sliced almonds, toasted

2 tablespoons sesame seeds, toasted

Cut wonton wrappers into ½-inch-wide strips and separate on paper towels. Heat 2½ cups vegetable oil in a large, wide saucepan over medium heat. Fry the wonton strips, 5 or 6 at a time, gently turning over once with a slotted spoon, until golden, 10-15 seconds per batch. Transfer to paper towels to drain.

Put romaine in a large salad bowl. In a separate mixing bowl, whisk together soy sauce, lemon juice, sugar, vinegar, salt and pepper. Add sesame oil and remaining ¼ cup vegetable oil in a slow stream, whisking until the sugar is dissolved and the dressing is well blended. In a third bowl, combine chicken, green onions, orange segments, almonds and sesame seeds. Add ⅓ cup of dressing and toss to coat. Toss romaine with enough dressing to lightly coat. Add the chicken mixture and toss lightly. Top with fried wonton strips and serve. Makes 4 servings.

* Brands may vary by region; substitute a similar product

Sunkist

Endive, Apple and Walnut Trio
Diamond Foods

1 cup Kirkland Signature walnuts

¼ cup olive oil

¼ cup balsamic vinegar

1 teaspoon Dijon mustard

¼ teaspoon kosher salt

⅛ teaspoon freshly ground black pepper

4 Belgian endives, halved lengthwise and cut into 1-inch chunks

1 large apple, cut into 1-inch cubes (Braeburns work well)

1 cup crumbled blue cheese, divided

Butter lettuce leaves or arugula, for serving

Preheat oven to 350°F.

To toast walnuts, spread evenly on a baking sheet or in a shallow pan. Bake, stirring once or twice, until lightly browned and fragrant, 7-10 minutes. Set aside.

In a large bowl, whisk together oil, vinegar, mustard, salt and pepper. Add endive, apple, walnuts and half the blue cheese; toss well.

Arrange lettuce leaves or arugula on 4-6 chilled plates. Pile the endive mixture on top. Garnish with the remaining blue cheese. Serve immediately. Makes 4-6 servings.

Strawberry, Jicama and Arugula Salad with Miso Dressing
Naturipe

16 ounces Naturipe* strawberries, trimmed and quartered

1 cup julienned jicama

4 cups arugula

1 teaspoon toasted sesame seeds, for garnish

MISO DRESSING

3 tablespoons white miso paste (shiro)

2 tablespoons rice vinegar

1 tablespoon mirin (Japanese sweet rice wine)

2 teaspoons sugar

2 tablespoons orange juice

¼ teaspoon coarsely ground black pepper

2 tablespoons extra-virgin olive oil

To prepare the dressing, combine miso, vinegar, mirin and sugar in a small bowl and whisk until smooth. Add orange juice, pepper and oil; whisk until well incorporated.

In a large bowl, gently toss strawberries, jicama and arugula.

Drizzle the dressing over the strawberry mixture and toss to coat evenly.

Transfer to plates and garnish with toasted sesame seeds. Makes 6 servings.

* Brands may vary by region; substitute a similar product.

Grapefruit and Tangerine Salad
Greene River Marketing

¼ cup orange juice

3 tablespoons olive oil

2 tablespoons water

1-2 tablespoons honey

½ teaspoon ground pepper

¼ teaspoon salt

Red leaf and green
  leaf lettuce

2 Tropicana* grapefruit,
  peeled and sectioned

1 Tropicana* navel orange,
  peeled and sectioned

2 Tropicana* tangerines,
  peeled and sectioned

2 pears, cored and sliced

1 cup seedless grapes

In a jar or bowl, combine orange juice, oil, water, honey, pepper and salt; shake or stir well. Refrigerate for 1 hour.

Line a platter with lettuce. Arrange fruit over the lettuce. Drizzle with the dressing. Serve immediately. Makes 6 servings.

* Brands may vary by region; substitute a similar product.

Cranberry-Pecan Spinach Salad
Boskovich Farms

1 pound Boskovich Farms*
  Fresh 'n' Quick spinach,
  rinsed and torn into
  bite-size pieces

1 cup pecan pieces

¾ cup blue cheese
  crumbles (optional)

1 cup dried sweetened
  cranberries

DRESSING

¼ cup white wine vinegar

¼ cup cider vinegar

½ cup vegetable oil

½ cup white sugar

2 tablespoons toasted
  sesame seeds

1 tablespoon poppy seeds

2 teaspoons minced onion

¼ teaspoon paprika

In a large bowl, combine spinach, pecans, blue cheese and cranberries. Set aside.

To prepare the dressing, combine all ingredients in a medium bowl and whisk together.

Just before serving, pour the dressing over the spinach mixture and toss well. Makes 6-8 servings.

Tip: Toasted slivered almonds can be substituted for the pecans.

* Brands may vary by region; substitute a similar product.

Artisan Lettuce Celebration Salad

 Quick & Easy

Tanimura & Antle

6-count clamshell of Tanimura & Antle* Artisan Lettuce (use Petite Gem or Petite Oak variety for wedges, Petite Tango as plate décor)

¼ cup capers

½ cup diced Tanimura & Antle* Artisan Red Onion

½ cup croutons (see note)

¼ cup shaved Parmesan cheese

CHAMPAGNE VINAIGRETTE

2 teaspoons Dijon mustard

¼ cup champagne or white wine vinegar

1 teaspoon honey

¼ teaspoon ground black pepper

1½ tablespoons water

¾ cup extra-virgin olive oil

1 large shallot, finely chopped

Cut core end of lettuces to release the leaves; cut the heads in half lengthwise. Rinse and drain well.

To prepare the vinaigrette, whisk together mustard, vinegar, honey, pepper and water in a small bowl. Whisking constantly, slowly add oil. Stir in shallot.

Arrange the lettuce wedges on a serving platter. Top with capers, onions, croutons and Parmesan. Drizzle with vinaigrette to taste. Makes 4-8 servings.

Note: Make your own croutons with bread, butter and seasoning—just slice and bake at 350°F for 10-15 minutes, or until golden brown.

* Brands may vary by region; substitute a similar product.

Holiday Green Salad

 Quick & Easy

Foxy Vegetables

6 cups torn Foxy* iceberg lettuce (about 1 head)

6 cups torn Foxy* romaine hearts (about 2 heads)

2 green onions, thinly sliced

1 cup thinly sliced Foxy* celery (about 3 ribs)

¾ cup dried cranberries

¼ cup sliced almonds, toasted

DRESSING

¼ cup extra-virgin olive oil

¼ cup white wine vinegar

¼ cup white sugar

1 tablespoon minced fresh parsley

1 teaspoon hot pepper sauce

Pinch of salt and black pepper

In a large bowl, combine all lettuce greens, onions and celery.

To prepare the dressing, combine all ingredients in a small bowl and mix well.

Pour the dressing over the salad and toss gently until well coated. Add cranberries and almonds. Serve immediately. Makes 10 servings.

* Brands may vary by region; substitute a similar product.

Green and White Asparagus Salad

NewStar Fresh Foods/Gourmet Trading/Jacobs Malcolm & Burtt

1 bunch (2¼ pounds) green asparagus, trimmed

1 bunch (1¾ pounds) white asparagus, trimmed and peeled

6 tablespoons champagne vinegar

2 tablespoons whole-grain mustard

2 tablespoons honey

½ cup olive oil

Sea salt and freshly ground pepper

2 small heads frisée lettuce, cleaned and trimmed

Parmesan cheese shavings, for serving

In a pot of boiling salted water, blanch asparagus for 5-8 minutes, until just tender. Transfer to a cold-water bath.

In a small bowl, mix vinegar, mustard and honey. Slowly add oil and mix until blended. Depending on your preference, you can add more vinegar. Season to taste with salt and pepper.

To serve, arrange asparagus on each plate, add some frisée and shaved Parmesan, and drizzle with vinaigrette. Makes 12 servings.

Tips: The asparagus can also be grilled over medium heat for 2 minutes on each side, or until just tender. If white asparagus is not available, use all green.

JACOBS MALCOLM & BURTT

Dijon-Balsamic Asparagus Salad

Altar Produce

Olive oil

1 pound fresh Altar Produce* green asparagus, cut diagonally into ¾-inch pieces

8 celery stalks, cut diagonally into ¼-inch pieces

2 carrots, shredded

¼ cup finely chopped fresh Italian parsley

¼ cup finely chopped fresh cilantro

1 jalapeño, seeded and finely chopped

DRESSING

4 teaspoons Dijon mustard

2 teaspoons soy sauce

1 teaspoon balsamic vinegar

¾ teaspoon dried oregano

¾ teaspoon dried tarragon

¾ teaspoon dried basil

Freshly ground pepper to taste

Juice of 1 lemon

3 tablespoons extra-virgin olive oil

Heat a small amount of oil in a sauté pan over medium-high heat. Add asparagus and pan-grill until tender and slightly browned.

In a large bowl, combine asparagus, celery, carrots, parsley, cilantro and jalapeño.

In a small bowl, combine all dressing ingredients, stirring to blend. Pour the dressing over the salad and toss lightly until evenly coated.

Refrigerate for 30 minutes before serving, or serve at room temperature. Makes 6-8 servings.

* Brands may vary by region; substitute a similar product.

ALTAR
PRODUCE LLC

Greek-Style Fruit Salad

Blossom Hill/Fillmore-Piru Citrus/Mas Melons & Grapes/Mulholland Citrus/Western Fresh Marketing

½ watermelon

8 fresh Mulholland Citrus* clementine mandarins, sectioned

½ Mas Melons* cantaloupe, cubed

2 large fresh Fillmore Citrus* blood oranges, cubed

1 pound fresh Mas Melons* table grapes (red or green)

5 fresh Blossom Hill* apricots, quartered

5 Western Fresh* black mission figs, quartered

4 cups plain Greek-style yogurt

4 tablespoons honey

¼ cup light brown sugar

½ cup chopped fresh mint

⅔ cup candied pecans, chopped

Scoop the flesh out of the watermelon, preserving the shell to use as a bowl. Cut the watermelon into bite-size pieces and set aside in the refrigerator.

In a large bowl, combine clementines, cantaloupe, oranges, grapes, apricots, figs, yogurt, honey and brown sugar. Toss gently to coat. Transfer to the watermelon bowl.

Garnish with mint and candied pecans. Chill for 30 minutes before serving. Place the watermelon pieces around the base of the bowl for serving. Makes 6 servings.

* Brands may vary by region; substitute a similar product.

Blueberry Watermelon Feta Salad

Naturipe

4 cups seedless watermelon chunks

2 cups Naturipe* blueberries, washed and drained

¼ cup chopped red onion

1 cup feta cheese crumbles

2 tablespoons lime juice

1 tablespoon minced fresh cilantro

Combine all ingredients in a large bowl. Toss gently to blend. Makes 6 servings.

Brands may vary by region; substitute a similar product.

Watermelon Feta Bowls

Dulcinea

1 tablespoon white balsamic vinegar

Pinch of sea salt

2 tablespoons olive oil

2 Dulcinea PureHeart mini-seedless watermelons, halved

¼ cup pistachios

¾ cup cubed feta cheese

In a small bowl, whisk together vinegar, salt and oil. Set aside.

Carefully cut the flesh from each watermelon half to create a bowl.

Cut the watermelon flesh into ¾-inch cubes.

Cut the rim of each watermelon half into a decorative V-shape pattern.

Place the watermelon cubes inside the watermelon halves. Top with pistachios and feta. Drizzle with dressing and serve. Makes 4 servings.

Composed Berry Salad

Andrew & Williamson/Curry & Company/SunnyRidge

Quick & Easy

2½ cups sliced fresh strawberries
2 cups fresh blueberries
2 cups fresh blackberries
⅓ cup cranberry-raspberry juice

1 tablespoon lemon juice
1 tablespoon sugar
Pinch of salt

Arrange strawberries lengthwise along the center of a medium platter. Group blueberries and blackberries, separately, on each side of the strawberries. In a small bowl, mix cranberry-raspberry juice, lemon juice, sugar and salt. Transfer to a sauce dish. Serve the berries with the dressing on the side. Makes 6 servings.

Recipe developed by Kati Neville.

Picnic Rice Salad with Fresh Fruit
The Oppenheimer Group/Sunny Valley International

½ cup plain yogurt
2 tablespoons lemon or lime juice
2 tablespoons honey
3 cups cold cooked white rice
1 Eastern ripe peach, peeled and diced

1 navel orange, peeled and diced
1 cup black or red seedless grapes, halved
Salt
¼ cup roasted sliced almonds
¼ cup chopped fresh mint (optional)

In a large bowl, combine yogurt, lemon or lime juice and honey; mix well. Stir in rice. Gently fold in peaches, oranges and grapes. Add salt to taste.

Cover and refrigerate until ready to serve. Garnish with almonds and mint just before serving. Makes 5-6 servings.

expect the world from us

FRANCE FREEMAN

Costco Buyer Tip
Mark DeCosta, Produce

I'm a fan of "super foods," and these recipes are packed with them. The term was made popular by Dr. Steven Pratt in a series of books, and many other experts have come up with their own lists. These foods are nutrient-rich, smart in terms of calories, and delicious. The blueberries and blackberries in the fruit salad are among the top super foods you can find. Also, the asparagus, snap peas, tomatoes and French green beans in the quinoa salad are great sources of vitamin A, B and C. For good health, keep super foods in your daily diet.

Fresh Garden Quinoa Salad
Alpine Fresh

1 pound Alpine Fresh* asparagus, stems trimmed

½ pound Alpine Fresh* French green beans, trimmed

½ pound Alpine Fresh* sugar snap peas

1½ cups quinoa, rinsed and drained

⅓ cup extra-virgin olive oil

2 tablespoons fresh lemon juice

Salt and freshly ground pepper

1-2 teaspoons grated lemon zest

2 tablespoons chopped fresh Italian parsley

1 cup Alpine Fresh* grape tomatoes, halved

¼ cup salted roasted pepitas/pumpkin seeds, for garnish

Cut green vegetables on the diagonal into 1-inch pieces. In a saucepan of boiling salted water, simmer the vegetables until bright green but crisp-tender, about 3-4 minutes. Drain, then place in a bowl of cold water for 1-2 minutes. Drain again and spread on a tray to cool. Pat dry.

Toast quinoa in a dry skillet over medium heat, stirring constantly, for about 4 minutes. Put toasted quinoa into a medium pot and add 3¼ cups water. Bring to a simmer, then reduce the heat to low, cover, and cook for 30-35 minutes. Remove from the heat and let sit, covered, for an additional 5 minutes, or until all the water is absorbed and the quinoa is tender. Set aside, uncovered, to let cool to room temperature. Fluff with a fork.

In a small bowl, whisk together oil, lemon juice, and salt and pepper to taste. Add lemon zest and parsley. In a large bowl, combine tomatoes, asparagus, beans and peas with the quinoa. Add the dressing and toss. Serve at room temperature or lightly chilled. Garnish with pepitas/pumpkin seeds. Makes 8-10 servings.

Fruit & Panna Cotta Salad
Alpine Fresh

2 tablespoons honey

2 tablespoons lemon juice

1 tablespoon grated lemon zest, divided

2 teaspoons poppy seeds

1½ cups Alpine Fresh* fresh-cut or whole mangoes diced into ½-inch pieces

3 cups Alpine Fresh* fresh-cut pineapples diced into ½-inch pieces

2 cups Alpine Fresh* blueberries, rinsed and drained

2 cups Alpine Fresh* blackberries, rinsed and drained

PANNA COTTA

⅓ cup skim milk

1 (.25 ounce) envelope unflavored gelatin

2½ cups heavy cream

½ cup sugar

1½ teaspoons vanilla extract

To prepare the panna cotta, pour milk and gelatin into the cream in a saucepan, stirring until completely dissolved. Cook for 1 minute on medium heat, stirring constantly. Remove from the heat, stir in sugar and vanilla, and pour into a bowl. Cool, uncovered, to room temperature. When cool, cover with plastic wrap and refrigerate until set (about 2 hours).

Whisk together honey, lemon juice, 1 teaspoon zest and poppy seeds. Combine the fruit in a large bowl and drizzle with honey-lemon dressing, gently tossing to coat. Spoon about ¼ cup panna cotta into individual bowls or glasses. Top with fruit. Sprinkle with lemon zest. Makes 8-10 servings.

Recipes developed by Christine W. Jackson, food stylist.

* Brands may vary by region; substitute a similar product.

Three-Grape Sweet Pasta Salad
Four Star Fruit

16 ounces *acini di pepe* pasta, or 2 cups pearl couscous

6 ounces pineapple juice

1 20-ounce can crushed pineapple

½ cup sugar

2 tablespoons flour

2 large eggs, beaten

4 teaspoons lemon juice

½ cup chopped toasted pecans

8 ounces lite whipped dessert topping

4 cups Four Star Fruit* red, green and black grapes (or any combination)

Mint leaves, for garnish

Cook pasta or couscous according to package directions, yielding 3-4 cups. Drain and rinse in cold water.

Place the pineapple juice in a saucepan. Drain the juice from the can of pineapple into the saucepan; reserve the pineapple. Add sugar, flour and beaten eggs to the saucepan and whisk to blend. Cook over medium heat, stirring, until thickened. Remove from the heat and add lemon juice.

Add the pasta to the sauce and stir to blend. Refrigerate for at least 6 hours.

Add drained pineapple, pecans, whipped topping and grapes to the pasta. Fold to incorporate all ingredients.

Transfer to a large serving bowl. Garnish with mint. Makes 10-12 servings.

Recipe developed by Christine W. Jackson, food stylist.

* Brands may vary by region; substitute a similar product.

Quinoa Salad with Pomegranate
Windset Farms

1 cup quinoa

1¾ cups vegetable or chicken stock

2 Fresco* mini cucumbers, diced

½ pound Concerto* grape tomatoes, halved

1 pomegranate, seeds only

1 tablespoon chopped fresh Italian parsley

1 tablespoon chopped fresh mint

1 tablespoon chopped fresh cilantro

DRESSING

1 shallot, minced

1 garlic clove, minced

¼ cup fresh lemon juice (about 2 lemons)

½ cup extra-virgin olive oil

½ teaspoon kosher salt

1 teaspoon sugar

½ teaspoon chili powder

¼ teaspoon ground cumin

¼ teaspoon ground coriander

Heat a medium skillet over medium heat. Add quinoa and toast for 5 minutes, or until the quinoa starts to pop and turn light brown.

Meanwhile, heat stock to boiling in a medium saucepan. Add quinoa and simmer for 15 minutes, or until all the liquid is absorbed.

To prepare the dressing, whisk together all the ingredients in a small bowl.

In a large bowl, combine warm quinoa with cucumbers, tomatoes, pomegranate seeds, chopped herbs and the dressing.

Serve at room temperature. Makes 4-8 servings.

Recipe developed by Executive Chef Dana Reinhardt.

* Brands may vary by region; substitute a similar product.

Black Bean and Pineapple Salad Olé

Del Monte Fresh Produce

- 3 tablespoons fresh squeezed lime juice
- 3 tablespoons apricot preserves
- 1 tablespoon light olive oil
- 2 15-ounce cans black beans, rinsed and drained
- 2 cups Gold Extra Sweet Del Monte* pineapple chunks

- 2 medium ears of corn, cooked and kernels cut from cobs (about 1½ cups)
- ⅓ cup sliced roasted red bell pepper
- ⅓ cup diagonally sliced green onions
- ⅓ cup chopped fresh cilantro
- 1-2 teaspoons minced jalapeño pepper (optional)

To make the dressing, in a small bowl whisk together lime juice, preserves and oil. In a large bowl, combine the remaining ingredients. Add the dressing and toss well. Chill for 2-3 hours to blend flavors before serving. Makes 6-8 servings.

* Brands may vary by region; substitute a similar product.

Eat Healthy. Live Healthy.®

Potato and Avocado Salad with Bacon Dressing

Chilean Hass Avocados

6 bacon slices, finely chopped
2 teaspoons oil
¾ cup chopped onions
2 tablespoons flour
1 tablespoon sugar or honey
Salt
1 teaspoon celery seeds
⅓ cup white vinegar
1 pinch ground black pepper
2½ pounds potatoes, cooked and diced
4 Chilean* Hass avocados, cut into small cubes
2 tablespoons chopped fresh chives (optional)

In a large pan, cook bacon over medium heat until crisp. Remove from the pan and set aside.

Add oil to the same pan. Add onions and cook until they begin to brown. Sprinkle flour over the onions, stir to blend, and cook for 1 minute. Add sugar, salt, celery seeds and vinegar. Simmer for 6-7 minutes, or until the vinegar evaporates. Add pepper.

Add potatoes and crumbled bacon to the pan. Stir and heat for 1-2 minutes, or until the potatoes are heated through. Transfer to a bowl and let marinate until lukewarm.

Fold in avocados. Sprinkle with chives.
Makes 6-8 servings.

Brands may vary by region; substitute a similar product.

CHILEAN HASS AVOCADOS
SO GOOD. SO MANY WAYS.

Southwest Roasted Many-Potato Salad

Wallace Farms/Skagit Valley's Best Produce/Valley Pride

Cooking spray
2 pounds red, Yukon Gold and purple Washington* potatoes
2 tablespoons extra-virgin olive oil, divided
4 slices bacon, chopped
1 cup chopped white onion
1 medium red bell pepper, chopped
1 medium green bell pepper, chopped
1 jalapeño, chopped
1 teaspoon ground cumin
½ cup chopped green onions
2 tablespoons chopped fresh cilantro
1 tablespoon fresh lime juice
¾ teaspoon salt

Preheat oven to 450°F. Coat a baking sheet with cooking spray.

Scrub and rinse potatoes; cut into quarters. Toss potatoes with 1 tablespoon oil. Arrange in a single layer on the prepared baking sheet. Roast until browned and tender, about 18-20 minutes. Transfer to a bowl.

While the potatoes are roasting, heat a large nonstick skillet over medium-high heat. Add bacon and cook, stirring occasionally, until starting to brown, about 5 minutes. Stir in onion and cook for 2 minutes. Add bell peppers, jalapeño and cumin. Cook, stirring occasionally, until the peppers are crisp-tender, about 5 minutes. Add to the bowl with the potatoes.

Add 1 tablespoon oil, green onions, cilantro, lime juice and salt to the bowl. Toss and serve warm or at room temperature. Makes 8 servings.

Brands may vary by region; substitute a similar product.

Samish River
POTATOES

Best

VALLEY PRIDE
Premium Northwest Produce

Tuna and Mango Sashimi Salad

Freska Produce

- **16 ounces sashimi-quality tuna steak**
- **2 tablespoons finely chopped green onion, including some of the green**
- **2 tablespoons minced fresh cilantro**
- **3 tablespoons soy sauce**
- **1 tablespoon minced Thai chile**
- **1 teaspoon minced garlic**
- **2 tablespoons minced fresh ginger**
- **2 tablespoons Asian sesame oil**
- **1 tablespoon sesame seeds**
- **1 large ripe Freska* mango, peeled and cut into 1-inch cubes**

Cut tuna into 1-inch cubes and place in a medium bowl. Add green onion, cilantro, soy sauce and chile.

In a small bowl, combine garlic and ginger.

In a small saucepan, heat sesame oil until it starts to smoke. Pour over the garlic and ginger.

Combine the ginger and tuna mixtures and toss. Cover and refrigerate for 2 hours.

Meanwhile, place sesame seeds in a heavy pan over medium heat. Slowly toast the seeds, shaking the pan, until they are golden brown; set aside to cool.

Fold mango into the tuna mixture.

Serve on salad plates, sprinkled with sesame seeds. Makes 4 servings.

Recipe courtesy of Chef Allan Susser, The Great Mango Book.

* Brands may vary by region; substitute a similar product.

Citrus Ahi Tuna Tiradito

Seald Sweet

- **2 ounces ahi tuna, sliced thin**
- **2 tablespoons Key lime juice**
- **2 tablespoons Seald Sweet* fresh-squeezed Indian River grapefruit juice**
- **1 tablespoon Seald Sweet* fresh-squeezed orange juice**
- **1 teaspoon soy sauce**
- **1 teaspoon wasabi oil**
- **6 leaves fresh cilantro, finely chopped**
- **1 tablespoon sliced shallot**
- **1 small or ½ large avocado, peeled and sliced**
- **1 peeled and sectioned Seald Sweet* clementine or mandarin orange**

Place tuna on a serving plate, spreading out.

In a small bowl, mix lime, grapefruit, and orange juices, soy sauce and wasabi oil. Pour evenly over the tuna.

Sprinkle the tuna with cilantro and shallots. Top with sliced avocado and clementine or mandarin sections. Chill for about 10 minutes. Makes 2-4 servings.

Recipe courtesy of Chef Raymond Mumford, Costa d'Este resort.

* Brands may vary by region; substitute a similar product.

Seald Sweet INTERNATIONAL

Orange, Shrimp and Jicama Salad
Booth Ranches/Sequoia Orange

1½ pounds jicama, peeled and cut into thin strips

6-8 navel oranges, zested, peeled and sliced into ¼-inch rounds

20 large shrimp, peeled, cooked and chilled

12 red onion rings, sliced ¼ inch thick

Grated zest and juice of 4 limes

2 tablespoons chopped fresh cilantro

BELL PEPPER OIL

½ red bell pepper, seeded and chopped

½ cup olive oil

Salt to taste

CILANTRO OIL

1 cup coarsely chopped cilantro

½ cup olive oil

Salt to taste

To prepare the bell pepper oil, place all ingredients in a blender and blend until smooth; strain.

To prepare the cilantro oil, place all ingredients in a blender and blend until smooth; strain.

Arrange jicama, orange slices, shrimp and onion rings on 4 dinner plates or large, flat pasta bowls. Drizzle with lime juice, cilantro oil and bell pepper oil. Top with cilantro, orange zest and lime zest. Makes 4 entrée servings.

Tip: The jicama can be replaced with 1 pound of lightly blanched sugar snap peas.

Recipe created by Chef Bill Hassett, Booth Ranches, LLC.

Little Italy Tuna Pizza Salad
Kirkland Signature

2 7-ounce cans Kirkland Signature solid white albacore tuna, drained and flaked

2 tablespoons Dijon mustard

4 large (9-inch) pita breads

4 teaspoons Kirkland Signature extra virgin olive oil

3 tablespoons Kirkland Signature shredded Parmigiano Reggiano, divided

6 cups baby arugula or spring salad mix

½ medium red bell pepper, diced

½ medium yellow bell pepper, diced

20 small grape tomatoes (5 ounces)

½ cup prepared balsamic vinaigrette or Italian dressing

In a small bowl, gently combine tuna and mustard. Set aside.

Lightly coat the entire surface of each pita with oil and sprinkle the top side with 1 teaspoon Parmigiano Reggiano.

Heat a skillet over medium-high heat. Grill each pita, cheese side up, for about 1½-2 minutes, then flip and grill the other side for about 1½-2 minutes, or until the edges are toasted and crisp. Remove from the pan and place on a plate.

Top each pizza crust with arugula or salad mix, the tuna mixture, bell peppers and tomatoes. Drizzle with dressing and sprinkle with the remaining Parmigiano Reggiano. Makes 4 servings.

Chef's Choice

Earthbound Farm. ORGANIC

Food to live by.

Myra Goodman

Myra Goodman and her husband, Drew, founded Earthbound Farm in their Carmel Valley, California, backyard 27 years ago. Myra's cooking is inspired by the fresh, flavorful and healthy harvest of their organic farm, which led her to establish one of the country's first certified organic kitchens. Her latest cookbook is The Earthbound Cook: 250 Recipes for Delicious Food and a Healthy Planet (Workman Publishing, 2010).

Heirloom Lettuce Salad with Apples, Pecans and Gorgonzola
Earthbound Farm

Recipes developed by Myra Goodman

6 cups Earthbound Farm* organic heirloom lettuce leaves, torn into bite-size pieces, carefully rinsed and dried (or substitute Earthbound Farm organic spring mix or washed butter lettuce)

1 large or 2 small Earthbound Farm* organic apples, peeled, quartered, cored and thinly sliced

½ cup pecan pieces, toasted

½ cup crumbled Gorgonzola cheese

LIGHT BALSAMIC VINAIGRETTE

½ cup extra-virgin olive oil

2½ tablespoons balsamic vinegar

2 teaspoons minced shallot

2 teaspoons Dijon mustard

¼ teaspoon salt

Freshly ground black pepper, to taste

To prepare the vinaigrette, place all the ingredients in a glass jar and seal the lid tightly. Shake vigorously to combine. (The dressing can be refrigerated, covered, for up to 1 month. Let it return to room temperature and shake vigorously before using.)

Place lettuce in a large bowl and toss with half of the vinaigrette. Divide the lettuce among 4 salad plates.

Place apples in the same bowl, drizzle with a small amount of dressing, and toss to coat. Divide the apples among the salad plates.

Sprinkle pecans and cheese over the salads. Drizzle with additional dressing, if desired, and serve immediately. Serves 4 as a side salad.

Both recipes from The Earthbound Cook: 250 Recipes for Delicious Food and a Healthy Planet, *© 2010, Myra Goodman.*

* Brands may vary by region; substitute a similar product.

Orecchiette with Broccolette
Earthbound Farm

Coarse sea salt or kosher salt

4 cups (12 ounces) orecchiette pasta

10 ounces Earthbound Farm* organic broccolette, ends trimmed, stalks cut into 1½-inch pieces (4 cups), or substitute baby broccoli or broccolini

¼ cup olive oil

5 canned anchovies, mashed to a paste with a fork

4 fresh garlic cloves, peeled and minced

Pinch of dried red pepper flakes, or more to taste

Grated zest of 2 lemons, preferably Meyer lemons

1½ cups freshly grated Parmesan or Pecorino Romano cheese, divided

Bring 4 quarts water to a boil in a large covered pot over high heat. Add 2 tablespoons coarse sea salt and stir in orecchiette. Cook, stirring once or twice, for 6 minutes. Then add broccolette and cook until the pasta is al dente and the broccolette is tender, 6 more minutes.

A few minutes before the pasta and broccolette are cooked, pour olive oil into a large skillet (at least 12 inches in diameter) and heat over medium heat. When the oil is hot, add anchovies, garlic cloves and red pepper flakes. Cook, stirring frequently, until the anchovies dissolve and the mixture is hot, about 2 minutes.

Reserve 1 cup of the cooking liquid, then drain the pasta broccolette mixture into a colander. Transfer the mixture to the skillet and cook for 2-3 minutes, stirring frequently, adding some of the hot pasta cooking water to the skillet if the mixture seems dry. Add lemon zest and 1 cup of the cheese, stirring to coat.

Transfer the pasta to a warmed platter and sprinkle with the remaining ½ cup cheese. Serve hot. Makes 4 servings.

* Brands may vary by region; substitute a similar product.

Jamie Purviance

Costco member Jamie Purviance is a national grilling expert, a 2010 James Beard Award nominee, and author of the recently released Weber's Time to Grill *and several bestselling companion books. He has been a guest chef at the James Beard House in New York City, and has been featured on many TV shows, including NBC's* Today, *CBS's* Early Show *and* The Oprah Winfrey Show.

Grilled Pizzas with Sausage and Black Olives
Tarantino

Recipes developed by Jamie Purviance

2 links (½ pound) Tarantino*
  mild Italian sausage

1¼ pounds premade pizza dough

Olive oil

Salt

1 package (12 ounces) grape tomatoes

1 small eggplant, cut crosswise into
  ¼-inch slices

2 cups grated mozzarella cheese

24 Kalamata olives

Remove the sausage meat from the casings and break the meat into ½-inch chunks. In a small skillet, sauté the sausage over medium heat until the meat is cooked through. Remove the sausage with a slotted spoon and set aside. Prepare the grill for direct cooking over medium heat (350°F-450°F).

Divide the pizza dough into 4 equal pieces. Lightly brush four 9-inch squares of parchment paper on one side with oil. Flatten each piece of dough on a sheet of parchment paper. Each round should be about ¼ inch thick and 8 inches in diameter. Lightly brush the tops with oil and sprinkle with salt. Let the rounds sit at room temperature for 5-10 minutes.

Grill the tomatoes and eggplant over direct medium heat, with the lid closed as much as possible, until the tomato skins burst and the flesh becomes very soft and the eggplant is tender, turning once or twice. The tomatoes will take about 5 minutes, and the eggplant will take 8-10 minutes. Put the tomatoes in a bowl and crush with a spoon or fork. Cut the eggplant into a medium dice.

Place the dough on the cooking grate with the paper sides facing up. Grill over direct medium heat until the dough is well marked and firm on the underside, 2-5 minutes, rotating as needed for even cooking. Discard the parchment paper. Transfer the crusts to a work surface with the grilled sides facing up.

Evenly divide the tomatoes, cheese, eggplant, sausage and olives over the crusts. Return the pizzas to the grill and cook over direct medium heat, with the lid closed as much as possible, until the cheese is melted and the bottoms of the crusts are crisp, 2-5 minutes, rotating the pizzas occasionally for even cooking. Transfer to a cutting board and cut into wedges. Serve warm. Makes 4 servings.

All recipes adapted from Weber's Time To Grill, *by Jamie Purviance. Used with permission. ©2011 Weber-Stephen Products LLC.*

* Brands may vary by region; substitute a similar product.

Tomato and Sausage Strata
Tarantino

9 links Tarantino* breakfast sausage

½ tablespoon unsalted butter

8 cups cubed (¾-inch) Italian bread
  (or other crusty bread)

1 pint small grape tomatoes

1 roasted red pepper, peeled and
  cut lengthwise into ¼-inch slices

6 ounces mozzarella cheese,
  cut in ¼- to ½-inch cubes

8 large eggs

1⅔ cups whole milk

2 teaspoons finely chopped
  fresh rosemary

2 teaspoons finely chopped
  fresh oregano

½ teaspoon kosher salt

¼ teaspoon ground black pepper

½ cup grated Parmesan cheese

Prepare the grill for direct cooking over medium heat. Grill the sausages over direct medium heat until they are cooked through, about 8-10 minutes, turning occasionally. Set the sausages aside.

Grease a 12-inch cast iron skillet with the butter and add the bread cubes. Halve the cooked sausages lengthwise and then cut them crosswise into thin slices. Scatter the sausages, tomatoes, roasted pepper and mozzarella evenly over the bread. In a large mixing bowl, whisk the eggs, milk, rosemary, oregano, salt, and pepper. Drizzle the egg mixture into the skillet and mix thoroughly. Top with the Parmesan cheese, cover with foil, and refrigerate overnight.

Prepare the grill for direct cooking over medium-low heat. Remove the foil from the skillet and grill until the bread is toasted and the center of the strata is firm, 30-40 minutes (any liquid will re-absorb upon resting, but a knife inserted into the center of the strata should come out free of uncooked egg). Let cool for 10 minutes, then slice and serve warm. Makes 8 servings.

* Brands may vary by region; substitute a similar product.

Sausage-Stuffed Zucchini with Roasted Pepper Sauce
Tarantino

SAUCE

4 large plum tomatoes, about 1 pound total

1 small yellow onion, cut crosswise into ½-inch slices

2 small bell peppers, 1 red and 1 yellow

2 tablespoons *each* finely chopped fresh basil leaves and finely chopped fresh oregano leaves

2 garlic cloves

2 tablespoons red wine vinegar

1 teaspoon kosher salt

¼ teaspoon ground black pepper

¼ cup extra-virgin olive oil

4 medium zucchini, about 2 pounds total, each cut in half lengthwise

4 links (1 pound) Tarantino* mild Italian sausage, casings removed

1 cup shredded Romano cheese

⅓ cup panko bread crumbs

Prepare the grill for direct cooking over medium heat (350°F-450°F). Grill the tomatoes, onions and peppers until the tomatoes are blistered and the skins are split, the onions are soft, and the peppers are blackened and blistered, turning every few minutes. The tomatoes and onions will take 8-10 minutes; the peppers 10-15 minutes. Place the peppers in a bowl and cover tightly with plastic wrap to allow the skins to steam and loosen for about 10 minutes.

When cool enough to handle, pull the skins from the tomatoes and cut out the stem ends. Remove and discard the outermost rings from the onion slices if they are dried and charred. Peel, core and seed the peppers.

Pulse the tomatoes, onions, peppers, basil, oregano, garlic, vinegar, salt and pepper in a food processor until a semi-smooth sauce is created. With the motor running, slowly add the oil. Transfer the sauce to a medium saucepan and heat over low heat to warm through and thicken for a few minutes, stirring occasionally.

With the cut sides of the zucchini facing up, lightly score the flesh ⅛ to ¼ inch in from the edges all the way around. Using a small spoon or melon baller, and using the scored edges as guides, carefully scoop out and discard the flesh and seeds, leaving what looks like a boat with uniformly thick walls.

In a medium bowl gently combine the sausage meat, cheese, bread crumbs and ½ cup of the tomato and pepper puree. Divide the mixture evenly among the zucchini boats, spreading it and lightly pressing it to fill the shells completely.

Grill the stuffed zucchini over direct medium heat until the sausage is cooked through and no longer pink, about 15 minutes. Using a wide spatula, carefully remove them from the grill. Serve on a bed of rice or pasta, if desired, and top each with some of the warm sauce. Pass any remaining sauce. Makes 4-6 servings.

* Brands may vary by region; substitute a similar product.

FAITH ECHTERMEYER

DELANO FARMS

Connie Guttersen

Dr. Connie Guttersen, R.D., Ph.D., is a renowned registered dietitian and culinary professional, New York Times bestselling author of The Sonoma Diet and a nutrition instructor at the Culinary Institute of America. Dr. Guttersen has spent her career focusing on developing flavorful and nutritious approaches to healthy eating and weight reduction. Her latest book is The New Sonoma Cookbook (Sterling, 2011).

Grilled Moroccan Pork Tenderloin Kabobs recipe on page 92

Grilled Moroccan Pork Tenderloin Kabobs

Delano Farms

Recipes developed by Connie Guttersen

2 tablespoons chopped fresh
  flat-leaf parsley

2 tablespoons lemon juice

1 tablespoon extra-virgin olive oil

8 cloves garlic, minced
  (4 teaspoons minced)

1 tablespoon chopped fresh oregano
  or 1 teaspoon dried oregano, crushed

1½ teaspoons coriander seeds, ground,
  or 1 teaspoon ground coriander

1 teaspoon paprika

1 teaspoon grated fresh ginger

½ teaspoon freshly ground
  black pepper

¼ teaspoon kosher salt

¼ teaspoon cayenne pepper
  or crushed red pepper

¼ teaspoon ground turmeric

1 1-pound pork tenderloin,
  cut into 1-inch cubes

2 cups Delano Farms* red,
  black or green seedless grapes
  (or some of each)

For marinade, in a large bowl stir together parsley, lemon juice, oil, garlic, oregano, coriander seeds, paprika, ginger, black pepper, kosher salt, cayenne pepper and turmeric until combined. Add pork cubes and grapes. Stir gently until pork and grapes are coated. Cover and marinate in the refrigerator for 1-2 hours.

On eight 12-inch skewers, alternately thread pork and grapes, leaving a ¼-inch space between pieces. For a charcoal grill, place kabobs on the rack of an uncovered grill directly over medium coals. Grill for 10-12 minutes or until pork is just slightly pink in center, turning occasionally to brown evenly. (For a gas grill, preheat grill. Reduce heat to medium. Place kabobs on grill rack over heat. Cover and grill as above.) Makes 4 servings.

Tips: If using wooden skewers, soak in enough water to cover for at least 1 hour before using. Also, you may substitute 1 pound skinless, boneless chicken breast halves for the pork. And try a variety of grapes for a colorful kabob.

Recipe courtesy of NewSonomaDiet.com.

* Brands may vary by region; substitute a similar product.

Grilled Moroccan Pork Tenderloin Kabobs photo on page 91

Grape & Arugula Salad

Delano Farms

2 cups arugula

2 cups romaine leaves, shredded

1 cup Delano Farms* red, green or
  black seedless grapes, cut in half

1 teaspoon lemon zest

Salt and pepper to taste

3 tablespoons Concord Grape Balsamic
  Vinaigrette (recipe at right)

¼ cup slivered almonds, toasted

2 tablespoons blue cheese, crumbled

GRAPE BALSAMIC VINAIGRETTE

½ cup unsweetened Concord
  grape juice

1 tablespoon balsamic vinegar

2 tablespoons extra-virgin olive oil

Salt and pepper to taste

To make the vinaigrette, place grape juice in a small saucepan. Reduce by half. Remove from heat and cool. (Note: Keep an eye on the reducing grape juice. It will burn if it reduces too far.)

Stir in balsamic vinegar and whisk in extra-virgin olive oil. Season with salt and pepper.

Place the arugula and romaine in a bowl. Add grapes and lemon zest. Season with salt and pepper, then dress with vinaigrette. Divide between 4 plates. Top with almonds and blue cheese. Makes 4 servings.

Tips: Cutting the grapes in half makes them easier to eat. Seasoning the greens before dressing allows them to take on the flavor of the salt and pepper more readily than after they are coated with vinaigrette. For variations, replace arugula with watercress, endive or red leaf lettuce.

Recipe courtesy of The New Sonoma Cookbook (Sterling, 2011).

* Brands may vary by region; substitute a similar product.

California Chicken Salad
Delano Farms

1 pound cooked chicken breast, cubed

2 Granny Smith apples, cored and chopped

1 cup celery, peeled and chopped (2 stalks)

½ cup scallions, chopped

2 tablespoons fresh flat-leaf parsley, chopped

¼ cup light dairy sour cream

¼ cup red wine vinegar

3 tablespoons mayonnaise or salad dressing

½ teaspoon kosher salt

¼ teaspoon freshly ground black pepper

¼ cup chopped walnuts, toasted

1 cup Delano Farms* red globe grapes, halved and seeded

6 cups mixed salad greens, torn

In a large bowl combine chicken, apples, celery, scallions and parsley.

In a small bowl, combine sour cream, red wine vinegar, mayonnaise, kosher salt and pepper. Add to chicken mixture. Stir in walnuts and grapes.

Divide greens among 6 serving plates; top with chicken mixture. Makes 6 servings.

Tip: Replace the sour cream with yogurt for a different taste.

Recipe courtesy of The New Sonoma Cookbook (Sterling, 2011).

* Brands may vary by region; substitute a similar product.

Jamie Oliver

Jamie Oliver is one of the world's best-loved television personalities and one of Britain's most famous exports. He has starred in seven television series, including ABC-TV's Emmy Award-winning Jamie Oliver's Food Revolution. *His latest cookbook project Is* Jamie Oliver's Meals in Minutes. *Oliver lives in London with his wife and four children. Visit* www.jamieoliver.com *for news, recipes, tips and more.*

Chicken Fajitas
Coleman Natural Foods
Recipes developed by Jamie Oliver

1 red bell pepper	Olive oil	**SALSA**
1 medium red onion	Sea salt and freshly ground black pepper	½–1 fresh red or green chile, to your taste
2 Coleman Organic* skinless, boneless chicken breasts	4 flour tortillas	15 ripe grape or cherry tomatoes
1 teaspoon smoked paprika	½ cup sour cream or natural yogurt	Small bunch fresh cilantro
Small pinch of ground cumin	1 cup guacamole	Sea salt and freshly ground black pepper
1 lime	4 ounces Cheddar cheese	1 lime
		Extra virgin olive oil

Put the grill pan on a high heat. Halve and seed the bell pepper and cut it into thin strips. Peel, halve and finely slice the onion. Slice the chicken lengthways into long strips roughly the same size as the bell pepper strips. Put the bell peppers, onion and chicken into a bowl with the paprika and cumin.

Squeeze over the juice of half a lime, drizzle over a lug of olive oil, season with a good pinch of salt and pepper, and mix well. Set aside to marinate.

To make the salsa, finely chop the chile and roughly chop the tomatoes and cilantro. Put the chile and tomatoes into a second bowl with a good pinch of salt and pepper and the juice of 1 lime. Add a lug of olive oil; stir in cilantro.

Use a pair of tongs to put all the pieces of bell pepper, onion and chicken into the preheated pan to cook for 6 8 minutes, until the chicken is golden and cooked through. As the pan will be really hot, keep turning the pieces of chicken and vegetables over so they don't burn—just lightly chargrill.

Warm the tortillas in a microwave or a warm dry frying pan. Divide the warmed tortillas among your serving plates. At the table, carefully serve the chicken and vegetables straight from the hot grill pan. Be sure to put it down on top of something that won't burn, like a chopping board. Before placing everything on plates, halve the remaining lime and squeeze the juices over the sizzling pan.

Serve with bowls of sour cream and guacamole alongside Cheddar, a grater and the fresh salsa. Makes 2 servings.

* Brands may vary by region; substitute a similar product.

Perfect Roast Chicken
Coleman Natural Foods

1 Coleman Organic* fresh whole chicken (from 3½ to 5 pounds)	Olive oil
2 medium onions	Sea salt and freshly ground black pepper
2 carrots	1 lemon
2 stalks celery	1 small bunch of fresh thyme, rosemary, bay, or sage, or a mixture
1 bulb of garlic	

Take the chicken out of the refrigerator 30 minutes before it goes into the oven. Preheat the oven to 475°F.

Wash and roughly chop the vegetables (no need to peel them). Break the garlic bulb into cloves, leaving them unpeeled. Pile all the vegetables and garlic into the middle of a large roasting pan and drizzle with olive oil.

Drizzle the chicken with olive oil and season well with salt and pepper, rubbing it all over the bird. Carefully prick the lemon all over, using the tip of a sharp knife. Put the lemon inside the chicken's cavity, with the bunch of herbs.

Place the chicken on top of the vegetables in the roasting pan and put it into the preheated oven. Turn the heat down immediately to 400°F and cook the chicken for 1 hour 20 minutes, or until the internal temperature is 165°F. **Note:** Cooking time varies depending on the size of the chicken.

Baste the chicken with pan juices halfway through cooking. When cooked, take the pan out and transfer the chicken to a board to rest for 15 minutes or so. Cover with aluminum foil and a kitchen towel until serving. Makes 4-6 servings.

From Jamie's Food Revolution *by Jamie Oliver © 2008, 2009. Photographs © David Loftus and Chris Terry 2008, 2009. Published by Hyperion. All Rights Reserved.*

Ellie Krieger

Ellie Krieger is the host of Healthy Appetite *and the author of the bestsellers* The Food You Crave *and* So Easy *and the brand-new* Comfort Food Fix. *A registered dietitian, she has a master's degree in nutrition from Columbia University. Krieger is a regular columnist for* Fine Cooking *and* Food Network *magazines and lives in New York City. Get more recipes and healthy living tips at www.EllieKrieger.com.*

Apple and Spinach-Stuffed Pork Chops with Mustard Wine Sauce

Rainier Fruit Company

Recipes developed by Ellie Krieger

2 tablespoons olive oil

1 small red onion, chopped

1 Rainier Fruit* Fuji apple, unpeeled, cored and cut into ½-inch pieces

1 large clove garlic, minced

3 cups lightly packed fresh baby spinach leaves (about 3 ounces)

½ cup prepared sauerkraut, drained

Four ¾-inch-thick center cut, bone-in pork loin chops (about 8 ounces each)

¼ teaspoon salt

½ teaspoon freshly ground black pepper

2 teaspoons all-purpose flour

1½ teaspoons ground turmeric

1 teaspoon caraway seeds

1 tablespoon Dijon mustard

½ cup fruity white wine, such as Riesling

1¼ cups low-sodium chicken broth

Heat 1 tablespoon of the oil in a large nonstick skillet over medium-high heat. Add the onion and cook, stirring occasionally, until softened, about 3 minutes. Add the apple and cook, stirring, until tender, about 4 minutes. Add the garlic and spinach and continue to cook until the spinach is just wilted, about 2 minutes. Stir in the sauerkraut until well combined. Transfer to a bowl and allow to cool.

Slice each pork chop horizontally to the bone, making a pocket for the stuffing. Stuff the spinach-apple mixture into the pockets, skewering to close with toothpicks, if necessary. Season the outside of the chops with salt and black pepper.

Heat the remaining 1 tablespoon oil in the skillet over medium-high heat. Add the pork chops and cook until just cooked through, 3 to 4 minutes per side. Transfer to a plate and tent with foil to keep warm.

Add the flour to the skillet and cook, stirring constantly, until a shade darker, about 1 minute. Add the turmeric and caraway and cook, stirring, 1 minute more. Whisk in the mustard, wine, and broth and simmer, whisking occasionally, until reduced and thickened, about 5 minutes.

Pour the mustard sauce over the pork and serve. Makes 4 servings.

Nutritional information: Each serving has 430 calories, 16 g total fat, 53 g protein, 13 g carbohydrates, 3 g fiber, 155 mg cholesterol, 530 mg sodium.

Both recipes from Comfort Food Fix *by Ellie Krieger (John Wiley & Sons, 2011).*

* Brands may vary by region; substitute a similar product.

Phyllo Cherry Turnovers

Rainier Fruit Company

3 tablespoons cornstarch

3 tablespoons fresh lemon juice

1 cup water

⅓ cup granulated sugar

1 pound Rainier Fruit* sweet cherries, pitted and halved (about 3 cups)

8 sheets frozen phyllo dough, thawed

3 tablespoons canola oil

Preheat the oven to 375°F. Place the cornstarch, lemon juice, water and sugar in a saucepan and whisk until the cornstarch is dissolved. Add the cherries, turn the heat to medium-high, and, stirring, bring to a boil. Reduce the heat to medium-low and simmer until the cherries have softened and the mixture has thickened, 10 to 12 minutes. Remove from the heat and let cool completely.

Place 1 sheet of the phyllo on a clean, dry work surface and brush lightly with some of the oil. Layer another sheet on top. Cut the phyllo stack in half lengthwise. Spoon about ¼ cup of the cherry filling onto one of the phyllo stacks about 2 inches from the top. Fold the top corner of the phyllo stack over the filling to form a triangle-shaped pocket. Continue to fold the pocket down the strip of phyllo in a way that maintains the triangle shape. Repeat with another ¼ cup of filling and the second stack of phyllo, then brush the outside of each triangle lightly with oil. Repeat with the remaining phyllo, filling and oil.

Place the turnovers on a baking sheet. Bake until crisped and browned, about 20 minutes. Serve warm or at room temperature. Makes 8 servings.

Tips: You can substitute Rainier Fruit* blueberries for the cherries in this recipe. Or, for a colorful and tasty option, use a mixture of blueberries and cherries.

Nutritional information: Each serving has 180 calories, 7 g total fat, 2 g protein, 31 g carbohydrates, 2 g fiber, 0 mg cholesterol, 95 mg sodium.

* Brands may vary by region; substitute a similar product.

Tony Seta

Master Chef Tony Seta is the creative force behind menus at numerous leading restaurants and food manufacturers across the country. He has worked closely with Gold Kist Farms in product development. Seta's passion is creating innovative signature dishes that thrill his clients and their consumers alike.

Fire Beer Marinade
Pilgrim's/Gold Kist Farms

Recipes developed by Tony Seta

The blend of chipotle in adobo, vinegar, onions and beer with pineapple fires up this dish!

6 slices pineapple (rings)

6 Gold Kist Farms* boneless, skinless chicken thighs (about 5 ounces each)

12 ounces prepared salsa, for serving

MARINADE

½ cup chopped canned chipotle peppers in adobo sauce

12 ounces beer

1 cup onions cut in small dice

2 tablespoons molasses

1 tablespoon kosher salt

¼ cup balsamic vinegar

¼ cup cider vinegar

¼ cup salad oil

To prepare the marinade, combine all ingredients in a bowl; blend well.

Place the pineapple rings and ½ cup of the marinade in a 1-quart resealable bag and seal.

Place chicken thighs in a 1-gallon resealable bag and cover with all but ½ cup of the remaining marinade. Marinate the chicken and the pineapple rings in the refrigerator for 3-4 hours.

Preheat the grill to 375°F.

Grill the chicken until it is golden brown on both sides and the internal temperature is 165°F, basting with the reserved marinade. While the chicken is grilling, grill the pineapple on both sides to a golden brown.

Place the chicken thighs on a platter with the grilled pineapple on top of or under the thighs. Serve with your favorite salsa. Makes 6 servings.

* Brands may vary by region; substitute a similar product.

Grilled Chicken Breasts San Antonio
Pilgrim's/Gold Kist Farms

4 8-ounce Gold Kist Farms* boneless, skinless chicken breasts

Canola oil

2 tablespoons barbecue spice

6 tablespoons Sweet Baby Ray's or other barbecue sauce

4 slices smoked Gouda cheese

Preheat the grill to 375°F.

Brush each chicken breast with oil on both sides, then season with barbecue spice.

Place the chicken breasts on a clean grill and cook to a golden brown on one side. Then turn over and cook for 2 minutes.

Brush the cooked side with barbecue sauce and cook for 2 minutes, then brush again with barbecue sauce and place a slice of cheese on each sauced chicken breast.

Grill the chicken breasts until the internal temperature is 165°F and the cheese has melted. Makes 4 servings.

Tip: Serve these chicken breasts on a bed of red onion cilantro coleslaw.

* Brands may vary by region; substitute a similar product.

CHRISTOPHER HIRSHEIMER

Lidia Matticchio Bastianich

Lidia Matticchio Bastianich is the author of the recently published Lidia's Italy in America. *She has written six other books, five of which have been accompanied by nationally syndicated public television series. She owns several award-winning restaurants and gives lectures on Italian cuisine throughout the country. For more, see www.lidiasitaly.com.*

Salmon with Mustard Sauce

SeaMazz

Recipes developed by Lidia Matticchio Bastianich

4 pieces SeaMazz frozen skinless salmon fillets, thawed

Flour for dredging

2 tablespoons vegetable oil

3 tablespoons unsalted butter

½ cup dry white wine

Salt and freshly ground pepper, to taste

2 tablespoons Dijon mustard

½ cup fish stock (see tips)

Juice of ½ lemon

¼ cup heavy cream

Lightly flour the salmon. In a large, non-reactive skillet, heat the oil, add the salmon and sauté over moderate heat until golden, turning once, about 3 minutes per side. Set the salmon aside and discard the oil from the pan.

Add the butter, wine and salt and pepper to the pan, and bring to a simmer. Add the mustard, fish stock and lemon juice. Simmer over moderately high heat for 5 minutes.

Gradually add the cream, stirring constantly, and simmer until slightly thickened, about 5 minutes. Add the salmon to the sauce and simmer until the fish is well coated and the sauce is reduced to ⅓ cup, about 3 minutes longer.

With a spatula, carefully transfer the fillets to serving plates. Strain the sauce, spoon a little over each fillet and serve the remainder in a sauceboat. Makes 4 servings.

Tips: If you don't make your own fish stock, you can find a packaged brand in some stores; or, a vegetable stock can be substituted in most fish recipes. This is a dish that could stand up to a light red wine. Otherwise, a lightly acidic white such as Pinot Grigio would be my choice.

Recipe adapted from La Cucina di Lidia, by Lidia Matticchio Bastianich and Jay Jacobs (Doubleday, 1990).

Roast Lobster with Bread Crumb Topping

SeaMazz

6 SeaMazz frozen lobster tails, thawed

1 cup dry bread crumbs

2 tablespoons chopped fresh Italian parsley

¾ teaspoon kosher salt

¼ cup plus 3 tablespoons extra-virgin olive oil

2 cups dry white wine

Lemon wedges for garnishing

Arrange a rack in the center of the oven, and heat it to 400°F. Cut the shells of the lobster tails lengthwise, pry the shells slightly open and loosen the meat. Arrange the lobster tails on a rimmed baking sheet, cut sides up.

Toss together the bread crumbs, chopped parsley and ¼ teaspoon of the salt in a bowl; drizzle in ¼ cup of olive oil, and toss well, until the crumbs are evenly moistened. Sprinkle the crumbs over the cut surfaces of the lobster halves, covering all the meaty parts. Pour the wine and the remaining 3 tablespoons olive oil into the pan around the lobsters (not on the crumbs); sprinkle the remaining salt into the wine and oil, and stir.

Tent the pan of lobsters loosely with a sheet of heavy aluminum foil (don't let it touch the topping), and carefully set the pan in the oven. Roast for 10 minutes, remove the foil, and roast another 10-12 minutes, until the lobster tails are cooked through and the crumbs are crisp and golden.

Serve the lobster tails immediately, placing one on each dinner plate, or all on a big platter to share family-style. Spoon any juices in the pan over the tails; place lemon wedges on the plates or platter. Makes 6 servings.

Recipe adapted from Lidia Cooks from the Heart of Italy, by Lidia Matticchio Bastianich and Tanya Bastianich Manuali (Alfred A. Knopf, 2009).

Spaghetti with Breaded Shrimp
SeaMazz

1 pound spaghetti
1 cup all-purpose flour
2 large eggs
Kosher salt
2 cups fine dry bread crumbs
1 pound SeaMazz easy-peel U-15 or larger
   shrimp, thawed and peeled, tails left on
4 tablespoons unsalted butter
3 tablespoons olive oil
2 garlic cloves, sliced

2 cups small broccoli florets
2 cups sliced cremini mushrooms
1 cup 1-inch pieces asparagus
1 teaspoon kosher salt
Pinch peperoncino flakes
Vegetable oil, for frying
1 bunch scallions, finely chopped
1 cup grated Grana Padano
   or Parmigiano-Reggiano
1 lemon, cut in 6 wedges

Bring a large pot of salted water to boil for pasta. Slip the spaghetti into the pot and cook until al dente. Reserve 1½ cups of the pasta water.

Pour the flour into one shallow bowl, beat the eggs with a pinch of salt in another and spread the bread crumbs in a third. Season the shrimp with salt, then dredge them in the flour, tapping off the excess. Dip the shrimp in the egg, letting excess drip back into the bowl, then dredge them in the bread crumbs. Set the breaded shrimp aside.

To make the pasta sauce, melt 2 tablespoons of the butter in the olive oil in a large skillet over medium heat. Add the garlic and let sizzle for a minute until fragrant. Add the broccoli, mushrooms and asparagus and season with the salt and peperoncino. Sauté the vegetables, tossing occasionally, until they begin to wilt, about 3 minutes. Ladle in ½ cup pasta water, cover the skillet and let cook until the vegetables are almost tender, about 5 minutes.

Heat ½ inch vegetable oil in another skillet over medium heat. Fry the shrimp in batches until crispy and golden, about 3 minutes per side. Drain on paper towels and season with salt. Keep the shrimp warm while you finish the pasta.

Once the vegetables in the sauce are almost tender, uncover and add the scallions and 1 cup pasta water. Bring the sauce to a simmer and cook until reduced and the vegetables are tender, about 8-10 minutes.

Plop the pasta directly into the sauce. Add the remaining 2 tablespoons butter and toss to melt. Remove from heat and toss with the grated cheese.

Serve the pasta in bowls, topping each serving with 3 or 4 breaded shrimp. Serve with lemon wedges to squeeze over the shrimp. Makes 4-6 servings.

Recipe adapted from Lidia's Italy in America, *by Lidia Matticchio Bastianich and Tanya Bastianich Manuali (Alfred A. Knopf, 2011).*

Garofalo

Matt Scialabba and Melissa Pellegrino

Matt Scialabba and Melissa Pellegrino are a husband-and-wife cooking and writing team who met while studying in Italy, where they learned the secrets of authentic regional cuisine. They are authors of The Italian Farmer's Table *(ThreeForks/Globe Pequot Press, 2010; www.theitalianfarmerstable.com). They are working on a sequel to be published in spring 2012.*

Gemelli with Braised Fennel, Raisins and Pine Nuts recipe on page 104

Gemelli with Braised Fennel, Raisins and Pine Nuts

Garofalo

Recipes developed by Matt Scialabba and Melissa Pellegrino

1 large fennel bulb with fronds attached	½ cup low-sodium chicken broth
1 tablespoon extra-virgin olive oil	¼ cup golden raisins
2 ounces pancetta, cut into ¼-inch dice	¼ cup pine nuts, toasted
1 leek, white and light green parts, trimmed, cleaned and thinly sliced	12 ounces Garofalo* organic gemelli (see note)
Kosher salt	Freshly ground black pepper
	Grated Parmigiano-Reggiano, for serving

Reserve ¼ cup chopped fennel fronds. Cut the fennel bulb in half, core it, and then thinly slice; set aside in a bowl.

Heat oil in a 12-inch straight-sided skillet over medium heat. Add pancetta and cook until it has rendered its fat and is starting to crisp, 5-8 minutes. With a slotted spoon transfer to a plate lined with paper towels. Pour off all but a thin layer of fat. Add the fennel and leeks and a pinch of salt. Cook, stirring occasionally, until the vegetables are lightly browned, 3-4 minutes.

Add chicken broth and bring to a simmer. Reduce the heat and cover with a lid. Cook the vegetables until they are meltingly tender, about 20 minutes. Remove the cover and add the pancetta to the pan along with the raisins and pine nuts. Cook until the flavors meld and the fennel mixture darkens slightly, 8-10 minutes.

Bring a large pot of well-salted water to a boil over high heat. Drop in gemelli and cook according to package directions. Reserve ½ cup of the cooking water. Drain the pasta well.

Toss the pasta with the fennel sauce, adding the reserved pasta water as needed. Toss in the reserved fennel fronds and season to taste with salt and pepper. Serve with grated Parmigiano-Reggiano on the side. Makes 4 servings.

Note: You can try other Garofalo cut pastas in this recipe.

* Brands may vary by region; substitute a similar product.

Gemelli with Braised Fennel, Raisins and Pine Nuts photo on page 103

Mushroom, Rosemary and Walnut "Pesto" with Spaghetti

Garofalo

¾ cup walnuts	3 tablespoons extra-virgin olive oil
1 garlic clove	Kosher salt and freshly ground black pepper
⅓ cup parsley leaves	1 pound Garofalo* spaghetti
1½ tablespoons chopped fresh rosemary	Grated Parmigiano-Reggiano, for serving
1½ pounds crimini mushrooms, stemmed and quartered	

In a food processor fitted with a blade attachment, pulse walnuts, garlic, parsley and rosemary until coarsely chopped. Add mushrooms and pulse until very finely chopped, but not a paste.

Heat oil in a 12-inch skillet over medium-low heat. Add the mushroom mixture, 1 teaspoon salt and a few grinds of pepper. Cook, stirring often, until the mushrooms darken and become fragrant, 5-7 minutes. Set aside in the pan.

Bring a large pot of well-salted water to a boil. Drop spaghetti into the water and cook according to package directions. Reserve 1 cup of pasta water and then drain the pasta.

Put the mushrooms over medium heat. Add ¼ cup of the reserved pasta water and scrape up any browned bits with a wooden spoon from the bottom of the pan. Add the spaghetti and toss to coat, adding pasta water, 1 tablespoon at a time, if the sauce seems dry. Serve with grated cheese on the side. Makes 6 servings.

* Brands may vary by region; substitute a similar product.

Garofalo

Baked Penne with Eggplant
Garofalo

Kosher salt

8 ounces Garofalo* organic penne

3 tablespoons extra-virgin olive oil

1 garlic clove, smashed

1 medium-sized eggplant (about 12 ounces), cut into ¼-inch pieces

1¾ cups shredded scamorza cheese or mozzarella, divided (see note)

1 cup ricotta

½ cup grated Parmigiano-Reggiano

1 28-ounce can whole plum tomatoes, crushed in a bowl with their juices

¼ cup sliced basil leaves

Bring a large pot of well-salted water to a boil over high heat. Drop in pasta and cook until just tender, 6 minutes. Drain the pasta and set aside.

Heat oil in a 12-inch skillet over medium heat. Add garlic and cook until lightly golden and the oil is fragrant, 1-2 minutes. Discard the garlic. Add eggplant and a pinch of salt and cook until just tender and lightly browned, 4-6 minutes.

Position a rack in the center of the oven and preheat the oven to 425°F.

In a large bowl mix together the eggplant, 1 cup shredded scamorza (or mozzarella), ricotta, Parmigiano and tomatoes. Add the pasta, basil and a pinch of salt and mix until combined. Spread the mixture out into a 13-by-9-inch baking dish. Top with the remaining ¾ cup scamorza.

Bake until the cheese is melted and browned, 25-30 minutes. Let cool for about 10 minutes before serving. Makes 6-8 servings.

Note: Scamorza is a firm Italian cow's-milk cheese.

* Brands may vary by region; substitute a similar product.

Mary Ann Esposito

Mary Ann Esposito is the host of the long-running PBS series Ciao Italia. *She is the author of 11 Italian cookbooks, including* Ciao Italia Pronto!, Ciao Italia Five-Ingredient Favorites, Ciao Italia Slow and Easy *and her latest,* Ciao Italia Family Classics. *She lives in Durham, New Hampshire, with her husband, Guy.*

Risotto with Pork Sausage and Greens

Premio

Recipes developed by Mary Ann Esposito

In my kitchen, a risotto made with beet greens and pork sausage is a requested favorite. I serve this as a main dish and team it with a salad and fresh fruit for a healthy and balanced meal.

½ pound beet greens, spinach, or Swiss chard, stemmed and washed

3 tablespoons extra-virgin olive oil, divided

1 garlic clove, minced

1 small onion, peeled and diced

½ teaspoon hot red pepper flakes or hot red pepper paste

½ pound Premio* mild or hot Italian sausages, casings removed

1½ cups Arborio rice

½ cup dry white wine

2 cups hot tomato juice

2½ to 3 cups hot chicken broth

½ cup grated Parmigiano-Reggiano cheese

Salt and black pepper

Drop the greens into a pot of boiling water and cook them just until wilted. Drain, cool, squeeze dry, and coarsely chop them. Set aside.

Heat 1½ tablespoons of the oil in a medium sauté pan and add the garlic and the greens. Cook for 2 minutes over medium heat. Transfer the mixture to a bowl and set aside.

In a heavy-bottomed, 2-quart saucepan, heat the remaining 1½ tablespoons olive oil over medium heat. When it is hot, stir in the onion, red pepper flakes, and sausage. Cook, breaking up the sausage, until the onion softens and the meat begins to brown slightly. Stir in the rice and mix to coat the rice well. Pour in the wine and stir until it evaporates.

Begin adding the tomato juice in ½-cup increments. Cook and stir, allowing the rice mixture to absorb each addition before adding more.

Add the broth in ½-cup increments, continuing to cook and stir until the rice mixture is creamy and the rice is still firm but cooked through. You may not need all the broth. Stir in the greens and grated cheese. Season with salt and pepper to taste and serve immediately. Makes 6 servings.

Both recipes adapted from Ciao Italia Family Classics, *to be published by St. Martin's Press in October 2012.*

* Brands may vary by region; substitute a similar product.

Sausage and Barley Soup

Premio

⅔ cup pearled barley

1 tablespoon extra-virgin olive oil

1 pound Premio* mild or hot Italian sausages

1 medium onion, chopped

2 celery stalks, thinly sliced

2 large carrots, thinly sliced

1 small fennel bulb (white part only), chopped

1 sweet red bell pepper, cored, seeded, and chopped

1 28-ounce can diced plum tomatoes

1 medium zucchini, cut in half lengthwise, then cut into thin half-moons

¼ cup minced flat-leaf parsley

¼ teaspoon hot red pepper flakes

Salt and black pepper

Put the barley in a large saucepan and cover it with 2½ cups of cold water. Bring to a boil, lower the heat, and cook until the barley is tender. Drain it in a colander and transfer to a bowl.

Heat the olive oil in a sauté pan over medium heat. Add the sausages and cook until browned. Transfer the sausages to a cutting board and allow them to cool for 5 minutes. Slice into ¼-inch-thick rounds and refrigerate until needed.

Put the onion, celery, carrots, fennel and bell pepper in a soup pot. Cover the ingredients with water by 2 inches. Bring to a boil then lower the heat to medium, cover, and allow the vegetables to cook until they soften.

Stir in the tomatoes and their juice and 2 cups of water. Bring to a boil, lower the heat to medium, and cook for 5 minutes. Stir in the zucchini, parsley and red pepper flakes and cook 2 minutes longer. Add the sausage and barley, cover, and cook about 5 minutes longer, just until everything is hot. Season with salt and pepper to taste and ladle into bowls. Makes 8 servings.

* Brands may vary by region; substitute a similar product.

Aaron McCargo, Jr.

Aaron McCargo, Jr., competed on and won The Next Food Network Star *in 2008, beating out thousands of culinary hopefuls for the ultimate dream job—his own Food Network show. On* Big Daddy's House, *McCargo shares his passion for big, bold flavors and fun, family cooking. Born and raised in Camden, New Jersey, he regularly speaks to youths at schools and community events, illustrating that they too can succeed despite the odds.*

Stuffed Pork Chops with Bacon

JBS Swift

Recipes developed by Aaron McCargo, Jr.

1 cup orange marmalade

¼ cup chopped scallions, white and green parts

¼ cup soy sauce

¼ cup spicy chile oil

9 ounces fresh baby spinach

6 slices hickory bacon, cooked and coarsely chopped (about ½ cup)

6 ounces smoked Gouda cheese, cut into small cubes

1 tablespoon chopped chipotle chile peppers in adobo sauce

1 5-pound rack of pork (8 ribs)

Kosher salt and freshly ground black pepper

2 tablespoons canola oil

In a small bowl, stir together the marmalade, scallions, soy sauce and chile oil. Set half the marmalade sauce aside for cooking and the other half for serving.

Prepare a hot fire in a charcoal or gas grill and oil the grill grates.

Steam the spinach in a steaming basket until wilted (or wilt it in a microwave oven). Transfer the spinach to a large bowl and add the bacon, cheese and chipotle chiles. Mix well.

Prepare the rack of pork by slicing it into 4 equal 2-bone chops. With a small, sharp knife, slit the side of each chop to create a pocket that goes nearly but not all the way through the chop. Wiggle the knife to open the pocket. Stuff each chop with the spinach filling. Secure the openings with toothpicks; season the chops with salt and pepper. Brush both sides of the chops with the canola oil. Grill the chops 15 minutes with the grill covered, turning 3 times.

Preheat oven to 350°F. Transfer the chops from the grill to a foil-lined shallow pan and loosely tent the chops with another piece of foil over the top.

Place the chops in the preheated oven and cook approximately 35 minutes or until the juices run clear and the internal temperature reaches 145°F. During the last 5 minutes of cooking, remove the foil and brush the chops with the marmalade sauce for cooking.

Remove the chops from the oven and let rest for 3 minutes before serving with the reserved sauce. Makes 4 servings.

Recipe adapted from Simply Done, Well Done, *by Aaron McCargo, Jr. (John Wiley & Sons, 2011).*

Easy Sautéed Pork and Pasta Dish

JBS Swift

2 cups canola oil

2 pounds boneless pork loin or pork tenderloin (see note)

2 tablespoons seasoned salt (such as McCargo's Seasoning Salt)

½ cup all-purpose flour

2 pounds fresh asparagus, trimmed, blanched for a minute in boiling water, and cut into 1-inch pieces

1 pound crabmeat, picked clean of any shells

½ cup chopped crispy bacon

3 cups heavy cream

¼ cup freshly squeezed lemon juice

3 tablespoons cold butter

¼ cup chopped fresh parsley

1 pound angel hair pasta, cooked according to package directions

In a large nonstick sauté pan over medium-high heat, preheat half the oil.

Season the pork slices with 1 tablespoon of the seasoned salt. On a large plate, mix together the flour with 1 tablespoon of the seasoned salt. Coat the pork slices with the seasoned flour.

Start to cook the coated pork slices in the oil without overcrowding for 2-3 minutes per side. Place the cooked pork on a rack-lined baking sheet. Cook the remaining pork slices, adding more of the oil to the pan as needed.

Pour the oil out of the pan and add the asparagus, crab and bacon. Cook, stirring with a rubber spatula if possible and being careful not to break up crabmeat, for 2-3 minutes. Add the cream and lemon juice and stir gently. Heat for 4-6 minutes, turn off the heat, and stir in the butter until melted. Stir in parsley.

Portion out the pasta between 4 plates, then top each with the pork and sauce. Makes 4 servings.

Note: If you're using pork loin, cut into 12 slices and pound each slice. If you're using pork tenderloin, cut it into 24 slices and pound each slice.

Alexandria Boswell

Longtime Costco member Alexandria Boswell of La Jolla, California, entered her Spinach-Stuffed Chicken Breasts recipe—a dish she perfected using Foster Farms fresh chicken from Costco—in Foster Farms' inaugural Fresh Chicken Cooking Contest. She won the $10,000 grand prize. Boswell has since opened a successful catering business. For more about Foster Farms' Fresh Chicken Cooking Contest, visit www.fosterfarms.com/cookingcontest.

Spinach-Stuffed Chicken Breasts
Foster Farms

Recipes developed by Alexandria Boswell

1 tablespoon olive oil
½ cup finely diced onions
10 ounces fresh spinach leaves
¼ cup chopped fresh dill
½ cup feta cheese crumbles
½ cup grated Monterey Jack

Salt
Ground black pepper
4 Foster Farms* fresh boneless, skinless chicken breasts
2 large eggs, beaten
1 cup panko (Japanese bread crumbs)
Olive oil cooking spray

Preheat oven to 375°F.

Warm oil in a large skillet over medium-high heat. Add onions and sauté until translucent, about 4 minutes. Add spinach, cover, reduce the heat to medium, and cook until the spinach is wilted.

Transfer the onions and spinach to a large bowl. Add dill, cheeses, ½ teaspoon salt and ½ teaspoon pepper; mix well to combine.

Sprinkle chicken with salt and pepper to taste. Place eggs and panko in separate bowls or plates. Coat a baking sheet with cooking spray and set aside.

Using a sharp knife, slit each chicken breast along the long side, cutting about ¾ of the way through. Stuff the breasts with equal amounts of the spinach mixture. Dip the breasts first in eggs and then in panko to coat.

Place the chicken on the prepared sheet and lightly coat with cooking spray. Bake for 45 minutes, or until the internal temperature is 165°F. Makes 4 servings.

* Brands may vary by region; substitute a similar product.

Mediterranean Turkey Pockets
Foster Farms

1 package (about 1½ pounds) Foster Farms* Fresh Ground Turkey
6 thick whole-wheat pita pockets

FETA CHEESE SPREAD
4 ounces feta cheese
¼ cup Greek yogurt or sour cream
5 pepperoncini, diced
⅛ teaspoon freshly

ground black pepper

OLIVE TAPENADE
3 tablespoons extra-virgin olive oil
2 tablespoons lemon juice
1 garlic clove, minced
4 basil leaves, chopped
1½ tablespoons capers
1¼ cups pitted olives (Niçoise, picholine, Kalamata)

CUCUMBER CARROT SLAW
1 cucumber, peeled
1 carrot, peeled
1 tablespoon red wine vinegar
½ tablespoon extra-virgin olive oil
⅛ teaspoon kosher salt
⅛ teaspoon freshly ground black pepper

To prepare the cheese spread, combine feta and yogurt in a blender. Blend together, adding a few tablespoons of water to loosen the mixture. Blend in pepperoncini and pepper. To prepare the tapenade, combine all ingredients in a food processor. Process for several seconds, until blended.

To prepare the slaw, use a mandoline or a knife to cut the cucumber and carrot in half and then into thin strips. Transfer to a bowl and add the remaining ingredients, stirring to coat.

Crumble and sauté the ground turkey in a pan over medium heat until well done.

Warm the pitas in a microwave or oven, wrapped in a wet paper towel. Cut an opening in each pita and place some slaw on the bottom. Spoon ground turkey, cheese spread, then tapenade into each pita and serve. Makes 6 servings.

Tip: Serve with a tomato, olive and mozzarella salad.

* Brands may vary by region; substitute a similar product.

Michael Psilakis

Chef Michael Psilakis has been lauded for both his traditional and reinterpreted Greek menus and is responsible for putting Modern Greek cuisine on the culinary map. Psilakis has accrued many of the food world's highest honors, including Chef of the Year from Bon Appétit and Esquire. His first cookbook, How to Roast a Lamb, *was published by Little, Brown in 2009.*

Sun-Dried-Tomato-Crusted Lamb Chops with Wilted Arugula and Tsatziki
The Lamb Cooperative

Recipes developed by Michael Psilakis

8 Australian loin lamb chops

Kosher salt and cracked
  black pepper

3 tablespoons extra-virgin
  olive oil, divided

2 shallots, finely chopped

6 cups (about 6 ounces)
  baby arugula leaves

⅓ to ½ cup tsatziki sauce
  (see note)

CRUST

¾ cup large, plump sun-dried tomatoes,
  roughly chopped

2 tablespoons oil-cured black olives, pitted

½ teaspoon minced rosemary

1 small sprig thyme, leaves only

½ teaspoon dry oregano, preferably Greek

1½ teaspoons Dijon mustard

1½ tablespoons extra-virgin olive oil

2 teaspoons red wine vinegar

About ½ teaspoon cracked black pepper

For the crust, in a food processor, combine all the ingredients and puree to a very smooth, thick paste, about 45 to 60 seconds. Reserve.

For the lamb, preheat the oven to 400°F. Season the lamb liberally on all sides with kosher salt and pepper. Preheat a sauté pan over medium high heat, add 1 tablespoon olive oil and brown the chops well on all sides.

Discard the oil in the pan. Transfer the chops to an oven-safe dish and place it in oven. Roast the chops for 5-6 minutes. Remove the chops from the oven and smear the sun-dried tomato crust over the top. Allow to rest for 5 minutes before serving.

Meanwhile, reheat the sauté pan over medium-high heat and add 1 tablespoon of olive oil. Add the shallots and sauté for about 1½ minutes. Add the arugula and wilt briefly, about 30 seconds. Divide the arugula among 4 plates and top with a spoonful of tsatziki sauce.

Serve the lamb next to the arugula and tsatziki. Finish with a drizzle of 1 tablespoon olive oil. Makes 4 servings.

Note: Tsatziki is a delicious sauce made from yogurt, cucumbers and other spices. You can make your own or find commercial brands in some stores.

Grilled Lamb Chops
The Lamb Cooperative

I like to serve these chops as an appetizer, straight off the grill, while everyone is hanging out and chatting. Or, serve as an entrée with a Greek salad.

1 frenched Australian rack of lamb
  (8 ribs)

Kosher salt and cracked black pepper

2 lemons

Extra-virgin olive oil

1 tablespoon dry Greek oregano

SOUVLAKI MARINADE

1 cup extra-virgin olive oil

3 cloves garlic, smashed and chopped

3-4 sprigs thyme

1 fresh bay leaf or 2 dried leaves

2 sprigs rosemary

2 shallots, sliced

Kosher salt and cracked black pepper

Prepare the Souvlaki Marinade by combining all ingredients in a bowl; set aside.

Using a sharp knife, slice the rack of lamb between the bones to make 8 equal chops. Pat them dry with a paper towel. Marinate the chops in the Souvlaki Marinade, refrigerated, for 24 hours.

Preheat a charcoal or gas grill, or ridged cast-iron grill pan, until hot. Lift the chops from the marinade, letting all of it drain away. Season liberally with kosher salt and pepper.

Grill the chops until firm and char-marked, about 3 minutes on each side, depending on how you like the meat done. Rest the meat for a minute or two.

Arrange the chops on a serving platter. Squeeze fresh lemons over the top, drizzle with extra-virgin olive oil, and finish with a sprinkle of oregano. Makes 4 servings.

Recipes adapted from How to Roast a Lamb, *by Michael Psilakis (Little, Brown and Company, 2009).*

Roasted Leg of Lamb
The Lamb Cooperative

1 Australian boneless leg of lamb (about 5 pounds), netting removed and butterflied to flatten

Kosher salt and cracked black pepper

Extra-virgin olive oil

1½ cups water

1 tablespoon Dijon mustard

3 large sprigs rosemary

3 tablespoons blended oil (90 percent canola, 10 percent extra-virgin olive)

STUFFING

1½ cups large, plump sun-dried tomatoes, roughly chopped

¼ cup oil-cured black olives, pitted

1 teaspoon minced rosemary

Leaves only from 3 small sprigs thyme

1 teaspoon dry oregano, preferably Greek

1 tablespoon Dijon mustard

3 tablespoons extra-virgin olive oil

1½ tablespoons red wine vinegar

About 1 teaspoon cracked black pepper

In a food processor, combine all of the stuffing ingredients and puree to a smooth, thick paste, about 45 to 60 seconds. Reserve about 2 tablespoons.

Lay the lamb out on a work surface with the fattier side down. Season generously with kosher salt and pepper and spread an even layer of stuffing over it, pressing the stuffing down into the crevices. Drizzle with a little olive oil and roll the lamb up in a tight spiral, seasoning the fatty side with salt and pepper as you roll. Tie in 3 or 4 places crosswise and 1 or 2 places lengthwise (twist the string around itself 3 times before you pull it tight, so it won't loosen as soon as you let go).

Preheat the oven to 375°F. In a small roasting pan, whisk the reserved stuffing with the water and mustard. Add the rosemary sprigs. Place a rack in the pan; the grills of the rack should not touch the liquid.

Season the lamb on all sides very generously with kosher salt and pepper. In a large, heavy skillet, warm the oil over medium-high heat. Sear the lamb well on all sides, using tongs and leaning the meat up against the sides of the pan to sear the thinner sides and cut ends. Transfer the lamb to the rack seam-side up and roast for about 1 hour, basting every 15 minutes with the pan liquid. To determine doneness, insert a meat thermometer into the thickest part of the lamb: 132°F is medium rare, 137°F is medium.

Remove the lamb and let it rest for about 10 minutes. Slice ¼-inch-thick pieces, drizzle with the pan sauce, and finish with a little extra-virgin olive oil. Makes 6-8 servings.

Puratos
Reliable partners in innovation

Marcy Goldman

Marcy Goldman is a pastry chef and cookbook author, and the host of BetterBaking.com. She's written four cookbooks: The Baker's Four Seasons *(HarperCollins),* A Passion for Baking *(Oxmoor House),* A Treasury of Jewish Holiday Baking *and* The Best of Better Baking.com *(both Whitecap Books). At the helm of BetterBaking.com, Goldman fields home bakers' questions and tests mouthwatering recipes that are worth breaking your diet for.*

Chocolate Chunk Cookies 'n' Cream Cheesecake recipe on page 116

Chocolate Chunk Cookies 'n' Cream Cheesecake

Kirkland Signature/Puratos

Recipes developed by Marcy Goldman

CRUST

8 Kirkland Signature chocolate
  chunk cookies

⅓ cup unsalted butter, melted

CHEESECAKE FILLING

2½ pounds cream cheese, softened

¾ cup sugar

1 14-ounce can sweetened
  condensed milk

2 tablespoons all-purpose flour

1 tablespoon pure vanilla extract

5 large eggs

⅓ cup chocolate chips

10 Kirkland Signature chocolate chunk
  cookies, coarsely broken

⅓ cup chocolate syrup

TOPPING

Melted chocolate, for drizzling (optional)

Preheat oven to 350°F. Line a baking sheet with parchment paper. Lightly spray a 9- or 10-inch cheesecake or springform pan with nonstick cooking spray. Line the bottom with a circle of parchment paper (this makes it easier later to remove the cake for serving). Place the pan on the baking sheet.

To prepare the crust, place cookies in a food processor and pulse to grind into fine crumbs (but not too much—too long and the crumbs will clump). Turn out into the springform pan and drizzle on the melted butter to mix. Pat the crumbs evenly and firmly into the pan bottom.

To prepare the filling, in a large mixer bowl (or food processor), blend cream cheese and sugar until smooth. Add condensed milk, flour and vanilla, and then eggs, one at a time, to make a smooth batter. Scrape the bottom of the bowl often.

Pour half the batter into the pan. Top with half the chocolate chips and half the cookie chunks, and swirl on half the syrup. Top with the remaining batter and chocolate chips, cookie chunks and chocolate syrup. Swirl lightly to immerse the cookie pieces and chocolate chips.

Bake for about 55 minutes. The cake is ready when it is just firm to the touch but not cracked or browning. If it seems wet in the center or too jiggly, lower the oven temperature to 325°F and bake for 10-15 more minutes. Turn off the oven, leave the oven door ajar, and let the cake cool in the oven for 1 hour. Then refrigerate overnight.

Drizzle on melted chocolate, if desired, before serving. Makes 14-16 servings.

Chocolate Chunk Cookies 'n' Cream Cheesecake photo on page 115

Apple Spice Bread Pudding

Kirkland Signature/Puratos

6 Kirkland Signature apple spice
  crumb muffins

6 large eggs

1½ cups evaporated milk
  or whipping cream

2 teaspoons pure vanilla extract

Pinch of salt

1 cup sugar

½ cup unsalted butter, melted

2 tablespoons all-purpose flour

2½ teaspoons baking powder

1½ cups small-dice apples
  (peeled if desired)

1 large red apple, cut in thin slices

Caramel sundae topping, warmed

Preheat oven to 350°F. Generously spray a 3- to 4-quart ovenproof casserole/serving dish with nonstick cooking spray.

Prepare the muffins by cutting into coarse pieces, about 1 inch square. Set aside.

In a large bowl, whisk eggs, milk, vanilla, salt, sugar, butter, flour and baking powder. Add the muffin chunks and diced apples and blend well but gently, taking care to not break apart the muffin chunks. Let stand for 10 minutes.

Spoon into the casserole. Place apple slices decoratively on top.

Bake for 45-55 minutes, or until the muffin-filling (which becomes a custard) just begins to brown and appears lightly set. Remove from the oven and drizzle on warm caramel sauce. Cut into squares and serve warm, chilled or at room temperature with cream or crème anglaise. Makes 6-8 servings.

Tip: You can also prepare this one to two days ahead and refrigerate until you're ready to bake it.

Quiche Muffins
Kirkland Signature/Puratos

¾ cup all-purpose flour
1 tablespoon baking powder
3 tablespoons white wine
1 cup milk
½ cup half-and-half
¼ cup olive oil
8 large eggs
1¼ teaspoons salt, or to taste
¼ teaspoon black pepper
½ teaspoon garlic powder
¼ teaspoon onion powder
1 tablespoon minced fresh parsley

2 cups shredded sharp white or orange Cheddar cheese
1 cup crumbled Kirkland Signature goat cheese
¼ cup finely minced scallions or onion
½ cup minced sun-dried tomatoes
6 Kirkland Signature croissants, chopped (6-8 cups)

GARNISH

Shredded Cheddar cheese
Minced fresh parsley
Paprika
Olive oil or melted butter

Coat 12 large muffin cups with nonstick cooking spray and then line with paper muffin liners. Place on a large baking sheet lined with parchment paper. Preheat oven to 350°F.

In a large bowl, whisk together flour, baking powder, wine, milk, half-and-half, oil, eggs, salt, pepper, garlic powder, onion powder and parsley. Then fold in the cheeses, scallions and sun-dried tomatoes. Fold in croissants. Let stand for 30 minutes.

Mix again briefly. Using an ice-cream scoop, deposit batter into prepared muffin cups. Garnish the tops with shredded cheese, parsley, paprika and a small drizzle of olive oil.

Bake until firm to the touch, 30-35 minutes. Makes 12 large or 14-16 medium muffins.

Devin Alexander

Costco member Devin Alexander has maintained a weight loss of more than 55 pounds for close to 20 years and is committed to helping others find healthy comfort foods through her TV shows, bestselling cookbooks, foods and culinary products. She is the author of The Most Decadent Diet Ever!, The Biggest Loser Cookbook *series to accompany the hit NBC show,* Fast Food Fix, *and more. For more from Alexander, visit her website,* www.devinalexander.com.

Naked Apple Tart
FirstFruits

Recipes developed by Devin Alexander

In culinary school, I used to make a tart very similar to this one, only it had a crust with tons of butter. Now, I enjoy it naked—without a crust, that is. Note that the "tart" cooks for quite a while, allowing the apples to transform into layers of soft, sweet deliciousness.

Butter-flavored cooking spray

2 large FirstFruits* Granny Smith apples, peeled

¾ cup 100% apple juice (not from concentrate)

2 tablespoons coconut sugar (see note)

2 teaspoons unsalted butter, melted

1 teaspoon ground cinnamon

Preheat the oven to 425°F. Lightly mist a 10-inch ceramic or glass tart dish with cooking spray.

Cut the apples in half lengthwise and remove the cores. Slice each half lengthwise into very thin slices. Starting from the outer edges of the dish, arrange the apple slices, laying them horizontally, in tightly overlapping circles in the bottom of the dish, until all of the apple slices are used (they will make a rose or flower blossom pattern).

In a small mixing bowl, whisk together the apple juice, sugar, butter, and cinnamon until well combined (the sugar and cinnamon will not dissolve completely). Pour half of the apple juice mixture evenly over the apples. Reserve the remaining half.

Bake for 30 minutes. Pour the reserved mixture evenly over the apples. Bake for 25 to 30 minutes longer, or until the apples are very tender and the glaze has caramelized on the top and around the edges of the tart (it should look almost burnt—dark brown, but *not* blackened). Cool for 5 minutes, then divide among 4 serving plates or dishes and serve. Makes 4 servings.

Note: Coconut sugar comes from coconut palm blossoms and has a lower glycemic index than cane sugar.

Nutritional information: Each serving has 120 calories, trace protein, 27 g carbohydrates (21 g sugar), 2 g fat, 1 g saturated fat, 5 mg cholesterol, 3 g fiber, 20 mg sodium.

* Brands may vary by region; substitute a similar product.

Cherry-Vanilla Almond Parfait
FirstFruits

This parfait looks beautiful and impressive in a parfait glass, but it's also a great on-the-go snack if you construct it in a resealable plastic container.

⅔ cup fat-free, fruit juice–sweetened cherry vanilla or vanilla yogurt

1 tablespoon whole-grain, crunchy, high-fiber, low-sugar cereal

½ cup stemmed, pitted and quartered fresh FirstFruits* cherries

1 tablespoon finely chopped lightly salted dry-roasted almonds

Spoon ⅓ cup of the yogurt into the bottom of a parfait or wine glass. Top the yogurt evenly with half of the cereal, followed by ¼ cup of the cherries.

Repeat with the remaining yogurt, cereal and cherries. Top with the almonds. Serve immediately or cover with plastic wrap and refrigerate for up to 1 day. Makes 1 serving.

Nutritional information: Each serving has 224 calories, 11 g protein, 37 g carbohydrates (25 g sugar), 4 g fat, trace saturated fat, 0 mg cholesterol, 3 g fiber, 128 mg sodium.

Both recipes adapted from The Biggest Loser Dessert Cookbook, *by Devin Alexander © 2010 by Universal Studios Licensing LLLP. The* Biggest Loser™ *and NBC Studios, Inc., and Reveille LLC. Permission granted by Rodale, Inc., Emmaus, PA 18098.*

* Brands may vary by region; substitute a similar product.

CARAVAN INGREDIENTS | CSM Bakery Products | BAKEMARK

Lara Starr

Lara Starr is a cake-decorating teacher, marketeer, radio producer, card-carrying cheapskate, wife and mom. She is the author of two cookbooks, The Party Girl Cookbook *and* The Frugal Foodie Cookbook. *She has developed recipes for a variety of projects, including* Princess Cupcakes, Fortune Cupcakes *and* Wookiee Pies, Clone Scones *and other Galactic Goodies. See what she's cooking up at www.larastarr.com.*

Chocolate Almond Bonbons
CSM Bakery Products

Recipes developed by Lara Starr

This is a terrific way to use Costco cake left over from parties and events. When cake and icing are mixed together, they make a fudgy, trufflelike center for these pretty treats.

¼ Kirkland Signature chocolate half-sheet cake

4 cups (24 ounces) chocolate chips

1 tablespoon vegetable shortening

3 cups chopped almonds

In a large bowl, mix the cake with a wooden spoon until the cake, icing and filling are combined and uniform in color. Cover the bowl with plastic wrap and chill the mixture for at least 1 hour or overnight.

Using a tablespoon, measure out the dough and roll into balls, placing each one on a baking sheet. Freeze for at least 30 minutes, or cover with plastic wrap to freeze overnight.

While the cake balls are chilling, melt chocolate chips in a double boiler or in the microwave. Stir until smooth, then add shortening and stir until melted and blended with the chocolate.

Place chopped almonds in a shallow bowl or plate and set aside.

Remove 3 cake balls from the freezer. Drop 1 ball into the melted chocolate. Using a spoon, cover the ball completely with chocolate. With a fork, lift out the cake ball from the chocolate, tapping the fork against the bowl to remove excess chocolate. Lift the handle of the fork to let the chocolate-covered ball roll off the fork into the chopped almonds. Cover the ball completely with almonds. Set aside on a baking sheet or serving platter.

Continue with the remaining cake balls, removing only 3 at a time from the freezer.

Store, covered, in the refrigerator for up to a week. Makes 50 bonbons.

Tip: You can also use Kirkland Signature All American Chocolate Cake from the Costco Bakery for this recipe.

Berry Baked French Toast
CSM Bakery Products

Greet your brunch guests with the welcoming smells of baking blueberry muffins and cinnamon. You can prepare most of this easy casserole the night before, so you'll be free to enjoy the company of your family and friends.

1 tablespoon butter

6 Kirkland Signature blueberry muffins

3 large eggs

3 cups milk

1 teaspoon vanilla extract

1 tablespoon packed light brown sugar

¼ teaspoon ground cinnamon

Grease a 13-by-9-inch glass or ceramic baking pan with butter.

Slice a blueberry muffin into 6 slices. Place the slices, overlapping, down the shorter side of the prepared baking pan. Continue slicing and arranging the rest of the muffins.

In a medium bowl, whisk eggs, milk and vanilla. Slowly pour the egg mixture over the muffins, covering them evenly. Chill the prepared muffins for at least 1 hour, or cover with plastic wrap and chill overnight.

Preheat oven to 375°F.

Before baking, sprinkle brown sugar and cinnamon over the muffins. Bake, uncovered, for 30-35 minutes, or until the top is golden brown. Let the pan cool on a cooling rack for 10 minutes. Serve warm. Makes 8 servings.

Entrées

Grilled Herbed Sea Scallops on Orzo Salad with Feta
Atlantic Capes Fisheries

2 garlic cloves,
  finely chopped

1 tablespoon grated
  lemon zest

2 teaspoons fresh
  lemon juice

¼ cup olive oil

1 tablespoon minced fresh
  oregano leaves

1 tablespoon chopped
  fresh thyme leaves

Salt and pepper

1½ pounds Atlantic Capes
  sea scallops, thawed

Chopped parsley or green
  onions, for garnish

ORZO SALAD

2 cups orzo
  (rice-shaped pasta)

½ pound sugar snap
  or snow peas

1 garlic clove, minced

2 tablespoons fresh
  lemon juice

¾ cup chopped fresh
  parsley, divided

2 teaspoons fresh
  oregano leaves

Salt and pepper to taste

½ cup olive oil

1 teaspoon Dijon mustard

1 teaspoon honey

¼ cup red wine vinegar
  or rice wine vinegar

1 pint cherry tomatoes,
  cut in half

6 green onions,
  thinly sliced

⅓ cup feta cheese,
  crumbled

In a bowl, combine garlic, lemon zest and juice, oil, oregano, thyme, and salt and pepper to taste. Add scallops and toss to coat. Marinate in the refrigerator for no more than 10-12 minutes, then remove the scallops from the marinade.

Preheat the grill to medium-high.

To prepare the salad, cook orzo until al dente.

Blanch snap peas and chill.

Combine garlic, lemon juice, ¼ cup parsley, oregano, salt and pepper, oil, mustard, honey and vinegar in a blender. Whir until the dressing is emulsified.

Put orzo and snap peas in a large bowl and stir in tomatoes, green onions, ½ cup parsley and feta. Add half of the dressing and toss to coat. Add more dressing if needed, and salt and pepper to taste.

Grill the marinated scallops for about 2-4 minutes on each side, or until lightly browned but still translucent in the center. Do not overcook.

Place the orzo salad on a serving dish and top with the grilled scallops. Drizzle the scallops with the remaining dressing and garnish with chopped parsley or green onions. Makes 4-6 servings.

Seared Scallops and Sambuca Spinach Sauté
American Pride Seafoods

SCALLOPS

4 tablespoons olive oil

16 American Pride
  Seafoods* sea scallops,
  thawed

Salt and pepper

Large pinch of sugar

2 tablespoons lemon juice

SPINACH

3 tablespoons butter

½ onion, chopped

3 garlic cloves, minced

⅓ cup sambuca liqueur

⅓ cup heavy cream

⅓ cup coconut cream

1 pound spinach, washed
  and stemmed

⅓ cup grated
  Parmesan cheese

1 pound linguine, cooked
  and drained, for serving

To prepare the scallops, preheat a sauté pan over medium heat and add oil. Season scallops with salt and pepper to taste, sugar and lemon juice. When the pan and oil are hot, add the scallops and sear until cooked to taste, about 4-5 minutes on each side. Set aside.

To prepare the spinach, preheat a sauté pan over medium heat. Melt butter, then add onion and garlic. Cook until translucent.

Add sambuca, heavy cream and coconut cream. Cook until reduced by half.

Add spinach and sauté until wilted. Sprinkle the spinach with Parmesan.

Serve the scallops and spinach over the linguine. Makes 4 servings.

* Brands may vary by region; substitute a similar product.

Red Hot Shrimp with Pineapple and Cantaloupe

Chestnut Hill Farms/Legend Produce

2 tablespoons unsalted butter

1 medium onion, diced

1 tablespoon minced garlic

1 tablespoon minced fresh ginger

3 tablespoons Madras curry powder

2 teaspoons coarse salt

½ teaspoon freshly ground black pepper

2 cups canned coconut milk

2 cups water

2 large sweet potatoes, peeled and diced

1 large ear of corn, kernels cut from cob

1½ pounds raw jumbo shrimp, peeled and deveined

1 ripe pineapple, peeled and diced

½ ripe cantaloupe, scooped with a melon baller

3 tablespoons minced green onions

3 tablespoons chopped fresh cilantro

In a large, heavy saucepan, melt butter over medium heat. Add onions and garlic; sauté until aromatic, about 3 minutes.

Stir in ginger, curry powder, salt, pepper, coconut milk and water. Add sweet potatoes and corn. Bring to a simmer, then continue to simmer, uncovered, for 15 minutes.

Add shrimp, pineapple and cantaloupe. Simmer for 4-5 minutes, or until the shrimp are cooked.

Pour into a large serving bowl and garnish with green onions and cilantro. Makes 6 servings.

Grilled Thai Shrimp with Ginger and Fruit Pasta Salad

Sandridge Foods/Rikki Rikki

2½ pounds small (51/60) raw shrimp, peeled and deveined

¾ cup Rikki's Thai Rub,* divided

2 Fuji apples

16 wooden skewers, soaked in water for 2 hours

1¼ pounds Sandridge Foods Ginger and Fruit Pasta Salad*

2 tablespoons chopped fresh cilantro

Place shrimp in a bowl and add ½ cup rub. Toss to coat. Refrigerate for 2 hours.

Core apples and cut into ½-inch-thick wedges. Place in a bowl and cover with cold water.

Preheat grill to medium.

Thread the shrimp on skewers (about 8 shrimp per skewer).

Drain the apples, pat dry and return to the bowl. Add the remaining ¼ cup rub and stir to coat; set aside.

Grill the skewered shrimp for about 2 minutes on each side. Remove from the grill.

Grill the apples for 3 minutes on each side. Remove from the grill.

Place equal amounts of pasta salad in the center of 4-6 plates. Top each dish of pasta salad with several skewers of shrimp and the grilled apple wedges. Sprinkle with cilantro. Makes 4-6 servings.

* Brands may vary by region; substitute a similar product.

Cajun Shrimp Boil

Kirkland Signature

1 stick (4 ounces) butter
5 garlic cloves, minced
⅓ cup lemon juice
2 bay leaves, broken in half
½ teaspoon dried rosemary
½ teaspoon paprika
½ teaspoon dried basil
½ teaspoon dried oregano
½ teaspoon cracked pepper

½ teaspoon sea salt
½ teaspoon crushed red pepper
1 teaspoon Cajun seasoning
  or Old Bay seasoning
12 ounces warm beer
6 ounces water
2 pounds Kirkland Signature frozen
  easy-peel shrimp, thawed and peeled

Melt butter in a large Dutch oven over medium heat. Add garlic and sauté for 3 minutes. Add lemon juice, all the herbs and spices, beer and water. Lower the heat, cover, and simmer for 20 minutes. Bring the heat back up to medium and cook for another 5 minutes. Add the shrimp and cook for another 4-5 minutes, or until the shrimp is done. Serve over rice. Makes 6 servings.

Tip: For an appetizer option, skip the rice and serve with crusty French bread for dipping in the Cajun sauce. Makes 8-10 appetizer servings.

KIRKLAND *Signature*

Creamy Lemon-Shrimp Pasta

Kraft

2 cups penne pasta, uncooked

1½ pounds raw, deveined, peeled medium shrimp

½ cup chicken broth

6 ounces (¾ of 8-ounce package) Philadelphia* cream cheese, cubed

2 teaspoons grated lemon zest

1 tablespoon fresh lemon juice

¼ cup Kraft* grated Parmesan cheese

½ cup Kraft* shredded mozzarella cheese

1 tablespoon chopped fresh parsley

Cook pasta in a large saucepan as directed on the package, adding shrimp to the boiling water for the last 3 minutes.

Meanwhile, heat broth in a large skillet over medium heat. Add cream cheese, lemon zest and juice. Cook, stirring, for 3-4 minutes, or until the cream cheese has melted.

Drain the pasta mixture. Add to the cream cheese sauce with Parmesan; mix well.

Top with mozzarella. Cover and cook for 3-4 minutes, or until the mozzarella is melted. Sprinkle with parsley. Makes 6 servings.

Variation: Substitute boneless, skinless chicken breasts for the shrimp. Cut chicken into strips. Heat a large nonstick skillet over medium heat. Add chicken and cook, stirring, for 7-8 minutes or until done. Add to the sauce with the pasta and Parmesan.

Nutritional information: Each serving has 360 calories, 34 g protein, 21 g carbohydrates, 15 g total fat, 8 g saturated fat, 270 mg cholesterol, 1 g fiber, 590 mg sodium, 2 g sugar.

* Brands may vary by region; substitute a similar product.

Caribbean Sunshine Lobster
Pescanova USA

6 Pescanova* frozen spiny lobster tails

3 tablespoons salt

4 tablespoons butter

2 tablespoons extra-virgin olive oil

1 tablespoon garlic powder

1½ tablespoons sea salt

Dried basil

Lemon wedges (optional)

SPICY ISLAND SAUCE

1 cup ketchup

½ cup mayonnaise

1 teaspoon Old Bay seasoning

5 drops hot pepper sauce

¼ teaspoon white balsamic vinegar or lemon juice

Thaw lobsters in cold running water. Add 3 tablespoons salt to a large pot of water and bring to a boil. Drop lobsters into the boiling water. When the water returns to a boil, cook for 3 minutes. Transfer the lobsters to a bowl filled with iced water for 3 minutes.

To prepare the sauce, combine all ingredients in a bowl and stir until blended.

Preheat the broiler.

Melt butter in a small pot over medium heat. Add oil, garlic powder and sea salt. Heat, stirring, for 1 minute.

Set lobster tails on a cutting board, shell facing up and belly down. Slice through the shell and meat without cutting through completely. Open gently.

Place the tails on a baking sheet. Baste with the melted butter mixture. Sprinkle with basil. Broil for 3½ minutes. Serve with Spicy Island Sauce or lemon wedges. Makes 6 servings.

Recipe developed by Laura R. Garrido.

Brands may vary by region; substitute a similar product.

PESCANOVA

King Crab and Pasta with Bacon and Lobster Medallions
International Seafood Ventures

1 9- to 10-ounce frozen lobster tail, thawed

1 tablespoon olive oil, divided

4 servings linguine

½ cup chopped bacon or pancetta

½ cup chopped shallots

1 tablespoon chopped garlic

Salt and pepper

1 cup plus 4 tablespoons shredded Parmesan, divided

2 tablespoons cream

1 cup blanched peas

16 ounces king crab meat (from 3-4 crab legs)

4 tablespoons seasoned dry bread crumbs

2 tablespoons chopped fresh parsley

Preheat oven to 350°F.

Bake lobster for 20-30 minutes, or until cooked through. Remove from the shell, slice into medallions, drizzle with olive oil, and set aside.

Boil linguine, adding lobster and crab shells for flavor. Strain pasta to remove the shells, reserving 1 cup pasta water.

Cook bacon in a large sauté pan over medium-high heat until crisp. Add shallots, garlic and a pinch of salt and pepper. Cook, stirring, until translucent. Turn heat to low, and stir in pasta. Add 1 cup Parmesan and ½-1 cup pasta water to create a thickened sauce. Add cream and turn off the heat. Stir in peas and crabmeat.

Divide lobster among 4 plates. Top with pasta. Sprinkle with bread crumbs, parsley and Parmesan. Drizzle with olive oil. Add salt and pepper to taste. Makes 4 servings.

FRANCE FREEMAN

Costco Buyer Tip
Nathan De Atley, Seafoods

Dungeness crab is a unique species, found only in Pacific waters from Alaska's Aleutian Islands to Southern California. Known for its flavorful, sweet meat and texture, Dungeness crab is a long-standing favorite among Costco Seafood Roadshow shoppers. Shelling the crab is simple—and the reward is well worth the effort. I recommend the step-by-step instructions on the Pacific Seafood website, www.pacseafood.com.

Tomato and Roasted Garlic Dungeness Crab

Pacific Seafood Group

¼ cup olive oil

4 tablespoons roasted garlic

½ teaspoon crushed red pepper

4 whole Dungeness crabs, cooked, cleaned and cracked

2 tablespoons chopped fresh basil, divided

2 tablespoons chopped fresh parsley, divided

4 fresh tomatoes, diced

1 tablespoon tomato paste

Preheat oven to 450°F.

Heat oil in a large, heavy ovenproof roasting pan over medium-high heat. Stir in garlic and red pepper. Add crabs. Sprinkle with half the herbs and the diced tomato. Stir to combine.

Place the pan in the oven and roast the crabs until heated through, stirring once, about 12 minutes.

Using tongs, transfer the crabs to a platter. Add tomato paste to the pan and heat through to thicken the roasting juices.

Spoon the sauce over the crabs. Sprinkle with the remaining herbs and serve. Makes 4 servings.

PacificSeafood™

Seared Peppercorn Ahi Tuna Steaks

Quick & Easy

Western United Fish Company

1 tablespoon butter

2 tablespoons canola oil

1 teaspoon whole peppercorns

2 8-ounce Western United ahi tuna steaks

1 teaspoon sea salt

¼ teaspoon hot paprika

4 cups arugula

1 medium avocado, peeled and sliced

In a medium skillet, melt butter with oil over medium-high heat. Add whole peppercorns to the skillet and cook for about 5 minutes, or until they soften.

Season ahi tuna steaks with salt and paprika. Place the steaks in the skillet and cook for 2 minutes per side, or until cooked to taste.

Place the ahi tuna steaks on a bed of arugula and garnish with avocado slices. Makes 4 servings.

Your Direct Source

Sesame-Crusted Ahi Tuna Steaks

Orca Bay

4 Orca Bay frozen ahi tuna portions, thawed

1 tablespoon sesame seeds

12 ounces (about 4 cups) green beans

Cooked rice, for serving

MARINADE

2 tablespoons lime juice (1 lime)

1 tablespoon reduced-sodium soy sauce

1 tablespoon mirin

2 tablespoons packed brown sugar (light or dark)

1 teaspoon finely minced fresh ginger

1 teaspoon finely minced fresh garlic (1 clove)

½ teaspoon cornstarch

½ teaspoon sesame oil

Pinch of crushed red pepper (optional)

Combine marinade ingredients in an ovenproof 10- to 12-inch nonstick skillet; stir to blend. Add thawed tuna, turn to coat, and refrigerate for 30 minutes.

Preheat oven to 425°F.

Remove the tuna from the refrigerator. Turn to coat and sprinkle the tops of the steaks with sesame seeds. Bake for 10-14 minutes, or until the fish flakes with a fork. Transfer the fish to plates.

Set the skillet and marinade on the stove over high heat. Add green beans and cook, turning frequently, for 4-5 minutes, or until the beans are tender-crisp and the marinade is reduced to a glaze. Serve with rice. Makes 4 servings.

ORCA BAY SEAFOODS, INC.

Grilled Albacore with Crispy Asian Slaw

Norpac Fisheries Export

1 tablespoon grated ginger
2 tablespoons sesame oil
4 tablespoons canola oil
4 tablespoons orange juice
1 tablespoon soy sauce
4 7-ounce albacore steaks

VINAIGRETTE

¼ cup water
¼ cup soy sauce
¼ cup mirin
⅓ cup canola oil
1 tablespoon sesame oil
Juice of 1 lime
2 teaspoons cornstarch

½ cup crushed pineapple
1 tablespoon grated ginger
1 garlic clove, minced
1 red chile, minced

CRISPY ASIAN SLAW

4 cups canola oil
8 wonton wrappers, thinly sliced
8 ounces snow peas
¼ cup grated ginger
½ Napa cabbage, thinly sliced
½ purple cabbage, thinly sliced
2 carrots, julienned
2 tablespoons chopped cilantro

Whisk together ginger, oils, juice and soy sauce. Place albacore in a flat baking dish, pour marinade over it, and refrigerate for 1 hour. Grill steaks until medium.

To prepare the vinaigrette, mix water, soy sauce, mirin, oils, lime juice and cornstarch in a saucepan. Bring to a boil, stirring lightly. Strain. Return to the pan and add pineapple, ginger, garlic and chile. Simmer for 8 minutes. Let cool. For best results, make in advance to infuse flavors.

To prepare the slaw, heat oil to 350°F and deep-fry wonton strips until golden brown; set aside. Blanch snow peas in boiling salted water for 30 seconds, chill in ice water, then cut into thin strips. In a large bowl, combine snow peas, ginger, cabbage, carrots, cilantro and all but ¼ cup vinaigrette; chill. Just before serving, gently mix in wonton strips.

Place slaw on plates and top with albacore. Drizzle with vinaigrette. Makes 4 servings.

FRANCE FREEMAN

Costco Buyer Tip
Scott O'Brien, Freezer Foods

Tilapia is a wonderful fish for many reasons. As you can see in this recipe, it bakes beautifully, working perfectly for any number of recipes calling for a lighter fish. It's also quick and easy on the grill—great for fish tacos. And its mild taste is ideal for those who don't like strong-tasting fish, such as kids. Healthwise, tilapia is an excellent source of protein, minerals and vitamins, yet low in calories and saturated fats. It's also helpful to know that the supplier, Regal Springs, is highly dedicated to the cleanest fish-raising practices and sustainability.

Baked Tilapia with Lemon, Garlic and Lavender
Kirkland Signature/Regal Springs

4 Kirkland Signature/Regal Springs frozen tilapia fillets, thawed

4 garlic cloves, crushed to a paste

1 teaspoon curry powder

1 tablespoon freshly grated lemon zest

½ teaspoon salt, plus more to taste

Ground pepper, to taste

1 teaspoon olive oil or other oil, plus more for drizzling

1 pound mixed vegetables, chopped or sliced into bite-size pieces

Lavender blossoms (optional; see note)

Cooked rice, for serving

Preheat oven to 375°F.

Place thawed fillets in a baking dish lined with parchment paper.

In a bowl, combine garlic, curry powder, lemon zest, salt, pepper and oil. Rub this mixture into the fillets.

Arrange vegetables around the fillets. Sprinkle the vegetables and fillets with additional oil, lavender, and salt and pepper to taste.

Bake for 15 minutes, or until the fish is just cooked through. The vegetables may still be very firm, which is a nice contrast to the softness of the fish.

Serve with rice. Makes 4 servings.

Note: Lavender blossoms can be found in the spice aisle at well-stocked grocers.

Tandoori Marinated Tilapia with Mango Salsa

Tropical Aquaculture

1 cup plain yogurt
1 teaspoon ground cumin
1 teaspoon ground coriander
1 teaspoon garam masala
1 teaspoon chili powder
½ teaspoon cayenne powder
1 teaspoon garlic powder,
  or 1 minced garlic clove
1 teaspoon minced fresh ginger
1 teaspoon salt

4 fresh Ecuadorian Tropical Brand* tilapia fillets
1-2 tablespoons butter

MANGO SALSA
3 ounces hearts of palm, diced
1 kiwi, peeled and diced
1 mango, peeled and diced
1 cucumber, peeled, seeded and diced
Zest of ½ lime
Juice of 1 whole lime
Salt and pepper, to taste

In a small bowl, combine yogurt, cumin, coriander, garam masala, chili powder, cayenne, garlic powder, ginger and salt; mix until well blended. Place fish in a non-reactive dish and lightly salt. Cover with the yogurt mixture and marinate in the refrigerator for at least 2 hours. Meanwhile, make the salsa. Mix all the ingredients together and let sit for 1 hour. To finish up, heat butter in a large skillet over medium-high heat. Shake any excess marinade off the fish and sauté for 4-5 minutes per side, or until cooked through. Serve topped with the salsa. Makes 4 servings.

Recipe created by Best Moon Catering for Tropical Aquaculture Products.

* Brands may vary by region; substitute a similar product.

TROPICAL
AQUACULTURE PRODUCTS, INC.

Grilled Citrus Rosemary Catfish
Consolidated Catfish Producers

4 fresh U.S. farm-raised
  catfish fillets

Juice of 2 lemons

Lemon pepper seasoning

CITRUS SAUCE

Grated zest and juice
  of 1 lime

Grated zest of 1 lemon

Grated zest of 1 orange

6 ounces pineapple juice

½ cup packed light
  brown sugar

1 tablespoon chopped
  fresh rosemary

¼ teaspoon salt

Preheat the grill.

To prepare the sauce, combine all ingredients in a small saucepan. Bring to a boil, then reduce the heat and simmer for 5 minutes.

Place catfish in a shallow dish and spoon lemon juice over each fillet. Sprinkle with lemon pepper seasoning. Let sit for 5 minutes.

Place catfish fillets on the well-oiled grill, skin side up, for 3-4 minutes. Carefully flip over and grill for 2-3 more minutes, or until the fish flakes easily when tested with a fork.

Transfer the catfish to a serving plate and spoon warm Citrus Sauce over the fillets. Makes 4 servings.

Striped Bass with Citrus Asian Marinade
PAFCO

1 whole striped bass
  (1-4 pounds), cleaned

Grilled lime halves and
  cilantro leaves, for
  serving (optional)

CITRUS ASIAN MARINADE

Grated zest and
  juice of 1 lime

5 garlic cloves

1 teaspoon chopped
  fresh ginger

¼ cup oyster sauce

¼ cup soy sauce

2 teaspoons
  chili-garlic sauce

2 tablespoons packed
  light brown sugar

1 tablespoon fish sauce

¼ teaspoon ground
  black pepper

1 tablespoon chopped
  fresh cilantro

1 green onion, chopped

Thoroughly rinse fish and pat dry. Cut 3 slits into the flesh on each side.

To prepare the marinade, combine all ingredients in a food processor and puree.

Place the fish in a nonreactive baking dish and coat with half of the marinade. Marinate in the refrigerator for about 1 hour.

Grilling: Preheat grill to medium-high and grease well. Grill the fish for 18-20 minutes, turning halfway through cooking.

Oven roasting: Preheat oven to 400°F. Line a sheet pan with foil and grease the foil. Place the fish on the pan. Roast for 15-20 minutes.

The fish is done when the internal temperature is at least 145°F and it flakes easily with a fork.

Drizzle the fish with more marinade before serving. Garnish with grilled lime halves and cilantro. Makes 2-4 servings.

MICHAEL FALCO

Costco Buyer Tip
Annette Alvarez-Peters, Wine

Balance is the key when pairing wine and food. The weight or body, the acids and the strength of flavors should be closely matched to create balance and prevent either item from overpowering the other. A refreshing Oregon Pinot Gris with delicate fruit flavor or a Chablis with stone fruit and mineral notes pairs nicely with this type of fish. Both wines are high in acidity, to complement the natural oils in the hake and the creaminess of the cheese.

Crispy Cheese-Topped Hake Fillets
Ocean Fresh Seafoods

1 pound frozen hake fillets	2 teaspoons crushed fresh garlic
1 teaspoon salt	2 cups fresh bread crumbs
1 teaspoon freshly ground black pepper	2 cups grated Cheddar cheese, plus more for topping
6 tablespoons butter	¼ cup chopped fresh Italian parsley
2 large leeks, thinly sliced	2 teaspoons dry mustard

Preheat oven to 350°F.

Place hake fillets in a greased glass baking dish. Season with salt and pepper.

Melt butter in a large sauté pan over medium-low heat. Add leeks and garlic; cook, stirring, until tender, about 5 minutes. Add the remaining ingredients and mix well.

Spoon the mixture over the fillets and top with extra cheese.

Bake the fish for 25-30 minutes, or until the topping is golden brown.

Makes 4-6 servings.

Tip: Serve with potato wedges and herb salad.

Fresh Flounder Piccata
North Coast Seafoods

8 2- to 4-ounce fresh
North Coast Seafoods*
flounder fillets

Salt and pepper

5 tablespoons
all-purpose flour

4 tablespoons vegetable oil

2 teaspoons freshly
minced garlic

2 tablespoons drained
small capers

½ cup white wine

Juice of 1 lemon

3 tablespoons butter

1 tablespoon chopped
fresh parsley

Season fish with salt and pepper to taste and then dust with flour.

Heat oil in a heavy frying pan over medium heat. Shake off excess flour and brown the fish, about 2 minutes on each side.

Remove the fish from the pan and pour off any oil and burnt flour. Add garlic and capers to the pan and cook for a minute or two.

Pour wine and lemon juice into the pan, turn up the heat, and cook to reduce the liquid by half. Turn down the heat and stir in butter and parsley.

Return the fish to the pan to warm. Taste the sauce and add salt and pepper if needed. Serve the fish with the sauce over the top. Makes 4 servings.

* Brands may vary by region; substitute a similar product.

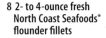

Halibut with Mustard Nut Crust
S.M. Products (BC) Ltd.

4 tablespoons butter,
softened, divided

¼ cup whole-grain mustard

½ cup hazelnuts,
finely chopped

4 6-ounce halibut fillets

Sea salt

Cayenne pepper

3 tablespoons chopped
fresh thyme

1½ cups dry white wine,
at room temperature

Preheat oven to 500°F.

Prepare the crust mixture by combining 3 tablespoons butter with mustard and hazelnuts.

Season halibut with salt and cayenne pepper to taste. Spread the crust mixture evenly over the top of each piece of halibut.

Melt the remaining 1 tablespoon butter and add to an ovenproof pan large enough to hold the fish in one layer. Place the fish in the pan. Sprinkle with thyme and pour in enough wine to come halfway up the sides of the fillets and not touch the crust.

Bake for about 10-15 minutes, or until the fish is flaky and the crust is bubbly. Serve immediately. Makes 4 servings.

S.M. Products

WOONIA

Pummelo Mojo over Grilled Halibut

Sunkist Growers

2 8-ounce halibut steaks

3 tablespoons vegetable oil

Grated zest and juice of 2 fresh Sunkist* pummelos (see note)

Grated zest and juice of 2 fresh Sunkist* limes

1 small red onion, thinly sliced

1 garlic clove, minced

2 tablespoons white balsamic vinegar

Sea salt and freshly ground pepper

Place halibut in a large nonreactive bowl or pan. Combine oil, zests, juices, onion, garlic and vinegar; pour over the fish. Marinate in the refrigerator for 20-30 minutes. Preheat the grill to medium-high. Remove the fish from the marinade and place on the grill. Pour the marinade into a saucepan. Grill the fish for about 7 minutes per side, or until it flakes easily. Transfer to a serving platter.

Bring the marinade to a boil over medium-high heat. Pour the hot marinade over the fish to serve. Season to taste with salt and pepper. Makes 4 servings.

Note: Sunkist* grapefruit, Oro Blanco or Melo Gold can also be used.

* Brands may vary by region; substitute a similar product.

Sunkist

FRANCE FREEMAN

Costco Buyer Tip
Bill Mardon, Seafoods

Nutritionists advise us that we should incorporate fish regularly in our diets because of the benefits of omega 3 fatty acids and low levels of saturated fats. Salmon and cod are both versatile and can be prepared in a variety of ways. Salmon can be grilled, baked, broiled or barbecued—try it grilled on a cedar plank with a little brown sugar. Cod can be grilled, baked, broiled, pan fried, used in fish tacos and, of course, deep fried as fish and chips.

Ginger Steamed Salmon with Vegetables
Copper River Seafoods

4 portions Kirkland Signature*
   wild Alaskan sockeye salmon
   (about 6 ounces each), thawed
4 tablespoons soy sauce
1 teaspoon ground black pepper
4 garlic cloves, peeled

¼ cup sliced fresh ginger
4 teaspoons sliced green onions
2-3 cups fresh vegetables cut
   in bite-size pieces (broccoli,
   green onions, carrots)
1 teaspoon toasted sesame oil

Marinate salmon in soy sauce and black pepper for 10-15 minutes.

Place the salmon in a steamer. Top each portion with garlic, ginger and green onions. Steam for about 10 minutes.

Add the cut vegetables and steam for 3 minutes, or until cooked to taste.

Sprinkle with sesame oil and serve immediately. Makes 4 servings.

Product available on a seasonal basis.

Fried Pacific Cod Spring Rolls
Copper River Seafoods

2 pounds Kirkland Signature* boneless,
   skinless Pacific cod portions, thawed
16 ounces bean thread noodles
   (clear noodles), soaked in water
   for 30 minutes, drained and cut
   into 1-inch pieces
2 sweet onions, chopped
2 pounds green cabbage, thinly sliced

2 carrots, thinly sliced
1 teaspoon salt
½ teaspoon ground black pepper
3 tablespoons soy sauce
30 spring roll wrappers
1 egg yolk, lightly beaten
Vegetable oil for deep-frying

Chop cod into 1-inch cubes. Place in a bowl and add noodles, onions, cabbage, carrots, salt, pepper and soy sauce; stir to blend.

Fill spring roll wrappers with the cod mixture. Rub some egg yolk on the edges to seal.

Working in batches, deep-fry in oil on medium-high heat until golden, about 5 minutes. Makes 6-7 servings.

Brands may vary by region; substitute a similar product.

Salmon Delight

True Nature Seafood

Quick & Easy

1 tablespoon sea salt
2 tablespoons garlic pepper seasoning
2 tablespoons lemon juice
½ cup extra-virgin olive oil, divided

2 tablespoons sesame seeds
2 tablespoons capers
1 fresh salmon fillet (8-10 ounces)

Preheat oven to 350°F or grill to 350-400°F.

In a small bowl, combine salt, garlic pepper, lemon juice, ¼ cup oil, sesame seeds and capers. Stir to blend. Spread over the salmon.

Wrap the salmon in aluminum foil coated with the remaining oil.

Bake for about 15-20 minutes, or until cooked to taste, opening the foil during the last 5 minutes of cooking to brown the fish. Makes 3-4 servings.

TRUE NATURE SEAFOOD

Glazed Salmon with California Avocado Slaw

California Avocado Commission

3 tablespoons soy sauce

1 garlic clove, peeled

1 teaspoon peeled and finely chopped fresh ginger

2½ tablespoons honey

1 teaspoon toasted sesame oil

¼ cup seasoned rice vinegar

¼ cup olive oil, plus more for sautéing

4 5-ounce salmon fillets

¼ cup sliced water chestnuts, cut into thin strips

1 medium carrot, shredded

1 red bell pepper, thinly sliced

3 cups shredded Napa cabbage

Salt and ground black pepper

1 ripe fresh California Avocado, peeled, seeded and cut into ¼-inch cubes

Place soy sauce, garlic, ginger, honey, sesame oil, vinegar and olive oil in a food processor or blender. Blend until creamy smooth. Place salmon fillets in a shallow dish and pour half of the soy sauce mixture over the top, turning to coat on all sides.

In a medium bowl, combine water chestnuts, carrot, bell pepper and cabbage.

Toss with the remaining soy sauce mixture. Season to taste with salt and pepper. Add avocado and toss to combine. Set aside.

Heat a small amount of olive oil in a large nonstick skillet over medium-high heat. Place the salmon skin-side up in the pan and cook until nicely browned, about 6 minutes. Turn the salmon over and cook about 6 minutes longer, or until cooked through. To serve, spoon some slaw over each fillet. Makes 4 servings.

Nutritional information: Each serving has 390 calories, 32 g protein, 26 g carbohydrates, 17 g fat (2.5 g saturated fat, 5 g polyunsaturated fat, 8 g monounsaturated fat), 80 mg cholesterol, 6 g fiber, 380 mg sodium.

Recipe provided by the California Avocado Commission.

Rose's Pesto Salmon Fillets in Phyllo Pastry

Marine Harvest

¼ cup pine nuts

10 garlic cloves, peeled

2 ounces fresh basil leaves

¼ cup olive oil

2 6-ounce portions Marine Harvest fresh boneless, skinless Atlantic salmon

2 phyllo sheets

¼ cup butter, melted

Preheat oven to 350°F.

In a food processor, combine pine nuts, garlic, basil and oil. Blend to a paste.

Rub salmon fillets evenly with the pesto. Place each fillet on a phyllo sheet and wrap the phyllo around the salmon. Transfer to a baking pan and brush evenly with melted butter.

Bake for 15 minutes, or until the pastry is browned. Makes 2 servings.

Recipe courtesy of Fred Rose, Rose's Country Catering, Campbell River, British Columbia.

Salmon Burgers with Grilled Pineapple and Teriyaki Sauce

Trident Seafoods

4 Trident Seafoods* frozen salmon burgers

4 whole pineapple slices

4 tablespoons teriyaki sauce

4 sesame seed buns

4 slices red onion

Grill salmon burgers according to package directions, along with the pineapple slices. After one side cooks, flip the burgers and pineapple and brush each with the teriyaki sauce.

Place the burgers on the buns. Top with pineapple and red onion slices. Makes 4 servings.

* Brands may vary by region; substitute a similar product.

Captain Jack's Salmon Rub
Multiexport Foods

2-3 pounds fresh Multiexport*
farmed salmon fillets (skinless)

RUB
2 tablespoons kosher salt
**3 tablespoons lightly packed light
brown sugar**
2 tablespoons dried parsley

1 tablespoon garlic powder
1 tablespoon paprika
1 tablespoon fresh ground pepper
1 tablespoon ground dill weed
1 teaspoon ground coriander
1 teaspoon ground cumin

Place salmon fillets in a baking dish. Mix all the rub ingredients in a small bowl. Sprinkle the desired amount of rub onto the fillets.

Baking: Preheat oven to 400°F. Place the seasoned salmon in the baking dish on the middle rack of the oven and bake for 15 minutes, or until the salmon is opaque and flakes easily with a fork. The internal temperature should be 145°F.

Grilling: Preheat grill to medium-high. Place the seasoned salmon on a pre-soaked cedar plank and cook for 20-30 minutes, or until the salmon is opaque and flakes easily with a fork. The internal temperature should be 145°F. Serve on the cedar plank for a great presentation. Makes 4-6 servings.

* Brands may vary by region; substitute a similar product.

Multiexport Foods

Tuscan Chicken with Pan-Fried Penne and Triple Tomato Sauce

Kirkland Signature/Tyson

2 tablespoons minced garlic, divided

Grated zest and juice of 1 lemon

½ cup hand-torn basil, divided

½ cup olive oil, divided

4 Kirkland Signature frozen chicken breast fillets, thawed

¼ cup minced onion

¼ cup sun-dried tomato strips

2 cups cherry tomatoes

1½ cups white wine

2 cups canned crushed tomatoes

¼ cup heavy cream

6 cups fully cooked penne

¾ cup thinly sliced crimini mushrooms

1 cup Brussels sprout leaves

In a large resealable bag, combine half the garlic, lemon zest and juice, ¼ cup basil and ¼ cup oil with chicken. Marinate in the refrigerator for 1-2 hours.

In a well-oiled saucepan over medium-low heat, combine remaining garlic, onion and sun-dried tomato; cook until fragrant. Add cherry tomatoes and cook until blistered. Add wine and reduce by half. Add crushed tomatoes and cream; simmer until hot.

In a large well-oiled nonstick skillet over medium heat, cook chicken, covered, for 3 minutes. Turn and cook until internal temperature is 165°F. Remove from the pan.

Heat remaining oil in the skillet. Add penne and mushrooms; cook, stirring, until penne is crispy and mushrooms have browned. Fold in Brussels sprouts, ¼ cup basil and warm tomato sauce.

Serve penne topped with sliced chicken. Makes 4 servings.

Chicken Noodle Strudel

Top Ramen

2 3-ounce packages Chicken Flavor Top Ramen

1 egg, beaten

1 teaspoon sesame oil

2 cups sliced cooked chicken breast

1 cup chopped red bell pepper

1 cup broccoli florets

1 8-ounce can crushed pineapple in syrup

1 tablespoon sugar

1 tablespoon vinegar

2 teaspoons cornstarch

Broccoli and red pepper, for garnish (optional)

Preheat oven to 350°F. Grease a 10-inch pie plate.

Cook noodles in 3 cups boiling water for 3 minutes. Drain. Mix beaten egg into the noodles. Place half of the noodles in the pie plate.

Heat oil in a sauté pan over medium heat. Add chicken and cook for 5 minutes. Add bell pepper and broccoli; sauté for 3 additional minutes. Stir in the noodle seasoning packet, pineapple and juice, sugar, vinegar and cornstarch. Cook for 3-5 minutes, until thickened.

Spread the chicken mixture evenly over the noodles in the pie plate. Top with the remaining noodles.

Bake for 20 minutes. Garnish with broccoli and red pepper. Makes 6-8 servings.

Chicken with Clementines and Olives
Duda Farm Fresh Foods

6-7 Dandy* clementines

1 28-ounce can
plum tomatoes

¼ cup rice or wheat flour

1 teaspoon smoked paprika

Salt and ground
black pepper

8 chicken thighs (skin on)

3 tablespoons extra-virgin
olive oil

1 large onion, thinly sliced

3 garlic cloves, chopped

½ teaspoon ground
cinnamon

¾ cup whole green olives

Cooked rice or polenta,
for serving

Peel and section 2 clementines. Juice enough of the remaining clementines to make ¾ cup juice. Set aside.

Drain tomatoes, reserving 1 cup of the liquid from the can. Set aside.

Place flour, paprika, 1 teaspoon salt and ⅛ teaspoon pepper in a paper bag and shake to blend. One at a time, add chicken thighs to the bag and shake to coat with the seasoned flour. Place the coated chicken on a plate. Discard the remaining flour.

Heat oil in a large, heavy skillet over medium-high heat. Add the chicken in 1 layer, skinned side down, and cook until golden brown, 5 minutes. Turn and cook the thighs until the second side is browned, about 3 minutes. Transfer to a plate.

Add onions and garlic to the pan. Cook until the onions are translucent, 4 minutes, stirring often. Pour in the clementine juice, reduce the heat to medium, and scrape the pan to gather up all the browned bits. Cook until the juice is reduced by half, about 3 minutes. Stir in cinnamon.

Return the chicken to the pan, skinned side down. One at a time, add the tomatoes by squeezing them in your fist over the pan. Pour in the reserved tomato liquid. Simmer for 10 minutes, uncovered, then turn the chicken. Add clementine sections and olives. Cook until the juices run clear when a thigh is pierced with a knife and the chicken is no longer pink near the bone, about 5 minutes.

Serve with rice or polenta. Makes 4 servings.

Note: You can use boneless, skinless chicken cuts with this recipe. Adjust cooking times accordingly.

Brands may vary by region; substitute a similar product.

Roasted Chicken Breasts with Grape, Orange and Feta Salsa
Sunkist Growers

4 boneless, skinless
chicken breasts

6 tablespoons extra-virgin
olive oil, divided

2 tablespoons curry powder

1½ cups Sunkist* grapes,
washed and halved

2 Sunkist* navel oranges,
peeled and segmented

½ red onion, sliced

½ cup crumbled feta cheese

¼ cup thinly sliced
basil leaves

Freshly ground pepper

Preheat oven to 375°F.

Place chicken in a medium bowl. Add 2 tablespoons olive oil and curry powder; toss to coat. Place the chicken breasts on a sheet pan and roast for about 10-15 minutes, or until cooked through.

In a mixing bowl, combine grapes, orange segments, onions, feta and basil. Toss with the remaining olive oil and season to taste with pepper.

Remove the chicken from the oven and let it rest for about 5 minutes. Slice each breast into 4 pieces and place on a serving plate. Top with salsa and serve. Makes 4 servings.

Brands may vary by region; substitute a similar product.

Sunkist

Chicken Dijon

Lea & Perrins

4 boneless, skinless chicken breasts, about 4 ounces each
Salt and pepper
¼ cup butter
½ cup Lea & Perrins Worcestershire sauce
½ cup sour cream
¼ cup Dijon mustard
1 tablespoon chopped fresh chives (optional)

Season chicken lightly with salt and pepper, if desired.

In a large skillet, melt butter over medium heat. Brown the chicken for 4-5 minutes on each side, pressing flat with a spatula.

In a small bowl, mix together Worcestershire sauce, sour cream and mustard. Spoon the sauce over the chicken and cook 2 minutes longer, or until cooked through.

Sprinkle with chives and serve warm. Makes 4 servings.

Heinz

Gilroy's Finest Saucy Garlic Chicken
Christopher Ranch

1 4-pound chicken, cut into 8 pieces
Salt and pepper
Olive oil
40 cloves Christopher Ranch* garlic or peeled garlic, or 10 tablespoons Christopher Ranch* chopped garlic
1¼ cups dry white wine
3 tablespoons chopped fresh Italian parsley
3 sprigs fresh thyme
2 sprigs fresh tarragon
Cooked rice or linguine, for serving

Generously season chicken with salt and pepper. Heat 3 tablespoons oil in a large, heavy skillet (with lid) over medium heat. Brown the chicken pieces on all sides, working in batches if necessary. When browned, remove and set aside.

Gently press garlic with the flat side of a knife to slightly break the cloves; remove peel. Add a little more oil to the skillet if necessary. Add garlic and sauté until golden, about 4 minutes. Do not burn. If using chopped garlic, lightly sauté just until warm. Add wine and herbs; bring to a boil.

Return the chicken to the pan and reduce the heat to medium-low. Cover and simmer, turning the pieces every few minutes, until the chicken is cooked through, about 30 minutes. Transfer the chicken to a serving dish; spoon the garlic sauce over all.

Serve with rice or linguine. Makes 4-6 servings.

* Brands may vary by region; substitute a similar product.

Grilled Chicken and Nectarine Kabobs

Trinity Fruit

MARINADE

1 cup honey

½ cup lemon juice

¼ cup deli mustard

¼ cup olive oil

¼ cup Worcestershire sauce

1 cup teriyaki sauce

3 garlic cloves, minced

3 pounds boneless, skinless chicken thighs, cut into bite-size cubes

3 fresh yellow-flesh California nectarines, sliced into ¼-inch-thick pieces

1 zucchini, cut into ¼-inch-thick slices

1 red bell pepper, sliced into 2-inch cubes

1 yellow bell pepper, sliced into 2-inch cubes

1 large white onion, sliced into 2-inch cubes

14 12-inch bamboo skewers, soaked in water for 30 minutes

In a large, shallow container, mix marinade ingredients. Set aside a small amount of marinade to brush on the kabobs while cooking.

Add chicken to the marinade, turning to coat. Cover the dish and refrigerate, turning the chicken occasionally, for at least 1 hour. Preheat a gas or charcoal grill.

Thread the chicken, nectarines, zucchini, bell peppers and onions onto the skewers.

Place the kabobs on the grill over medium heat. Cook for 9-11 minutes, turning occasionally and brushing with the reserved marinade, or until the chicken is no longer pink in the center. Makes 10-12 servings.

Recipe created by Casey Jones.

Corn Salsa with Peppery Chicken

Del Monte Foods

4 skinless, boneless chicken breasts

½ teaspoon coarsely ground pepper

Chopped fresh cilantro or parsley, for garnish (optional)

Flour tortillas, for serving (optional)

CORN SALSA

2 teaspoons olive oil

½ cup chopped onion

1 small garlic clove, finely chopped

1 15¼-ounce can Kirkland Signature whole-kernel golden sweet corn, drained

1 14½-ounce can Del Monte or S&W organic diced tomatoes

1 teaspoon cornstarch

1 15-ounce can black beans, rinsed and drained

Preheat the broiler.

Sprinkle chicken with pepper. Place on unheated rack of broiler pan. Broil 4-5 inches from the heat for 12-15 minutes, turning once, or until the chicken is no longer pink or the internal temperature is 165°F.

To prepare the salsa, heat oil in a medium saucepan over medium heat. Add onion and garlic; cook for 2 minutes, or until the onion is tender. Stir in corn, undrained tomatoes and cornstarch. Cook and stir until slightly thickened and bubbly. Cook and stir 2 minutes more. Stir in beans and cook until heated through.

Spoon the salsa onto plates. Top with chicken. Sprinkle with chopped fresh cilantro or parsley and serve with tortillas. Makes 4 servings.

Moon Gate Orange Chicken

Florida Growers/Noble Worldwide

2 Florida* tangerines

3 green onions, cut into ¼-inch pieces

⅓ cup soy sauce

¼ cup sugar

1 cup Florida* tangerine juice or juice from 3-4 fresh tangerines

Vegetable oil for deep-frying, plus 2 tablespoons for stir-frying

2 pounds boned, skinned chicken breasts and thighs, cut in bite-size pieces

1 tablespoon shredded fresh ginger or 1 teaspoon ground ginger

¼ teaspoon hot pepper sauce

Score the peel of 1 tangerine into quarter sections; remove the peel. Remove all white membrane and cut the zest into long, thin strips. Peel the second tangerine. Separate both tangerines into segments. Set aside.

In a small bowl, combine green onions, soy sauce, sugar and tangerine juice. Set aside.

Pour oil to a depth of 3 inches into a large, heavy saucepan. Heat to 375°F. Working in batches, fry chicken for about 4 minutes, or until no longer pink. Remove with a slotted spoon and drain on paper towels.

Heat 2 tablespoons oil in a large skillet over medium-high heat. Add ginger, hot pepper sauce and tangerine peel strips; stir-fry for 1½ minutes. Add chicken pieces and stir-fry for 3 minutes. Add tangerine juice mixture and stir-fry for 3 minutes. Transfer to a heated serving dish.

Garnish with tangerine segments. Makes 8 servings.

* Brands may vary by region; substitute a similar product.

Stuffed Chicken Breasts

Kirkland Signature/Sunsweet

Nonstick cooking spray

1 cup herb-seasoned croutons

½ cup chicken stock

1 tablespoon butter

1 cup peeled, cored and chopped Granny Smith apple

½ cup chopped onion

½ cup chopped walnuts

1 tablespoon chopped fresh rosemary, plus more for topping

12 Kirkland Signature/Sunsweet pitted dried plums (prunes), chopped

Salt and freshly ground pepper

4 boneless, skinless chicken breasts

Preheat oven to 375°F. Coat an 11-by-7-inch baking dish with cooking spray.

Place croutons in a medium bowl. Pour stock evenly over the croutons; let stand for 5 minutes.

Meanwhile, melt butter in a medium skillet over medium heat. Add apple and onion; cook for 10 minutes, stirring frequently, until very soft.

Add apple mixture, walnuts, rosemary and dried plums to the croutons and mix well. Season to taste with salt and pepper.

Cut a slit in each chicken breast to form a large pocket. Fill with the stuffing mixture and transfer to the prepared baking dish. Season to taste with salt, pepper and rosemary.

Bake for 1 hour, or until the chicken is cooked through. Makes 4 servings.

Chicken Broccoli Divan
Eat Smart

1½ pounds Eat Smart*
broccoli florets, cut into
bite-size pieces

1 32-ounce package
chicken broth or
reduced-sodium broth

1 tablespoon butter

1 tablespoon olive oil

1½ pounds boneless,
skinless chicken breasts,
cut into bite-size pieces

1 cup chopped onion

¼ cup flour

⅓ cup dry sherry or
dry white wine

2 teaspoons Dijon mustard

4 ounces Neufchatel
(⅓ less fat) cream cheese

1½ cups shredded
reduced-fat sharp
Cheddar cheese, divided

Salt and freshly
ground pepper

2 cups plain croutons
(or any flavor), crushed

Preheat oven to 400°F. Lightly grease a 13-by-9-inch baking dish.

Cook broccoli in boiling water for 2-3 minutes. Drain well and set aside.

Place chicken broth in a medium saucepan over medium-high heat; cook until reduced to 2 cups.

Melt butter and oil in a large skillet over medium-high heat. Add chicken and onion; cook for 5 minutes, or until the chicken is nicely browned.

Stir in flour and cook for 1 minute. Add the reduced broth, sherry, mustard and cream cheese; cook, stirring, until the mixture is smooth.

Stir in broccoli, then stir in ¾ cup shredded cheese a little at a time, cooking until the cheese is melted. Season to taste with salt and pepper. Transfer the broccoli mixture to the prepared pan and sprinkle with crushed croutons.

Bake for 15 minutes. Top with the remaining cheese and cook 5 minutes longer, or until the mixture is bubbly and the topping is browned. Makes 8 servings.

Tip: In a hurry? Use diced or coarsely shredded rotisserie chicken meat in place of chicken breasts; just omit that cooking step and stir into the sauce.

Brands may vary by region; substitute a similar product.

Tuscan Chicken Torta
General Mills

1 15- to 16-ounce can
cannellini beans,
rinsed and drained

1⅓ cups Original
Bisquick mix

⅓ cup Italian dressing

1½ cups diced
cooked chicken

1 9-ounce box Green Giant
frozen chopped spinach,
thawed and squeezed
to drain

1 cup shredded mozzarella
cheese (4 ounces)

3 large eggs

1¼ cups milk

⅓ cup slivered almonds,
toasted

Preheat oven to 375°F.

Mash beans in a medium bowl. Stir in Bisquick mix and dressing. Spread over the bottom and 2 inches up the sides of an ungreased 9-by-3-inch springform pan. Bake for 10-12 minutes, or until set.

Layer chicken, spinach and cheese over the crust.

Combine eggs and milk in a bowl and mix until blended. Pour over the cheese. Sprinkle almonds evenly over the top.

Bake, uncovered, for 50-55 minutes, or until golden brown and a knife inserted near the center comes out clean. Let stand for 10 minutes. Loosen the edges of the torta and remove the sides of the pan. Makes 6 servings.

Nutritional information: Each serving has 465 calories, 31 g protein, 42 g carbohydrates, 22 g fat, 6 g saturated fat, 150 mg cholesterol, 6 g fiber, 700 mg sodium.

Herb-Roasted Cornish Hens

McCormick

2 whole Cornish hens
(about 1¼ pounds each)

2 tablespoons olive oil

2 teaspoons McCormick
Gourmet Collection
garlic salt

2 teaspoons McCormick
Gourmet Collection
paprika

2 teaspoons McCormick
Gourmet Collection rose-
mary leaves, crushed

1 teaspoon McCormick
Gourmet Collection
thyme leaves

½ teaspoon McCormick
Gourmet Collection
coarse grind black pepper

Preheat oven to 350°F.

Place hens on a rack in a shallow roasting pan.
Brush with oil.

Mix all of the spices and herbs in a small bowl.
Rub evenly over the entire surface of the hens.

Roast in the oven for 1-1¼ hours, or until the
hens are cooked through (an internal temperature
of 165°F). Makes 4 servings.

Pistachio and Mustard Seared Lamb

Wonderful Pistachios

8 rosemary sprigs,
leaves picked off

2 tablespoons yellow
mustard seeds

1 bunch (8-10 sprigs) fresh
thyme, leaves removed

12 garlic cloves,
crushed and chopped

½ cup extra-virgin olive oil,
plus more for drizzling

2 tablespoons sherry
wine vinegar

3 pounds lamb loins,
trimmed

Coarse sea salt

Freshly ground black pepper

½ cup Wonderful Pistachios
kernels, crushed

Cooked brown rice
or flageolet beans,
for serving

In a small bowl, combine rosemary leaves,
mustard seeds, thyme leaves, garlic, oil and
vinegar; mix to blend.

Coat each lamb loin liberally with the herb oil.
Season to taste with salt and pepper. Marinate
in the refrigerator overnight.

When you are ready to cook, preheat the oven
to 350°F.

Remove the lamb from the marinade and brush
off excess. Roll each loin in pistachios, just
enough to coat.

Preheat a large sauté pan over high heat, add
a drizzle of olive oil, and sear each loin. Finish in
the oven to an internal temperature of 135°F
for medium-rare (150°F for medium). Let the
meat relax for 10-15 minutes before cutting. It
will continue to cook as it stands.

Serve over brown rice or flageolet beans and
drizzle with olive oil. Makes 4 servings.

Wonderful® PISTACHIOS

Onion-Crusted Rib Veal Chops with Oven-Dried Tomatoes

Plume De Veau

2 cups vegetable oil

1 large Spanish onion, sliced thin

Salt, black pepper and onion powder

1 cup all-purpose flour, for dredging

4 Plume De Veau* rib veal chops

2 egg whites beaten lightly with 1 tablespoon dry sherry

OVEN-DRIED TOMATOES

1 large vine-ripened tomato, sliced in ⅛-inch slices (8 slices)

1 tablespoon extra-virgin olive oil

1 sprig fresh thyme, leaves removed and chopped

Pinch of salt

To prepare the tomatoes, preheat oven to 200°F. In a bowl, lightly toss all ingredients together. Lay out on a baking sheet and bake for 2 hours, or until the tomatoes are slightly dry to the touch.

Heat vegetable oil in a saucepot to 350°F. Allow enough room for the onions. Season onions to taste with salt, pepper and onion powder. Toss in flour, shaking off excess.

Add onions to the hot oil and fry until light golden brown. Remove from the pot and lay on paper towels to absorb excess oil. When the onions are cool enough to handle, chop coarsely and place in a pan large enough to dredge a veal chop.

Preheat oven to 350°F. Lightly season veal chops with salt and pepper. Dredge in egg whites and then coat with onions.

Lay the chops on a baking sheet and bake for about 20 minutes, or until cooked to desired doneness or medium. To serve, place 2 slices of tomato on each plate and top with a veal chop. Makes 4 servings.

Tip: These can be served with a drizzle of reduced veal stock or red wine demi-glace.

* Brands may vary by region; substitute a similar product.

Sautéed Loin Veal Chops with Spicy Cauliflower
Plume De Veau

TEMPURA BATTER
1 cup all-purpose flour
1 cup cornstarch
1 tablespoon
  baking powder
2 eggs
2 egg yolks
1 bottle light beer

Vegetable oil for
  deep frying

1 cup cauliflower florets
4 Plume De Veau*
  loin veal chops
Salt and pepper
2 tablespoons
  vegetable oil
1 tablespoon peanut oil
1 tablespoon sesame oil
1 tablespoon
  chopped garlic
¼ cup chopped shallots

1 tablespoon chopped
  fresh ginger
½ cup chopped
  green onions
¼ cup roughly chopped
  cilantro leaves
1 teaspoon sambal oelek
  (red chili paste)
1 tablespoon sweet
  rice vinegar
¼ cup soy sauce

Preheat oven to 350°F. To prepare the tempura batter, mix flour, cornstarch and baking powder in a bowl. In another bowl, beat eggs and egg yolks. Stir in beer. Add the dry ingredients and stir until blended. Keep chilled until ready to use.

Heat oil for deep frying to 350°F. Dip cauliflower in tempura batter. Fry until crisp and golden brown. Remove from the oil and place on paper towels to drain.

Season veal chops to taste with salt and pepper on both sides. Heat 2 tablespoons vegetable oil in a large ovenproof sauté pan over medium-high heat. Add the chops and sauté on both sides until light brown. Transfer to the oven and cook for 15-20 minutes, or until medium-rare. Remove from the oven and keep warm.

In a separate pan, heat the peanut and sesame oil over high heat. Add garlic, shallots and ginger; sauté until the shallots are browned. Add green onions and cilantro; heat for 30 seconds. Add sambal oelek, vinegar, soy sauce and cauliflower. Toss briefly. Top the veal chops with the cauliflower mixture and serve. Makes 4 servings.

* Brands may vary by region; substitute a similar product.

Osso Buco with Port, Shallots, Carrots and Orange

Plume De Veau

½ cup extra-virgin olive oil

4 Plume De Veau* veal osso buco (shanks) (about 4 pounds)

Salt and black pepper

Flour, for dredging

8 whole shallots, peeled

1 garlic clove, peeled

1 cup baby carrots

2 celery stalks, cut in pieces

¼ cup tomato paste

1 bay leaf, 1 sprig fresh thyme, 1 sprig fresh rosemary, 2 leaves fresh basil

1 cup port wine

½ cup red wine

2 cups hot veal stock (chicken stock can be substituted)

1 teaspoon finely grated orange zest

In a saucepot, heat oil over medium heat. Season veal with salt and pepper to taste and dredge in flour. Add to the pan and lightly brown on all sides. Remove from the pan.

Add shallots, garlic, carrots and celery to the pan, then add salt and pepper to lightly season. Sauté until lightly browned. Add tomato paste and herbs; sauté for 1 minute. Add port and red wine; cook until reduced by half. Add veal stock; bring to a simmer.

Return the veal to the pot and cook, covered, over very low heat until the meat starts to fall away from the bone, about 2-3 hours. Remove the meat and vegetables from the pot. Cover and keep warm.

Place the pot over medium heat and cook until the liquids are reduced by half. Adjust the seasoning.

Serve the veal with sauce, vegetables and orange zest. Makes 4 servings.

Brands may vary by region; substitute a similar product.

Veal Cutlets with Applewood Bacon, Napa Cabbage and White Grapes

Plume De Veau

2 ounces applewood-smoked bacon, chopped

6 tablespoons unsalted butter, divided

1 tablespoon chopped shallots

2 cups shredded Napa cabbage

¼ cup white wine – Sauvignon Blanc or Pinot Grigio

¼ cup veal or chicken stock

Salt and pepper

¼ cup halved white grapes

4 Plume De Veau* veal cutlets, pounded lightly

In a large sauté pan, cook bacon over medium heat until light brown. Remove the bacon from the pan and pour off the grease.

Add 1 tablespoon butter to the pan. Add shallots and sauté for 1 minute. Add cabbage and sauté until wilted.

Add wine and stock; cook until reduced by half. Return the bacon to the pan. Season to taste with salt and pepper. Remove from the pan and keep warm.

Heat 1 tablespoon butter in the pan. Add grapes and sauté until hot. Remove from the pan and keep warm.

Season cutlets with salt and pepper to taste. Place the pan over very high heat. Add 2 tablespoons butter and heat until light brown. Add 2 cutlets and sauté for ½ minute on each side. Remove to a plate. Add 2 tablespoons butter and cook the remaining cutlets.

To serve, spoon the cabbage onto dinner plates and top with the veal cutlets and grapes. Makes 4 servings.

Brands may vary by region; substitute a similar product.

Roasted Pork with Walnuts and Grapes

California Walnuts

1 cup chopped Kirkland Signature walnuts

2 tablespoons chopped fresh rosemary

1 teaspoon salt

½ teaspoon pepper

2 pounds pork tenderloin

6 tablespoons honey, divided

3 cups seedless grapes (red and green)

½ cup balsamic vinegar

1 tablespoon spicy brown mustard

3 garlic cloves, minced

Preheat oven to 375°F.

In a bowl, stir together walnuts, rosemary, salt and pepper.

Pat pork dry and brush with 4 tablespoons honey. Place on a low-rimmed baking sheet and press the walnut mixture onto the top and sides. Surround the pork with grapes. Roast for 30 minutes, or until the internal temperature is 160°F. Let stand for 5 minutes before slicing.

Meanwhile, combine the remaining 2 tablespoons honey, vinegar, mustard and garlic in a small saucepan and simmer for 5 minutes. Drizzle over the sliced pork and grapes. Makes 4-6 servings.

Prime Rib of Pork with Oven-Roasted Grapes

Pandol Bros., Inc.

3-pound pork rib roast

Salt and freshly ground black pepper

2 tablespoons grapeseed oil

1 cup red wine (Burgundy)

1 shallot, minced

1 cup veal stock

2 tablespoons butter

ROASTED GRAPES

2 cups Pandol* red seedless grapes

⅛ teaspoon crushed red pepper

Splash of grapeseed oil

Pinch of kosher salt and black pepper

To prepare the grapes, preheat oven to 400°F. Toss grapes with red pepper, oil, salt and pepper. Place on a baking sheet and roast for 8-10 minutes. Set aside.

Reduce oven temperature to 350°F.

Season pork with salt and pepper to taste. Heat oil in a heavy pan over medium-high heat and sear the roast on all sides. Transfer to a roasting pan and roast for about 1 hour, or until the internal temperature is 150°F.

Meanwhile, prepare the sauce. Discard the rendered fat left in the pan. Deglaze the pan with wine over medium heat. Add shallots and reduce by half. Add veal stock and reduce by half, until slightly thickened. Season to taste with salt and pepper. Add the roasted grapes and butter.

When the roast is removed from the oven, let it rest for 15 minutes. Slice between the bones. Serve with the sauce. Makes 4-6 servings.

* Brands may vary by region; substitute a similar product.

Roasted Raspberry Chipotle Pork Tenderloin

Fischer & Wieser

½ cup olive oil

2 teaspoons minced fresh rosemary leaves, plus 4-5 sprigs for garnish

1 tablespoon minced garlic

1 teaspoon sea salt

1½ teaspoons freshly ground black pepper

2 1-pound pork tenderloins, trimmed

1¾ cups Fischer & Wieser's The Original Roasted Raspberry Chipotle Sauce

¼ cup fresh raspberries, for garnish

Preheat oven to 425°F. In a small bowl, whisk together oil, rosemary, garlic, salt and pepper. Place tenderloins on a baking sheet and rub generously all over with the seasoned oil. Roast, uncovered, until the internal temperature is 155°F, about 20-25 minutes. Remove the meat from the oven and set aside, loosely covered with foil, for 10 minutes, to rest and allow the internal temperature to rise to 160°F.

While the meat is resting, heat raspberry chipotle sauce in a small saucepan until just heated through, not to boiling. Slice the meat into ¼- to ½-inch slices; fan out on a serving plate. Pour the heated sauce over the slices. Garnish with rosemary sprigs and raspberries. Serve hot. Makes 6 servings.

FISCHER & WIESER

Apple-Pear Pork Tenderloin
Oneonta Starr Ranch Growers

2 pork tenderloins
Salt and pepper
3 tablespoons olive oil
3 shallots, sliced
3 garlic cloves, sliced
½ cup dry white wine
(or vegetable broth)
1½ cups apple cider
3 Starr Ranch Growers*
Braeburn or Granny
Smith apples, cored and
cut into ⅛-inch slices
(with skin)
2 Diamond Starr Growers*
Bosc pears, cored and
cut into ⅛-inch slices
(with skin)
3 tablespoons butter

Preheat oven to 450°F.

Season pork with salt and pepper to taste. Heat oil in a frying pan over medium-high to high heat. Add pork and sear on all sides. Add shallots and garlic; sauté until tender, about 1-2 minutes. Add wine or broth and stir until deglazed. After the browned bits have surfaced, add cider, apples and pears; stir.

Transfer all ingredients to a baking dish. Cover and bake for about 45-60 minutes, or until the internal temperature is 165-170°F.

Remove the pork from the pan and keep warm. Remove the apple and pear pieces from the pan with a slotted spoon and place in a bowl.

Pour the sauce from the baking dish back into the frying pan, bring to a boil over medium-high to high heat, and cook until reduced by half. Whisk in butter. Add the apple and pear pieces, stirring gently.

Place the pork on a serving dish and slice on the bias. Top with the apple-pear sauce. Makes 6-8 servings.

* Brands may vary by region; substitute a similar product.

ONEONTA
STARR RANCH
growers

Mushroom-Stuffed Pork with Mandarin Oranges
Festival

2 4-ounce cans Festival*
sliced mushrooms, drained
6 tablespoons butter,
divided
1 shallot, minced
2 teaspoons minced
fresh sage
1 teaspoon minced
fresh oregano
1½ teaspoons minced
fresh thyme
Salt and pepper
2½-pound boneless
pork loin roast
3½ teaspoons olive oil
1½ pounds fingerling
potatoes, cut in half
2 pounds sweet onions,
sliced
2 small leeks, sliced
⅓ cup dry white wine
(or mandarin juice)
2 11-ounce cans Festival*
mandarin oranges,
drained
3 tablespoons chopped
fresh parsley

Preheat oven to 350°F.

Sauté mushrooms in 2 tablespoons butter over medium-high heat until golden brown. Cool, then add shallot and herbs. Chop fine. Add salt and pepper.

Make a hole through center of pork lengthwise, wiggling the knife to widen. Stuff with mushroom mixture. Sear in oil over medium-high heat.

Boil potatoes in salted water until tender. Cool in cold water. Melt 2 tablespoons butter over low heat in the pork pan, add potatoes, and toss to coat. Transfer to a roasting pan, top with pork, and roast for 45 minutes, or until the internal temperature is 160°F.

Caramelize onions in 2 tablespoons butter over medium heat. Add leeks and wine; cook until the wine evaporates. Add mandarins, parsley, salt and pepper; heat to warm.

Slice pork and top with the orange mixture. Makes 6 servings.

Recipe developed by Chef Tyler Hefford-Anderson.

* Brands may vary by region; substitute a similar product.

FESTIVAL
A celebration of quality!

Pork Chops with Apples and Bacon
Farmland Foods

½ cup walnut pieces

8 slices Kirkland Signature* bacon, cut into ½-inch pieces

1 cup chopped sweet yellow onion

4 Farmland* center-cut boneless pork chops (about 1 inch thick)

Ground ginger

Rubbed dried sage

1 large Granny Smith apple, cored and cut into 1½-inch pieces

½ cup dried cranberries

¼ teaspoon apple pie spice

¾ cup apple cider

¼ cup maple syrup

In a large skillet, toast walnuts over medium-high heat, stirring often. Remove from the skillet and set aside.

Add bacon to the skillet and cook for about 5 minutes. Add onions and continue cooking until the bacon is done and the onions are browned and tender. Remove from the skillet, reserving the grease.

Season pork chops on both sides with ginger and sage to taste. Place in the skillet and cook in the bacon grease over medium-high heat until browned, about 2 minutes per side. Remove the chops and carefully drain the grease from the skillet. Return the chops to the skillet. Add apple, dried cranberries, bacon and onions. Sprinkle with apple pie spice. Pour cider and maple syrup over all.

Cover and simmer over medium-low heat for 5 minutes. Turn the chops and cook for 5 minutes, or until the internal temperature is 155°F.

Serve the chops topped with the apple-bacon mixture. Garnish with toasted walnuts. Makes 4 servings.

* Brands may vary by region; substitute a similar product.

Tri-Tip with Roasted Carrots and Potatoes
Cargill Meat Solutions

1 2- to 4-pound Morton's of Omaha Steakhouse Classic Tri-Tip Roast (premarinated)

2 pounds carrots, peeled

3 pounds fingerling potatoes, washed

1 lemon, halved

2 tablespoons olive oil, divided

Kosher salt

Ground black pepper

Preheat oven to 425°F.

Remove tri-tip roast from the package and place on a rack in a shallow roasting pan with the fat side up.

Toss carrots, potatoes and lemons in 1 tablespoon oil. Season to taste with salt and pepper. Place on a foil-covered sheet pan with the lemon halves cut side up.

Set the meat pan in the center of the oven and the vegetable pan above it. Roast for about 50 minutes, or until the internal temperature of the meat is 145°F and the carrots and potatoes are tender.

Let the meat rest for 15 minutes before slicing across the grain into ¼-inch slices.

Serve the sliced meat with the whole carrots and fingerling potatoes. Finish the dish by squeezing lemon juice over the beef and drizzling with the remaining olive oil. Makes 6–8 servings.

Spicy Korean Barbecue Rib-Eye Skewers with Asian Slaw
Kirkland Signature/Tyson

1 cup kimchi

1 tablespoon minced garlic

½ cup soy sauce

2-inch piece fresh ginger

4 Kirkland Signature rib-eye steaks, each cut into 6 strips lengthwise

24 skewers

DIPPING SAUCE

¼ cup Korean chili paste

¼ cup honey

1 cup bulgogi sauce

ASIAN SLAW

¼ cup Korean chili paste

¼ cup honey

½ cup rice vinegar

2 tablespoons fish sauce

2 cups shredded cabbage

½ cup shaved cucumber

½ cup shaved radish

½ cup shaved red onion

½ cup shaved pear

¼ cup shaved green onion

¼ cup fresh cilantro leaves

In a food processor, blend kimchi, garlic, soy sauce and ginger until a paste forms. Rub the paste over the steak strips. Refrigerate for 2-3 hours.

Preheat the grill to medium-high.

To make the dipping sauce, combine all ingredients and stir until blended. Set aside.

To make the slaw, combine chili paste, honey, vinegar and fish sauce in a large bowl. Mix until blended. Add the remaining ingredients and toss to coat. Set aside.

Thread the steak strips onto the skewers and grill for 2-3 minutes on each side.

Serve the skewers with the slaw and dipping sauce. Makes 4 servings.

Pot Roast with Cranberry Pomegranate Sauce

Mazola

½ cup all-purpose flour

2 teaspoons Mazola Chicken Flavor Bouillon

½ teaspoon ground black pepper

2½-3 pounds boneless beef chuck roast

¼ cup Mazola corn oil

1½ cups diced onions

1 cup pomegranate juice

1½ cups dried cranberries, divided

1 tablespoon brown sugar

1 tablespoon Worcestershire sauce

2 teaspoons balsamic vinegar

Preheat oven to 350°F.

In a shallow bowl, combine flour, bouillon powder and pepper. Thoroughly dredge roast in the flour mixture.

Heat oil in a large Dutch oven over medium-high heat. Brown the meat for 3-5 minutes on each side, or until well browned; remove from the pan.

Add onions to the pan juices and cook for 2 minutes. Stir in pomegranate juice and half of the cranberries; bring to a boil and cook for 1 minute. Add sugar, Worcestershire sauce and vinegar, stirring until the sugar is dissolved.

Return the roast to the pan, turning to coat with sauce. Cover the pan and roast in the oven for 75 minutes. Stir well; add remaining cranberries. Cover and cook for 15-30 minutes, or until the meat is tender (check for doneness at an internal temperature of 145°F).

Remove from the oven and let rest for 10 minutes. Transfer the meat to a platter, slice and top with sauce. Makes 6-8 servings.

Mazola.

Beef Pot Roast with Noodles

Cargill Meat Solutions

1 Morton's of Omaha Beef Pot Roast with Gravy (about 2½ pounds)

16 ounces egg noodles

3 tablespoons butter, divided

1 pound button mushrooms, sliced

1 yellow onion, diced

1 10¾-ounce can condensed cream of mushroom soup

1 cup milk

2 cups sour cream

2 teaspoons white vinegar

Ground black pepper to taste

Kosher salt to taste

Remove beef pot roast from the package and shred the meat with 2 forks.

Bring 2 quarts of salted water to a boil for the noodles.

Heat 2 tablespoons butter in a nonstick sauté pan over medium heat. Add shredded pot roast to the pan and cook until the beef becomes deep brown and slightly crispy. Then turn the meat over and repeat. Remove from the pan once both sides are browned.

Cook noodles according to package directions once the beef is cooked.

Melt the remaining butter in the sauté pan over medium heat. Sauté mushrooms and onions for 2-3 minutes. Add remaining ingredients and heat until simmering. Add the reserved crispy beef shreds. Season to taste.

Serve over the egg noodles. Makes 6 servings.

Mom's Organic Meatloaf
Organic Ranchers

2 eggs
⅔ cup organic whole milk
1 teaspoon salt
½ teaspoon ground pepper
4 slices bread, crust removed,
   torn into pieces
¾ cup grated carrots
1 onion, minced

2 tablespoons Worcestershire sauce
1 cup grated Cheddar cheese
2 pounds Organic Ranchers*
   85/15 ground beef ⬤Organic

TOPPING
½ cup organic ketchup
2 tablespoons mustard
2 tablespoons brown sugar

Preheat oven to 350°F.

Combine eggs and milk in a large bowl and beat lightly. Add salt and pepper. Add bread and mix until well soaked and broken down. Add carrots, onions and Worcestershire sauce; mix well. Add cheese and beef, stirring until well blended.

To prepare the topping, combine ketchup, mustard and brown sugar in a small bowl and stir to blend. Set aside.

Pack the beef mixture into a 9-by-5-inch loaf pan. Bake for 30 minutes, then add the topping. Bake for another 30-45 minutes, or until the internal temperature is 160°F. Makes 8 servings.

* Brands may vary by region; substitute a similar product.

Rigatoni with Lamb Sauce
Kirkland Signature/Olde Thompson

1 tablespoon olive oil

1 small onion, minced

1 carrot, peeled and minced

1 celery stalk, minced

2 garlic cloves, minced

⅓ cup red wine

1 pound ground lamb

1¼ cups whole milk

1 teaspoon plus 2 tablespoons Kirkland Signature sea salt, plus more to taste

½ teaspoon Kirkland Signature Malabar ground pepper, plus more to taste

½ teaspoon Kirkland Signature Saigon cinnamon, plus more to taste

2 teaspoons dried oregano

2 tablespoons tomato paste

1 28-ounce can diced tomatoes

1 pound rigatoni

¼ cup grated Parmesan cheese, plus more for serving

Heat oil in a large skillet over medium-high heat. Add onion, carrot and celery. Cook until the vegetables have softened, about 4 minutes. Add garlic and cook until fragrant, about 30 seconds.

Add wine and cook until reduced by half.

Add lamb, milk, 1 teaspoon salt and pepper, stirring to break up the meat. Cook, stirring occasionally to crumble the meat, until most of the liquid has evaporated, about 20 minutes.

Stir in cinnamon, oregano, tomato paste and diced tomatoes; return to a simmer. Reduce the heat to medium and cook until the sauce has thickened, about 12-15 minutes. Season to taste with additional salt, pepper and cinnamon.

Meanwhile, bring 4 quarts of water to a boil. Add 2 tablespoons salt to the water. Add rigatoni and cook until al dente. Drain the pasta, reserving ¼ cup of the cooking liquid.

Toss the pasta with Parmesan, reserved cooking liquid and meat sauce. Serve with additional Parmesan. Makes 4-6 servings.

Parmigiano Reggiano Risotto with Prosciutto, Mushrooms and Peas

Kirkland Signature/Arthur Schuman/Citterio

6-8 cups chicken broth

4 tablespoons butter, divided

3 tablespoons extra-virgin olive oil, divided

1 yellow onion, minced

1 garlic clove, minced

1 pound mushrooms, sliced

2 cups Arborio rice

10 ounces frozen peas, defrosted

½ cup Cello rich and creamy mascarpone

½ cup grated Kirkland Signature Parmigiano Reggiano, plus shavings for garnish

6 ounces Citterio* prosciutto (about 12 slices), each slice cut into 3 long pieces (reserve 6 pieces for garnish)

3 tablespoons chopped fresh parsley

Salt and pepper

In a saucepan, bring chicken broth to a boil, then reduce to a simmer.

In a Dutch oven, heat 2 tablespoons butter and 2 tablespoons oil over medium-high heat. Add onions and garlic; sauté until soft, then remove from the pan and set aside. Add 2 tablespoons butter and 1 tablespoon oil to the pan. Add mushrooms and sauté until soft and just brown. Set aside with the onions and garlic.

Add rice to the pan, stirring constantly to prevent sticking. Add a large ladleful of hot chicken broth, reduce the heat to medium-low, and cook, stirring, until all the liquid is absorbed. Continue the process, adding broth one ladleful at a time. After 20 minutes, add peas, mushrooms and onions. Continue to add broth and cook until the rice is tender.

Remove the pan from the heat. Stir in mascarpone, grated Parmigiano Reggiano and prosciutto. Add parsley and salt and pepper to taste.

Transfer to a serving dish. Using a peeler, shave 6-8 curls from the wedge of Parmigiano Reggiano directly on top. Garnish with the reserved prosciutto slices. Serve immediately. Makes 4-6 servings.

* Brands may vary by region; substitute a similar product.

Sausage and Chicken Cacciatore
New York Style Sausage

¼ cup olive oil

4 links New York Style*
  Italian sausage,
  cut in half crosswise

8-10 ounces boneless
  chicken breast, cut in
  bite-size pieces

8-10 ounces boneless
  chicken thigh meat,
  cut in bite-size pieces

4 teaspoons thinly
  sliced garlic

½ cup onions cut in
  1-inch squares

1 cup halved mushrooms

1 cup green bell peppers
  cut in 1-inch squares

1 cup zucchini cut in
  ¼-inch slices

Pinch of salt

Pinch of ground pepper

¼ cup dry white wine

½ cup chicken stock

4 cups marinara sauce

1 pound spaghetti
  (or any other pasta)

Heat oil in a large nonstick skillet over medium heat. Add sausage and cook until lightly browned all over, 2-3 minutes.

Add all chicken and sauté for 2-3 minutes.

Add garlic, onions, mushrooms and bell peppers. Turn up the heat slightly and sauté for 3-4 minutes.

Add zucchini, salt and pepper.

Turn the heat to high, add wine, and light with a match to burn off the alcohol.

Add chicken stock and cook until slightly reduced, about 2 minutes.

Add marinara sauce, reduce the heat, and simmer for about 5 minutes.

Meanwhile, cook spaghetti according to package directions.

Place the spaghetti in a large serving bowl and top with the sauce. Makes 4-6 servings.

Brands may vary by region; substitute a similar product.

Spicy Pasta Provençal
McCormick

8 ounces spaghetti

¼ cup olive oil

2 garlic cloves,
  finely chopped

1 pint cherry tomatoes,
  quartered

½ cup pitted Kalamata
  olives, coarsely chopped

2 tablespoons capers

2 teaspoons McCormick
  Gourmet Collection
  Tuscan Italian Seasoning

⅛ teaspoon McCormick
  Gourmet Collection
  crushed red pepper
  (or to taste)

2 tablespoons chopped
  fresh parsley

½ cup grated
  Parmesan cheese

Cook pasta according to package directions. Drain well.

Heat oil in a large skillet over medium-low heat. Add garlic; cook and stir for 1 minute, or just until fragrant. Add tomatoes, olives, capers, Italian seasoning and red pepper; cook and stir for 3 minutes, or until the tomatoes begin to soften.

Place the pasta in a large serving bowl. Add the tomato mixture and parsley; toss well. Sprinkle with Parmesan. Makes 4 servings.

Bolognese in Peppers
Organic Ranchers

½ cup basmati rice

2 tablespoons olive oil, divided

2 tablespoons minced carrots

2 tablespoons minced celery

½ pound Organic Ranchers* ground beef ♥Organic

¼ pound pancetta or lightly smoked bacon, diced

1½ cups prepared marinara sauce

¼ cup dry red wine

½ teaspoon crushed red pepper flakes

⅓ cup heavy cream

¼ cup grated Parmesan cheese, divided

¼ cup grated Romano cheese, divided

6 bell peppers (any color), cut in half lengthwise, seeds removed

Preheat oven to 375°F. Cook rice according to package directions, until tender and fluffy. Set aside. Heat 1 tablespoon oil in a large skillet over medium-high heat. Add carrots and celery; cook, stirring, until tender. Add ground beef and pancetta; cook until browned and crumbled. Drain off any excess liquid and return the pan to the heat.

Add marinara sauce, wine and red pepper flakes; simmer for 10 minutes. Stir in cream, half of the Parmesan and Romano, and rice. Simmer for 5 minutes, or until most of the liquid has been absorbed.

Place peppers in a shallow baking dish. Fill with the beef mixture. Drizzle with the remaining oil and top with the remaining cheese. Bake, uncovered, for 30 minutes, or until the peppers are tender. Serve hot. Makes 4 servings.

Brands may vary by region; substitute a similar product.

The
Katama
Company

Crispy Fried Spinach Cheese Ravioli with Pesto Sauce

Cibo Naturals/Monterey Gourmet Foods

¼ cup canola oil

¼ cup (½ stick) butter or margarine

1 36-ounce package fresh Monterey Pasta Spinach & Cheese Ravioli

1 22-ounce jar Kirkland Signature by Cibo Naturals Pesto Sauce

¼ cup grated Parmesan cheese (optional)

⅛ teaspoon salt (optional)

Pinch of ground black pepper or red pepper flakes (optional)

Add a portion of the oil and butter to a large (12-inch) skillet and heat over medium heat. When the butter begins to foam, add about ¼ of the ravioli. Sauté on one side for 2 minutes, or until they are golden brown and begin to develop bubbles on the surface. The heat should not be above a medium range, so as to brown the ravioli but not burn it.

When the first side is browned, turn the ravioli over. When they are golden brown, remove from the pan and place on a dry paper towel to absorb excess oil.

Repeat the above process until you've cooked enough ravioli to meet your needs. Place the ravioli on a platter and drizzle with pesto sauce or serve the sauce in a bowl for dipping.

For extra flavor, combine grated Parmesan, salt and pepper. Lightly toss the ravioli in the mixture before serving. Makes 10 servings.

CIBO NATURALS

MONTEREY PASTA COMPANY

Asian Noodle Salad
Chicken of the Sea

4 cups cooked lo mein noodles or spaghettini

1¼ cups bottled low-fat Asian dressing, divided

1 medium head Napa or Chinese cabbage, shredded

1 cup shredded red cabbage

1 cup shredded carrots, plus more for garnish

Half of an 8-ounce can sliced water chestnuts

1 cup sliced green onions

1 7-ounce can Chicken of the Sea chunk light tuna in water, drained

Toasted black or white sesame seeds, for garnish (optional)

Mandarin orange slices, for garnish (optional)

In a bowl, toss noodles with a third of the dressing. Evenly divide the noodles among 4 plates; set aside.

In the same bowl, mix together cabbages, carrots, water chestnuts and green onions. Gently fold tuna and the remaining dressing into the mixed vegetables, blending well.

Top the noodles with the tuna salad mixture. Garnish with shredded carrots, sesame seeds and mandarin orange slices, if desired. Serve immediately. Makes 4 servings.

Spinach and Cheese Stuffed Shells
Classico

12 jumbo pasta shells

1 10-ounce package frozen chopped spinach, thawed and well drained

1 cup low-fat ricotta cheese

½ cup freshly grated Parmesan cheese

1 egg white, slightly beaten

2 tablespoons milk

1 32-ounce jar Classico* Tomato & Basil Pasta Sauce, or 4 cups

½ cup shredded mozzarella cheese

Preheat oven to 350°F. Cook pasta al dente according to package directions and drain.

In a medium bowl, mix together spinach, ricotta, Parmesan, egg white and milk. Stuff each shell with about 2 tablespoons of the cheese mixture.

Spoon about 1½ cups of pasta sauce into an 8-by-8-inch baking dish and spread evenly. Arrange the stuffed shells in the baking dish and spoon the remaining pasta sauce evenly over the top.

Cover tightly with aluminum foil and bake for 15 minutes. Remove the foil and sprinkle with mozzarella. Bake, uncovered, for an additional 15 minutes, or until heated through. Let rest for 5 minutes before serving. Makes 4 servings.

Tip: This classic meatless dish can be prepared ahead of time. Cover and store in the refrigerator until ready to bake.

* Brands may vary by region; substitute a similar product.

Alaskan Crab Melts
Alaska Glacier Seafoods

4 English muffins, split

⅓ cup mayonnaise

1 tablespoon prepared horseradish

¼ cup minced white onion

½ cup finely diced dill pickles

1 tablespoon dill pickle juice

1 pound Alaska Glacier Seafoods* Dungeness crab meat (2 whole crabs, shelled)

8 slices Cheddar cheese

Preheat oven to 350°F.

Place English muffins on a sheet pan and toast in the oven for about 10 minutes.

Meanwhile, mix mayonnaise, horseradish, onion, pickles and pickle juice in a medium bowl. Add crab and stir, breaking up any large chunks.

Remove the muffins from the oven and top with the crab mixture. Place a slice of cheese on each mound of crab. Return to the oven and bake until the crab mixture is warm and the cheese is melted, about 15 minutes. Makes 4 servings.

* Brands may vary by region; substitute a similar product.

Cod Sandwiches with Asian-Style Slaw
Trident Seafoods

8 portions Trident Seafoods* Panko Breaded Cod

4 cups shredded green and red cabbage

¼ cup diced onion

2 tablespoons chopped fresh cilantro

4 square ciabatta rolls

DRESSING

4 tablespoons sesame seed oil

2 tablespoons rice vinegar

2 tablespoons white and black sesame seeds

2 tablespoons finely sliced green onions

Bake cod according to package directions.

While the fish is baking, combine cabbage, onions and cilantro in a mixing bowl.

To prepare the dressing, combine all ingredients and whisk to blend. Add to the salad and stir to coat.

Warm the rolls in the oven.

To assemble, slice the rolls in half and place 2 fish portions on the bottom half of each roll. Top with the cabbage slaw and roll tops. Makes 4 servings.

* Brands may vary by region; substitute a similar product.

Tilapia Panini Sandwiches with Olive Caper Spread

Slade Gorton

2 portions Gourmet Bay*
  Sun Dried Tomato Tilapia

2 thin slices provolone cheese, cut in half

Butter, softened

2 square ciabatta rolls, cut in half

2 sprigs parsley, for garnish

2 lemon twists, for garnish

1 cup prepared pasta salad, for serving

To prepare the spread, place cream cheese in a food processor and mix until soft. Add mayonnaise and blend. Transfer to a bowl and stir in olives, capers and parsley. Add lemon juice and salt and pepper to taste. Makes enough for 6 sandwiches.

OLIVE CAPER SPREAD

½ cup cream cheese, softened

¼ cup mayonnaise

⅓ cup pitted Kalamata olives, minced

1 tablespoon capers, minced

2 teaspoons chopped parsley

1 teaspoon lemon juice

Salt and pepper

Preheat oven to 375°F. Place tilapia on a sheet pan and bake for 10-12 minutes, or until the internal temperature is 145°F. Place provolone on the fish and return to the oven for 1-2 minutes, until the cheese melts.

Lightly butter the ciabatta and toast on a panini grill. Spread olive spread equally on all the sandwiches.

Remove the fish from the oven and place on the bread. Close up the sandwiches and cut in half with a serrated knife. Garnish with parsley and lemon twist. Tastes great with a pasta salad. Makes 2 servings.

Brands may vary by region; substitute a similar product.

Fish Sticks in Baja Tacos

Trident Seafoods

8 Trident Seafoods*
  All Natural Breaded
  Fish Sticks

4 flour tortillas, warmed

4 cups shredded lettuce

1 cup shredded
  Cheddar cheese

4 tablespoons prepared
  pico de gallo

4 tablespoons chopped
  fresh cilantro

Bake fish sticks according to cooking instructions on the bag.

Place 2 fish sticks in each tortilla.

Add lettuce, cheese, pico de gallo and cilantro. Makes 4 servings.

Brands may vary by region; substitute a similar product.

Tilapia Wraps with Pico de Gallo
Rain Forest Aquaculture

1 cup plain yogurt

4 teaspoons fresh
  lemon juice

4 teaspoons finely chopped
  fresh chives

Salt and freshly
  ground pepper

4 tablespoons butter

14 ounces fresh Rain
  Forest Aquaculture*
  tilapia fillets, cut into
  1-inch strips

12 small flour tortillas

PICO DE GALLO

3 medium tomatoes, diced

½ mango, diced

1 red onion, finely chopped

3-4 tablespoons finely
  chopped fresh cilantro

3-4 tablespoons finely
  chopped garlic

1 teaspoon chili powder

¼ cup fresh lime juice

1 tablespoon olive oil

Salt and freshly
  ground pepper

To prepare the pico de gallo, mix tomatoes, mango, onion, cilantro and garlic in a bowl. Stir in chili powder, lime juice and oil. Add salt and pepper to taste.

In a small bowl, mix yogurt with lemon juice and chives. Season to taste with salt and pepper.

Melt butter in a large frying pan over medium-high heat. Add tilapia and cook for 1 minute per side, or until just cooked through. Season to taste with salt and pepper.

Fill the tortillas with tilapia, pico de gallo and a spoonful of the yogurt mixture. Makes 4 servings.

Brands may vary by region; substitute a similar product.

Rain Forest
AQUACULTURE

Bagels with Hot-Smoked Sockeye Salmon

 Quick & Easy

Trident Seafoods

4 bagels

4 tablespoons whipped cream cheese

12 cucumber slices

8 slices Trident Seafoods* peppered hot-smoked sockeye salmon

4 tablespoons diced red onions

Radish sprouts, for garnish

Cut bagels in half. Spread each bottom half with cream cheese.

Top each with 3 cucumber slices and 2 slices of smoked salmon.

Sprinkle with onions and radish sprouts. Close with bagel top. Makes 4 servings.

* Brands may vary by region; substitute a similar product.

Chicken Romaine Heart Wraps

Andy Boy

3 chicken breasts, cooked and sliced

1 Andy Boy* romaine heart, leaves separated

1 Hass avocado, sliced

2 red Roma tomatoes, cored, seeded and cut into strips

1 green onion, sliced

⅓ cup grated cheese (feta, Mexican blend or mozzarella)

CILANTRO PESTO

3 garlic cloves, peeled

Salt

1 bunch of cilantro

⅓ cup toasted pumpkin seeds

½ cup oil

¼ cup chicken stock (optional)

Freshly ground pepper

First, make the cilantro pesto by placing garlic and 1 teaspoon salt in a small food processor and pulse until finely chopped. Add cilantro leaves and pumpkin seeds and continue processing until creamy. With the motor running, slowly pour in oil, blending until it has a light, smooth texture. Add chicken stock if needed to thin. Season to taste with salt and pepper. Set aside.

In a bowl, combine chicken with the cilantro pesto.

Place some chicken in the center of each romaine leaf. Top with avocado, tomatoes and green onions. Sprinkle with cheese. Gently fold the bottom of the leaf upward and roll the sides over to wrap. Makes 6 servings.

Tip: The pesto can also be made with a mortar and pestle.

* Brands may vary by region; substitute a similar product.

Grape Chicken Caesar Salad Wrap

Anthony Vineyards

Quick & Easy

1 12-inch flour wrap/tortilla

⅓ cup sliced grilled chicken breast

⅓ cup red seedless grapes, stemmed and halved

1 tablespoon creamy Caesar salad dressing

1 cup shredded romaine lettuce

1 tablespoon shredded Parmesan cheese

Serve whole or cut in half at an angle. Makes 1 serving.

Tip: This can also be made with beef fajita meat or turkey.

Recipe provided by the California Table Grape Commission.

Lay out wrap (heat if desired) and layer the ingredients in the order listed.

Fold the lower third of the wrap up over the filling, then fold the outer edges inward. Continue rolling up to complete the roll.

ANTHONY
VINEYARDS

Chicken Salad with Dried Blueberries
Meduri Farms

2 cups cubed roasted chicken breast
¼ cup finely chopped celery
1 tablespoon finely chopped red onion
¼ cup sliced almonds
1 cup Kirkland Signature dried blueberries,
  chopped or left whole

¼ teaspoon salt
1 cup sour cream
1 tablespoon wasabi horseradish
4 large croissants
Sea salt potato chips, for serving

In a bowl, combine chicken, celery, onion, almonds, blueberries, salt, sour cream and wasabi. Mix until blended. Chill for 1 hour. Slice croissants in half lengthwise and fill with the chicken salad mixture. Serve with chips. Makes 4 servings.

Roast Beef Sandwiches with Horseradish Mayonnaise
La Brea Bakery

4 tablespoons prepared horseradish

½ cup mayonnaise

Kosher salt

Freshly ground black pepper

8 ¼-inch-thick slices La Brea Bakery
  Rosemary Olive Oil Loaf

Olive oil

1 pound roast beef, sliced

½ pound Havarti cheese, sliced

½ red onion, thinly sliced

½ cup arugula

In a small bowl, mix together horseradish and mayonnaise. Season to taste with salt and pepper. Set aside. Lightly brush each slice of bread on both sides with oil. In a moderately hot skillet, toast the bread on both sides until lightly golden brown.

Spread about 1 tablespoon of the horseradish mixture on each slice of bread. For each sandwich, place roast beef, cheese and onions on 1 slice of bread. Arrange arugula on top. Cover with another slice of bread. Makes 4 servings.

LA BREA BAKERY

Stack-the-Deck Club Sandwiches
West Liberty Foods

Cooking spray

12 slices firm white bread, divided

1 5-pound Kirkland Signature Meat and Cheese Platter with Spicy Brown Mustard

12 stackers-style dill pickle slices

1 tablespoon ground pepper

6 slices light rye bread, toasted

2-3 tablespoons honey

1 apple, thinly sliced

1 cup prepared coleslaw

Preheat oven to 400°F. Lightly coat a large baking pan with cooking spray.

Place another large baking pan in the oven (not sprayed) while it is preheating.

Place 6 slices white bread on the sprayed pan. Spread the tops evenly with ⅓ cup mustard. Top with Swiss cheese slices and pickles. Sprinkle evenly with pepper.

Top each sandwich with a toasted rye slice. Spread evenly with ¼ cup mustard and drizzle with honey. Top with Cheddar slices and ham.

Arrange apples over the ham and spread evenly with coleslaw. Top with turkey slices, provolone slices and remaining white bread slices.

Carefully remove the hot pan from the oven. Place the pan of sandwiches in the oven and top with the preheated pan. Place a heavy skillet on top of the pan to press. Bake for 10 minutes, or until the cheese has melted.

Cut the sandwiches into halves or quarters. Makes 12 entrée or 24 appetizer servings.

WLF West Liberty Foods.

Southwestern Cheesesteak Sandwiches
National Beef

1 boneless beef chuck roast (about 3-4 pounds)

1½ teaspoons ground cumin

1½ teaspoons chipotle chile powder

2 tablespoons vegetable oil

1 large onion, sliced

1 poblano pepper, sliced

1 cup prepared thick-and-chunky salsa

1-2 cups beef stock

Salt and pepper

8 hoagie buns

8 ounces pepper jack cheese, shredded

Dry meat thoroughly with paper towels.

Combine spices, reserving 1 teaspoon. Rub 2 teaspoons of the spices on the roast.

Heat oil in a pot over medium heat. Add the roast and carefully sear. Remove from the pot.

Add onion, poblano and reserved 1 teaspoon spices to the pot; sauté until tender. Remove, let cool, and refrigerate.

Return the roast to the pot. Add salsa and enough beef stock to halfway cover the roast. Bring just to a boil, then reduce the heat, cover, and simmer gently until fork-tender (about 3 hours).

Remove the roast to a cutting board. Slice the beef and season to taste with salt and pepper.

Add onions and peppers to the liquid in the pot to reheat.

Preheat the broiler.

Split hoagie buns, top with cheese, and toast briefly under the broiler. Assemble the sandwiches with beef, onions and peppers. Makes 8 servings.

National Beef

Italian-Style Sirloin Sandwiches
Cargill Meat Solutions

RUB
- ⅓ cup Italian seasoning
- 2 tablespoons crushed red pepper
- 3 tablespoons onion powder
- 3 tablespoons garlic powder
- 1 tablespoon ground black pepper
- 3 tablespoons kosher salt
- 1 13-pound whole prime top sirloin steak (top butt)
- ¼ cup olive oil
- 1 quart beef stock
- 2 cups dry red wine
- 16 12-inch hoagie rolls, split in half
- 1 16-ounce jar giardiniera (Italian-style pickled vegetables)

To prepare the rub, in a small bowl, combine Italian seasoning, red pepper, onion powder, garlic powder, black pepper and salt. Rub the spices into the sirloin. Refrigerate, uncovered, overnight.

Preheat oven to 450°F.

Rub the sirloin with oil. Place on a rack in a roasting pan. Set in the oven and roast until deep brown, about 25-30 minutes. Reduce the oven temperature to 275°F.

Add beef stock and wine to the pan. Cover the beef with foil and cook for 2½-3 hours, or until the internal temperature is 135°F.

Remove from the oven, remove the foil, and let the meat rest for 30-45 minutes. Reserve the liquid from the pan and refrigerate until needed.

Slice the sirloin across the grain, the thinner the better.

Heat the reserved juices to a simmer. Add the meat slices and heat for 1 minute, then drain.

Place the sliced beef on the hoagies and top with giardiniera. Makes 16 servings.

Teriyaki Burgers
Mr. Yoshida's

- 1 pound lean ground beef
- ¼ teaspoon ground black pepper
- ½ cup Mr. Yoshida's Original Gourmet Marinade & Cooking Sauce,* divided
- 1 8-ounce can pineapple rings, drained
- 4 slices Cheddar or Swiss cheese
- 4 hamburger buns

Preheat the grill.

In a medium bowl, combine beef, pepper and ¼ cup Original Gourmet Sauce. Shape into 4 patties.

Grill the burgers and pineapple rings, basting with the remaining ¼ cup sauce during the last 1-2 minutes of grilling.

Place cheese on burgers, top each with a slice of pineapple, and transfer to the buns. Makes 4 servings.

* Brands may vary by region; substitute a similar product.

Cowboy-Style Burgers
Windset Farms

6 6-ounce beef, lamb, bison or turkey
 burgers (or portobello mushrooms)

Smoked Cheddar cheese

6 buns

Delicato* butter lettuce

Grilled red onions

DRY RUB

2 tablespoons *each* orange, red and
 yellow Dolce Super Sweet* baby bell
 peppers, dehydrated and ground
 (see note)

2 tablespoons garlic powder

2 tablespoons smoked garlic powder

2 tablespoons cracked black pepper

1 Gusto* hot pepper, split and seeded
 (optional)

2 tablespoons kosher salt

ROASTED TOMATOES

26-36 Campari tomatoes

Kosher salt

Black pepper

Olive oil

ROASTED PEPPER MAYO

1 red, yellow or orange Maestro*
 bell pepper

Mayonnaise, about 1 cup

Black pepper

To prepare the rub, blend all ingredients, using a mortar and pestle or coffee grinder.

To prepare the roasted tomatoes, preheat oven to 225°F. Halve tomatoes length-wise. Add salt and pepper to taste. Drizzle with oil. Place on a baking sheet, cut side up, and roast for 2-4 hours, or until they look like moist sun-dried tomatoes. Do NOT char.

To prepare the mayo, preheat oven to 400°F. Roast pepper on a baking tray until the skin blisters, 30-45 minutes. Let cool, then peel and seed. In a blender, combine equal parts pepper and mayonnaise and blend until smooth. Add black pepper to taste.

Grill patties, seasoning with dry rub after flipping. Melt cheese on top. Spread pepper mayo on buns. Add roasted tomatoes, lettuce and grilled onions. Top with patties. Makes 6 servings.

Note: To dehydrate peppers, remove stem and seeds, then cut into strips. Place in a dehydrator overnight.

Recipe developed by Chef Ned Bell.

* Brands may vary by region; substitute a similar product.

Cajun Sloppy Joes
Kirkland Signature/Orleans International

Cooking oil

1 pound Kirkland Signature
 ground beef

1 onion, coarsely chopped

4 garlic cloves, minced

1 large jalapeño, halved
 and seeded

1 red bell pepper,
 coarsely chopped

1 10.75-ounce can
 light chicken gumbo
 soup, liquid drained
 and discarded

1½ cups homemade or
 prepared tomato sauce

2 tablespoons tomato paste

1 tablespoon red
 wine vinegar

1 tablespoon molasses

1 tablespoon
 Worcestershire sauce

1 teaspoon dry mustard

¼ cup prepared
 barbecue sauce

¾ teaspoon salt

Freshly ground black pepper

Cayenne pepper

Hot sauce

8 whole-wheat burger
 buns, buttered and
 grilled or toasted (this
 helps hold the moisture)

Spicy pickle chips and warm
 potato chips, for serving

Heat a large nonstick skillet or Dutch oven over medium-high heat. Add enough oil to coat the pan. Add beef, onion, garlic, jalapeño and bell pepper. Cook, stirring to break up the meat, for 5-8 minutes, or until the meat is browned. Drain the drippings from the pan and discard.

Stir in drained soup, tomato sauce, tomato paste, vinegar, molasses, Worcestershire sauce, mustard, barbecue sauce and salt. Add black pepper, cayenne pepper and hot sauce to taste. Reduce the heat to low and simmer until the liquid is reduced and the mixture has thickened.

Fill the buns with the sloppy joe mixture. Serve with spicy pickle chips and warm potato chips. Makes 8 servings.

Three-Berry Pulled Pork
Kirkland Signature/Rader Farms

3-pound boneless
 pork shoulder

Salt and pepper

1 large onion, sliced

2 cups Rader Farms/
 Kirkland Signature
 Nature's Three Berries,
 thawed

½ cup hoisin sauce

2 tablespoons diced
 fresh ginger

3 garlic cloves, minced

6 dried mushrooms,
 crumbled

2 teaspoons hot sauce

3 tablespoons cider vinegar

1 large head Napa cabbage,
 shredded

10-12 large whole-wheat
 tortillas

BERRY SAUCE

3 cups Rader Farms/
 Kirkland Signature
 Nature's Three Berries,
 thawed

1 teaspoon grated
 lemon zest

3 tablespoons lemon juice

2 tablespoons sugar

3 tablespoons Chambord
 (black raspberry liqueur)

Lightly season pork with salt and pepper. Layer onions in a slow cooker. Place the pork, fat side up, on the onions.

In a bowl, combine berries, hoisin, ginger, garlic, mushrooms, hot sauce and vinegar. Pour over the pork.

Slow-cook on low for 6-7 hours. Remove the pork and scrape off the top layer of fat. Shred the meat.

Add cabbage to the slow cooker and simmer for 5-10 minutes. Stir in the shredded pork.

To prepare the sauce, strain berries and discard seeds. Mix berries, lemon zest and juice, and sugar in a saucepan; simmer over low heat until sugar dissolves. Add Chambord. Bring to a boil, then remove from the heat.

Spoon the sauce onto tortillas, add pork, and fold. Makes 10-12 servings.

Recipe developed by Deb Sklar.

FRANCE FREEMAN

Costco Buyer Tip
Melanie Silva, Bakery

This pulled pork sandwich is a delicious example of the great dishes you can create with any of the artisan breads at Costco—particularly with items offered in our deli cases. For example, toast slices of Panné Provincio French baguette and top with artichoke dip, tapenade or salsa. Or top toasted bread with marinara, a slice of fresh mozzarella and a leaf of fresh basil and bake it until the cheese begins to melt. And you can never go wrong with dipping the bread in a blend of Kirkland Signature olive oil and balsamic vinegar.

Pulled Pork Banh Mi Sandwich
Panné Provincio

VEGETABLE MÉLANGE
2 cups rice wine vinegar
½ cup sugar
¼ cup salt
1 medium carrot, julienned
½ cucumber, julienned
¼ red onion, julienned
½ jalapeño, julienned
2 tablespoons thinly sliced
  fresh cilantro

1 Panné Provincio French baguette,
  sliced in half horizontally
2 tablespoons olive oil
4 romaine leaves, thinly shredded
24 ounces prepared pulled pork
1 lime, cut into wedges
Fresh cilantro leaves, for garnish

SWEET AND SPICY SAUCE
2 tablespoons Sriracha sauce (see note)
¼ cup mayonnaise
4 tablespoons Thai sweet chili sauce

To prepare the vegetable mélange, combine vinegar, sugar and salt in a small saucepan. Bring to a boil and cook until the salt and sugar have dissolved.

In another bowl, combine carrot, cucumber, onion, jalapeño and cilantro. Pour the hot vinegar mixture over the vegetables and refrigerate for at least 4 hours. When ready to use, drain excess liquid from the vegetables before placing on the sandwiches.

To prepare the sauce, combine all ingredients in a small bowl. Blend well and refrigerate until ready to use.

Preheat oven to 350°F.

Drizzle baguette with oil. Toast in the oven for 5 minutes.

Remove the bread from the oven and assemble the sandwich in the following order: baguette bottom half, sweet and spicy sauce, shredded romaine, pulled pork, vegetable mélange, baguette top.

Cut the sandwich into slices and garnish with lime wedges and cilantro.
Makes 4-6 servings.

Note: Sriracha is a Thai hot sauce typically made with chili peppers, garlic, sugar, salt and other ingredients. Look for it wherever you would find spicy sauces in your local store.

Greek Salad Pitas with Olive-Garlic Tapenade

Gold Coast Packing/Babé Farms

1½ cups seeded and finely diced English cucumber

1¼ cups seeded and finely diced Roma tomatoes

¾ cup crumbled feta

½ cup finely diced radishes

2 tablespoons extra-virgin olive oil

1 tablespoon red wine vinegar

1 teaspoon dried oregano

Freshly ground black pepper

4 whole-wheat pitas, warmed and sliced in half

2 cups lightly packed Gold Coast* spinach

2 cups lightly packed Babé Farms* Organic Spring Mix ♥Organic

OLIVE-GARLIC TAPENADE

1 garlic clove

½ cup pitted Kalamata olives

1 tablespoon extra-virgin olive oil

1½ teaspoons red wine vinegar

To prepare the tapenade, chop garlic in a food processor. Add olives, oil and vinegar. Process until spreadable but still chunky.

In a large bowl, combine cucumber, tomatoes, feta and radishes. Add oil, vinegar, oregano and a few grinds of pepper; toss to combine.

Divide the tapenade among the pitas, spreading it evenly inside the pocket. Stuff each pita half with about ½ cup of the combined salad greens and ½ cup of the salad mixture. Makes 4 servings.

* Brands may vary by region; substitute a similar product.

BLT Pizza
Kirkland Signature

5 slices bacon, cooked, cut in half

1 Kirkland Signature frozen cheese pizza

1 large vine-ripened tomato, thinly sliced

4 ounces romaine lettuce, shredded

⅓ cup mayonnaise

Lay bacon pieces evenly over frozen pizza.

Bake the pizza according to package directions.

When the pizza is cooked, remove it from the oven and place on a cutting board. Evenly distribute tomato slices over the bacon.

In a bowl, toss romaine with mayonnaise until evenly coated (DO NOT do this step until you are ready to eat the pizza). Evenly top the pizza with the dressed lettuce. Makes 8-10 servings.

Cape Cod BBQ Chicken Pizza
Chairmans Foods

Quick & Easy

- 1 12-inch precooked pizza crust
- 5 tablespoons sweet barbecue sauce
- ½ cup Comfort Cuisine Cape Cod Chicken Salad
- ½ cup fresh baby spinach
- ¼ red bell pepper, cut in thin strips
- ¼ yellow bell pepper, cut in thin strips
- ¼ cup shredded mozzarella cheese
- 2 teaspoons coarsely chopped cilantro (optional)
- 2 teaspoons thinly sliced green onion (optional)

Preheat oven to 350°F.

Using a pizza stone or greased cookie sheet, bake the pizza crust for 5-8 minutes, or until it starts to get crispy and firm; remove from the oven.

Spread barbecue sauce evenly over the crust.

Add chicken salad, evenly distributing over the crust.

Next, add spinach and bell peppers.

Top it off with mozzarella and return to the oven for another 8-10 minutes, or until the cheese has melted and browned a bit.

Garnish with cilantro and green onions. Makes 4-6 servings.

Peach Pizza
Fowler Packing

- Prepared dough for 1 pizza
- 1 ripe peach, thinly sliced
- 1 teaspoon balsamic vinegar, plus more for dressing greens
- ½ red onion, thinly sliced
- 1 tablespoon olive oil
- 1 teaspoon fresh thyme leaves
- 1 cup grated Manchego cheese (see note)
- 4 slices prosciutto
- Fresh basil leaves and arugula, for garnish

Preheat the grill. Preheat oven to 350°F.

Divide the dough into quarters and roll each piece into a 6-inch round. Grill the dough over medium-high heat for 3-5 minutes on each side.

On the stove, sauté peaches with vinegar in a sauté pan over high heat until they are soft.

In a second sauté pan, sweat onions in oil over high heat until they are translucent. Stir in thyme.

Layer cheese, prosciutto, peaches and onions on the pizza rounds. Bake in the oven for 10 minutes.

Toss basil and arugula lightly in balsamic vinegar and place on the pizzas. Makes 4 servings.

Note: Manchego is a Spanish sheep's-milk cheese.

Desserts

Chocolate Mousse with Wine-Soaked Cherries

Chelan Fresh Marketing

MOUSSE

6 ounces semisweet chocolate, chopped (plus extra for shaving)

4 large egg yolks

¼ cup cold water

3 tablespoons granulated sugar, divided

1 teaspoon vanilla extract

5 ounces (about ½ cup plus 1 tablespoon) pasteurized egg whites

1 cup heavy cream

WINE-SOAKED CHERRIES

½ cup red wine (pinot or rosé)

½ cup granulated sugar

Grated zest of 1 lemon

¾ pound Chelan Fresh* sweet red cherries, pitted

WHIPPED CREAM

½ cup heavy whipping cream

2 teaspoons granulated sugar

1 teaspoon vanilla extract

To prepare the mousse, melt chocolate in a glass bowl in a microwave oven at medium (50%) power until melted, about 2-3 minutes, stirring about halfway through the cooking time.

In a small bowl, mix egg yolks and water. Pour the mixture into the top pan of a small double boiler. Cook over simmering water, whisking constantly, until the mixture bubbles at the edges. Remove top pan from heat and continue to whisk to cool, about 1 minute.

Whisk in 2-3 teaspoons of melted chocolate until smooth. Whisk in 2 tablespoons sugar, then the remaining chocolate, about 1 tablespoon at a time, until incorporated. Stir in vanilla; refrigerate.

In a medium bowl, beat egg whites with the remaining 1 tablespoon of sugar until stiff peaks form; set aside. In a large chilled bowl, beat cream until stiff peaks form. Gently fold the whipped cream, then the whites mixture, into the chocolate mixture.

Spoon the mousse into individual serving bowls or 1 large bowl. Cover and refrigerate overnight.

To prepare the cherries, combine wine, sugar and lemon zest in a large saucepan and bring to a boil over medium heat. Add cherries, reduce the heat to medium-low, and simmer until slightly reduced, about 10 minutes. Set aside and let cool.

To prepare the whipped cream, combine all ingredients and whip.

To serve, top the mousse with cherries, whipped cream and shaved chocolate. Makes 6 servings.

* Brands may vary by region; substitute a similar product.

Rugala Trifle

Dawn Foods

1 3.4-ounce package vanilla pudding

12 Kirkland Signature Rugala, chocolate and raspberry

¾ cup sweet sherry

1 pint fresh raspberries

Chocolate fudge syrup

Whipped cream (optional)

Prepare pudding according to package directions. Slice 2 rugala in half and set aside.

Chop the remaining rugala. Place in a bowl, add sherry, and let soak for 5 minutes.

Spoon the pudding into 4 clear individual serving dishes. Layer with raspberries, then the soaked rugala. Repeat.

Top with the reserved sliced rugala. Drizzle with chocolate syrup. Serve with whipped cream. Makes 4 servings.

Dawn®
FOOD PRODUCTS, INC.

Caramelized Apple or Pear Parfaits with Macadamia Nut Crisp

Columbia Marketing International

6 large CMI* apples or pears, peeled, cored and chopped into 1-inch chunks

1 tablespoon lemon juice

⅔ cup sugar

1 teaspoon grated lemon zest

⅛ teaspoon salt

¼ teaspoon ground allspice

Whipped cream, for serving

Ground cinnamon, for garnish

MACADAMIA NUT CRISP

⅓ cup flour

¼ cup packed light brown sugar

¼ cup granulated sugar

¼ teaspoon ground cinnamon

¼ teaspoon ground nutmeg

¼ teaspoon salt

5 tablespoons butter, slightly softened

¾ cup chopped macadamia nuts

In a medium saucepan, combine apples or pears with lemon juice and toss to coat. Add sugar, grated zest, salt and allspice. Bring to a simmer over medium heat. Cook until the fruit is soft and most of the juices have evaporated, stirring occasionally. The remaining juices should be syrupy and beginning to caramelize. Remove from the heat and keep warm.

Preheat oven to 350°F.

To prepare the crisp, combine flour, brown sugar, granulated sugar, cinnamon, nutmeg and salt in a medium bowl. Add butter and rub into the dry ingredients until crumbly. Add nuts and toss to incorporate. Break up the mixture onto a cookie sheet and bake until golden brown, about 15 minutes. Remove and set aside.

In parfait or wine glasses, alternate layers of fruit, crisp and whipped cream, finishing with whipped cream on top and a dusting of cinnamon. Makes 4-6 servings.

Recipe courtesy of Chef David Toal of Ravenous Catering, Wenatchee, Washington.

* Brands may vary by region; substitute a similar product.

Layered Fruit Whip Dessert

Castle Rock Vineyards/Nature's Partner

1 6-ounce package lemon-flavored gelatin dessert

1 3.4-ounce package cheesecake-flavored instant pudding mix

24 ounces low-fat cottage cheese

16 ounces frozen whipped dessert topping, thawed

3 cups Castle Rock or Nature's Partner* red seedless grapes, washed

4 ripe Nature's Partner* kiwifruit, peeled and diced

2 ripe Nature's Partner* peaches, washed and diced

1 cup Nature's Partner* blueberries, washed

In a large mixing bowl, mix together gelatin, pudding mix, cottage cheese and whipped dessert topping. Refrigerate.

In a separate bowl, stir all fruit together, setting aside ½ cup each of grapes and diced kiwifruit for garnish (optional).

Using a clean glass trifle or serving bowl, layer the fruit and the gelatin mixture trifle-style, beginning with the fruit.

Refrigerate overnight. Garnish with the reserved grapes and kiwifruit, if desired. Makes 10-12 servings.

* Brands may vary by region; substitute a similar product.

Sunny Fresh Delight Fruit Parfaits
Bee Sweet/HMC Farms/Premier Citrus Marketing/AJ Trucco

2 tablespoons coconut shavings

½ cup walnut halves

1½ cups vanilla yogurt

3 ripe Bee Sweet Citrus murcott tangerines, cut into medium-sized chunks

2 ripe Premier Citrus Marketing grapefruits, cut into medium-sized chunks

4 ripe Trucco kiwifruits, cut into medium-sized chunks

2 ripe HMC Farms peaches, cut into medium-sized chunks

1 teaspoon ground cinnamon

For each serving, in a large cup or bowl make layers in the following order:

Layer 1: 1 teaspoon coconut, 1 tablespoon walnut halves, ¼ cup yogurt, several tangerine chunks and several grapefruit chunks.

Layer 2: 1 teaspoon coconut, 1 tablespoon walnut halves, ¼ cup yogurt, several kiwi chunks and several peach chunks.

Layer 3: ¼ cup yogurt, a few pieces each of tangerine, grapefruit, kiwi and peach, and a few walnut pieces.

Sprinkle the top with 1 teaspoon coconut and ½ teaspoon cinnamon. Makes 2 servings.

Chocolate Cherry Cheesecake Trifle

Primavera

CAKE

1 cup egg whites

Pinch of salt

1 teaspoon cream of tartar

1¼ cups sugar

1 teaspoon vanilla extract

1 cup flour

⅓ cup pitted and finely chopped Primavera* fresh sweet cherries, divided

CHEESECAKE FILLING

16 ounces cream cheese, softened

¼ cup sugar

¼ cup half-and-half

¼ cup pureed Primavera* fresh sweet cherries

1½ cups finely chopped Primavera* fresh sweet cherries

1½ cups shaved chocolate

1 cup prepared whipped cream

Preheat oven to 325°F. To prepare the cake, with an electric mixer, beat egg whites with salt and cream of tartar until they begin to foam. Add sugar and beat until stiff peaks form. Mix in vanilla. Carefully fold in flour.

Pour half of the batter into an ungreased 9-inch tube pan and top with half of the chopped cherries. Pour in the remaining batter and sprinkle on the remaining cherries. Bake for 50 minutes, or until a toothpick comes out clean. Let cool before removing from the pan. To prepare the filling, blend cream cheese and sugar with an electric mixer until smooth. Add half-and-half and pureed cherries.

To assemble, cut the cake into 1- to 1½-inch cubes. In a trifle dish, place an even layer of cake cubes and cheesecake filling. Sprinkle with chopped cherries and shaved chocolate. Repeat layers until the trifle dish is full, finishing with whipped cream and the remaining cherries and chocolate on top. Makes 6-8 servings.

Brands may vary by region, substitute a similar product.

PRIMAVERA

Buttery Shortbread and Cherry Parfaits

J&J Snack Foods

1 cup jarred Morello cherries, drained
⅓ cup sugar, divided, plus more to taste
1 cup heavy cream
½ teaspoon almond extract
8 ounces mascarpone cheese

4 large martini glasses
8 Kirkland Signature Chocolate Dipped
   All Butter Shortbread Cookies
1 4-ounce bar Ghirardelli semi-sweet
   chocolate, grated

In a large bowl, mash cherries with a fork until no whole ones remain. Mix in 4 teaspoons sugar, or to taste. Set aside.

In a clean mixing bowl, whip cream until almost stiff peaks form. Beat in ¼ cup sugar and almond extract. Fold in mascarpone.

To assemble, using half of the mascarpone mixture, put a base layer in each glass.

Place 2 shortbread cookies back to back, with the icing facing out, in the center of each glass and push down into the mascarpone base.

Spoon equal amounts of the mashed cherries into each glass around the cookies.

Top with the remaining mascarpone mixture and garnish with grated chocolate. Makes 4 servings.

Tip: The parfaits can be made up to 3 hours before serving and refrigerated.

Golden Peach Cobbler

SunWest

⅔ cup sugar, divided
1¼ cups flour, divided
Salt
5 cups peeled, sliced ripe fresh SunWest* peaches
1 tablespoon lemon juice
4 tablespoons butter, divided
1 tablespoon ground cinnamon
1½ teaspoons baking powder
½ cup milk

Preheat oven to 400°F.

In a small bowl, combine ½ cup sugar, 2 tablespoons flour and a dash of salt; mix well.

Place peaches in a medium bowl. Sprinkle with lemon juice. Add the sugar mixture and stir to coat. Place in a buttered 9-inch baking dish, dot with 1 tablespoon butter, and sprinkle with cinnamon.

In a medium bowl, combine the remaining flour, 1 tablespoon sugar, baking powder and ¼ teaspoon salt. Cut 3 tablespoons butter into the flour mixture until it resembles coarse cornmeal. Add milk and mix until the dry ingredients are moistened. Spoon 9 rounded mounds of dough over the peaches. Sprinkle with the remaining sugar.

Bake for 30 minutes, or until the topping is golden brown. Makes 9 servings.

* Brands may vary by region; substitute a similar product.

Blueberry Cherry Cobbler

Grower Direct Marketing/Victoria Island Farms

1¼ cups Grower Direct* pitted fresh cherries
1¼ cups Victoria Island Farms* blueberries
¾ cup sugar
¾ cup warm water
Vanilla ice cream, for serving

BATTER
6 tablespoons butter
1 cup all-purpose flour
1 cup sugar
1 teaspoon baking powder
1 cup milk

Preheat oven to 350°F.

In a bowl, mix cherries, berries, sugar and water. Set aside.

To prepare the batter, melt butter and swirl in the bottom of a 12-by-9-inch baking dish.

In a bowl, combine flour, sugar, baking powder and milk; mix well. Pour this mixture on top of the butter. Spread the fruit mixture with its liquid evenly over the batter.

Bake for about 1 hour, or until slightly browned on top.

Serve warm with ice cream. Makes 6-8 servings.

* Brands may vary by region; substitute a similar product.

Sautéed Bing Cherries over Chocolate Ice Cream

Morada Produce

3 cups pitted Morada Produce*
 Bing cherries
Juice of ½ lemon
¼ cup butter

⅓ cup packed brown sugar
3 tablespoons Triple Sec
 or cherry brandy
Chocolate ice cream, for serving

In a glass bowl, toss together cherries and lemon juice. Melt butter in a frying pan over medium heat. Add cherries and brown sugar. Sauté until the cherries have softened and the brown sugar is caramelized.

Remove the pan from the heat. Stir in liqueur. Serve over your favorite chocolate ice cream. Makes 6 servings.

Tip: You can scoop the ice cream into stemmed glasses for a beautiful presentation.

* Brands may vary by region; substitute a similar product.

M O R A D A
Produce Company

Cherry Almond Tartlets
M&R Company

6 or 12 paper baking molds
  (2.5- or 4-inch diameter)

Nonstick cooking spray

2 cups sliced almonds, divided

1 cup flour

⅓ cup butter

2 tablespoons honey

**3 cups M&R* cherries, pitted,
  halved and divided**

½ cup water

2 teaspoons cornstarch

½ teaspoon almond extract

**¼ cup dark chocolate
  (chips or chopped bar)**

CREAM CHEESE FILLING

**4 ounces Neufchatel cheese
  or cream cheese, softened**

2 teaspoons honey

1½ cups light whipped topping

Preheat oven to 375°F. Coat baking molds with cooking spray.

In a food processor, combine 1¾ cups almonds, flour and butter. Blend until the nuts are finely chopped. Drizzle in honey and blend until a dough forms. Fill the bottom and sides of each mold with dough, pressing it with the back of a spoon to evenly distribute (about ¼ inch thick). Bake for 10 minutes, or until lightly browned around the edges. Cool on a rack.

To prepare the filling, blend cream cheese and honey. Add whipped topping and stir until evenly blended. Place a spoonful of filling in each cooled crust. Refrigerate while making the topping.

In a blender, puree 1 cup cherry halves, water and cornstarch. Pour into a small saucepan, set over medium heat, and bring to a boil. Cook, stirring, until it is thickened and shiny. Remove from the heat. When cool, fold in the remaining cherries and almond extract.

Spoon cherries and sauce onto each tartlet. Sprinkle with almonds. Melt chocolate and drizzle over each tartlet. Makes 6-12 servings.

Recipe developed by Christine W. Jackson, food stylist.

* Brands may vary by region; substitute a similar product.

Red, White and Blue Banana Splits

Dole

- 1½ cups sliced Dole* strawberries
- 1 tablespoon sugar
- 3 medium Dole* bananas, peeled and cut in half lengthwise
- 1½ cups fresh Dole* Tropical Gold pineapple cut into small chunks
- 6 small scoops vanilla sorbet, or any flavor
- ½ cup blueberries or raspberries
- Mint leaves, for garnish (optional)

In a medium bowl, mash strawberries with sugar. Set aside.

Arrange banana halves in 3 banana split dishes. Place pineapple chunks along the center of each dish.

Place 2 scoops of sorbet on top of each. Spoon mashed strawberries over the sorbet. Top with blueberries. Garnish with mint, if desired. Makes 3 servings.

* Brands may vary by region; substitute a similar product.

Grape Delight

Stevco

- 2 pounds green seedless grapes
- 2 pounds red seedless grapes
- 6 ounces fat-free vanilla Greek yogurt
- ¼ teaspoon ground nutmeg
- 2 ounces fat-free cream cheese, softened
- 1 teaspoon vanilla extract
- 2 tablespoons agave nectar or honey
- ½ cup light brown sugar
- 1 cup pecans, finely chopped

Wash grapes, remove the stems, and drain.

In a large bowl, whip together yogurt, nutmeg, cream cheese, vanilla and agave nectar until smooth.

Fold the grapes into the mixture until coated. Pour into a serving bowl.

Place brown sugar in a small bowl, breaking up any lumps. Stir in pecans. Sprinkle over the grapes to cover completely. Cover and chill overnight. Makes 10-12 servings.

My Blueberry Boys Fruit Pizza Pie
Townsend Farms

CRUST
½ cup butter, softened
¾ cup sugar
1 large egg
1¼ cups flour
1 teaspoon cream of tartar
½ teaspoon baking soda
¼ teaspoon salt

FILLING
1 8-ounce package cream cheese, softened
½ cup sugar
2 teaspoons vanilla extract
4 cups Townsend Farms* fresh or frozen blueberries

TOPPING
½ cup sugar
Pinch of salt
1 tablespoon cornstarch
½ cup orange juice concentrate, thawed
2 tablespoons lemon juice
¼ cup cold water

Preheat oven to 350°F. To prepare the crust, in a large bowl, cream butter and sugar until smooth. Mix in egg. In a separate bowl, combine flour, cream of tartar, baking soda and salt. Stir into the butter mixture until well blended. Press the dough into an ungreased 10- to 12-inch pizza pan. Bake for 8-10 minutes, or until light brown. Let cool.

To prepare the filling, beat together cream cheese, sugar and vanilla. Spread over the crust. Arrange blueberries on top.

To prepare the topping, combine all ingredients in a saucepan. Bring to a boil over medium heat, then cook for 1-2 minutes, stirring constantly, until thickened. Let cool, but not set. Spoon over the blueberries.

Chill for 1 hour. Cut into wedges. Makes 6-8 servings.

Tip: Other fresh or frozen fruit can be added to the blueberries.

* Brands may vary by region; substitute a similar product.

Apple Caramel Pizza

Columbia Marketing International

1 tube refrigerated sugar cookie dough

1 8-ounce package cream cheese, at room temperature

½ cup packed light brown sugar

¼ cup creamy peanut butter

1 teaspoon vanilla extract

3 CMI* Fuji apples (or any preferred variety)

¼ cup caramel ice cream topping

½ cup chopped pecans

Preheat oven to 350°F. On a cookie sheet, roll out dough into a large cookie (about ¾ inch thick). Bake for about 17 minutes, or until light brown. Remove from the oven and let cool for 10 minutes.

In a mixing bowl, combine cream cheese, brown sugar, peanut butter and vanilla. Beat with a speed mixer until well blended. Spread the mixture evenly over the baked cookie pizza.

Peel and slice apples. Cut the slices into bite-size chunks and arrange evenly over the pizza. Microwave caramel topping for about 45 seconds, or until warm. Drizzle evenly over the apples. Sprinkle pecans over the apples.

Cut into wedges and serve immediately. Makes 8 servings.

Recipe courtesy of Chef David Toal of Ravenous Catering, Wenatchee, Washington.

* Brands may vary by region; substitute a similar product.

Granola Pear Crisp
Nature's Path Organic Foods

6 ripe pears (about 2 pounds), cored and sliced

1 tablespoon freshly squeezed lemon juice

¼ cup sugar

1 teaspoon pumpkin pie spice

2 cups Nature's Path* Pumpkin Flax Plus Granola ❂Organic

2 tablespoons unsalted butter, cut into bits

Ice cream or sorbet, for serving (optional)

Position rack in the center of the oven and preheat to 375°F.

In an 8-inch square baking dish, toss together pears, lemon juice, sugar and pumpkin pie spice.

Cover the pan tightly with aluminum foil and bake for 20 minutes.

Remove the foil and sprinkle granola evenly over the pears. Distribute butter on top.

Bake, uncovered, until the pears are tender and the top is lightly browned, 15-20 minutes longer.

Cool on a rack for 5-10 minutes.

To serve, spoon into dessert bowls. Top with a scoop of ice cream, if you wish. Makes 6-8 servings.

* Brands may vary by region; substitute a similar product.

Mango Brown Betty
Profood

5 cups Philippine Brand* dried mangoes cut in bite-size pieces

8 tablespoons butter, melted

2 cups plain dry bread crumbs

1½ cups packed light brown sugar

⅛ teaspoon ground cinnamon

Preheat oven to 350°F. Grease an 8-by-8-by-2-inch pan.

Place mango pieces in a bowl and cover with boiled hot water. Let stand for about 5 minutes, or until softened. Drain and set aside.

In a bowl, mix melted butter with bread crumbs.

In another bowl, blend brown sugar and cinnamon.

Place a layer of buttered bread crumbs in the bottom of the prepared pan. Add a layer of mangoes, followed by a layer of the brown sugar/cinnamon mixture. Continue layering, ending with a layer of buttered bread crumbs on top.

Bake for 25 minutes, or until the topping is medium brown. Makes 6-8 servings.

Tip: White sugar can be used instead of brown sugar, for a slightly sweeter taste.

* Brands may vary by region; substitute a similar product.

Old-Fashioned Apple Dumplings

Borton & Sons

Pastry dough for double-crust pie

6 large Borton* Granny Smith apples

½ cup butter, divided

¾ cup packed light brown sugar

1 teaspoon ground cinnamon

½ teaspoon ground nutmeg

3 cups water

2 cups granulated sugar

1 teaspoon vanilla extract

Preheat oven to 400°F. Butter a 13-by-9-inch pan.

On a lightly floured surface, roll pastry into a large rectangle, about 24 by 16 inches. Cut into 6 square pieces.

Peel and core apples, leaving the bottoms intact. Place an apple on each pastry square with the cored opening facing upward.

Cut butter into 8 pieces. Place 1 piece of butter in the opening of each apple; reserve the remaining butter for the sauce. Divide brown sugar between the apples, poking some inside each cored opening and the rest around the base of each apple. Sprinkle cinnamon and nutmeg over the apples.

With slightly wet fingertips, bring one corner of each pastry square up to the top of the apple, then bring the opposite corner to the top and press together. Bring up the 2 remaining corners and seal. Slightly pinch the dough at the sides to completely seal in the apple. Place in the prepared pan.

In a large saucepan, combine water, granulated sugar, vanilla and the reserved butter. Place over medium heat and bring to a boil. Boil for 5 minutes, or until the sugar is dissolved. Carefully pour over the dumplings.

Bake for 50-60 minutes, or until golden brown. Place each dumpling in a dessert bowl and spoon some pan sauce over the top. Makes 6 servings.

* Brands may vary by region; substitute a similar product.

Almond-Stuffed Nectarines and Peaches

Pride Packing Co./Fruit Patch

3 large Mary's Pride peaches

3 large Fruit Patch nectarines

12 amaretti (almond cookies)

½ cup sliced almonds, toasted

¼ cup sugar

½ cup unsalted butter, cut into 8 slices

½ cup sweet Marsala or Moscato

Ice cream, for serving

Preheat oven to 350°F.

Bring a saucepan filled with water to a boil. Dip peaches and nectarines into the boiling water for about 20 seconds, then remove and place in ice water to cool. The skin will slip off the fruit.

Cut fruit in half through the stem end and remove the pits. Place the cut halves, hollow side up, in a lightly buttered baking dish.

In a food processor, combine amaretti, almonds and sugar. Pulse a few times until crumbled. Add butter and process to form a paste. Divide the paste evenly among the fruit halves, mounding it in the hollows.

Bake for 20-30 minutes, basting occasionally with a little wine, until tender when pierced with a knife.

Serve warm or at room temperature with ice cream. Makes 6 servings.

Plum Clafoutis

WesPak

1 teaspoon plus
  1 tablespoon butter,
  divided

1½ pounds WesPak
  plums, thinly sliced
  (about 4½ cups)

3 tablespoons plus ¼ cup
  sugar, divided

3 eggs, separated

½ cup flour

1 cup heavy cream

2 teaspoons vanilla extract

2 tablespoons plum or
  almond liqueur (optional)

½ cup toasted almonds,
  for garnish

SAUCE

4 ounces white chocolate

¼ cup heavy cream

1 teaspoon vanilla extract

Preheat oven to 375°F. Grease a 9-inch baking dish with 1 teaspoon butter.

Melt 1 tablespoon butter in a 10-inch skillet over medium heat. Add plums and 3 tablespoons sugar. Cook until the plums are softened. Remove from the heat and let cool.

Place the plums in the prepared baking dish. Reserve the juices in the skillet.

In a blender, combine egg yolks, ¼ cup sugar, flour, cream, vanilla and liqueur; blend. Add the cooled plum juices from the skillet and blend thoroughly.

Beat egg whites until stiff; fold into the cream mixture. Pour over the plums.

Bake for 35 minutes, or until a toothpick inserted in the center comes out clean.

To prepare the sauce, melt chocolate with cream and vanilla over low heat.

Serve the clafoutis warm, drizzled with the sauce. Decorate with almonds. Makes 8 servings.

Hazelnut-Stuffed Pears

California Pear Advisory Board

¾ cup toasted hazelnuts,
  almonds or pecans

5 tablespoons packed
  light brown sugar

⅛ teaspoon salt

1½ tablespoons hazelnut
  or walnut oil

1½ tablespoons unsalted
  butter, melted

4 fresh California Bartlett
  or Bosc pears

¼-½ cup Frangelico,
  Amaretto or other
  liqueur

Preheat oven to 350°F.

Grind nuts with sugar and salt in a food processor. Add oil and butter. Pulse until the mixture is moist.

Slice each pear in half and remove the core and seeds with a paring knife, enlarging the middle of the pear for stuffing.

Mound the nut mixture in the fruit. Place the fruit halves, cut side up, in a baking dish. Pour liqueur over the top of each pear. Bake until the filling is lightly browned and the fruit is soft, about 25 minutes.

Serve warm, topped with pan juices and additional liqueur. Makes 4 servings.

Nutritional information: Each serving has 435 calories, 3.5 g protein, 52 g carbohydrates, 24 g fat, 12 mg cholesterol, 5 g fiber, 82 mg sodium, 41 g sugar.

Based on a recipe from Deborah Madison's Seasonal Fruit Desserts.

CALIFORNIA
PEARS

Peach Burritos
Kingsburg Orchards

2 large Kingsburg Orchards* peaches
   (yellow or white)
3 8-inch fresh flour tortillas

Ground cinnamon
1 tablespoon butter, divided

Thinly slice peaches and place along the center of each tortilla. Sprinkle a pinch of cinnamon over the peaches and then fold the tortilla like a burrito.

For each burrito, melt 1 teaspoon butter in a skillet over low heat. Place the burrito in the skillet and heat just until golden brown on each side. Heat the burrito for only a few minutes to ensure that the tortilla is cooked, but not too crispy. Remove from the heat and sprinkle with another pinch of cinnamon. Serve immediately. Makes 3 servings.

* Brands may vary by region; substitute a similar product.

Apples and Cream Cheesecake Dessert

Yakima Fresh

¾ cup all-purpose flour

1 teaspoon baking powder

½ teaspoon salt

1 3.4-ounce package dry vanilla pudding mix (not instant)

3 tablespoons butter or margarine, softened

1 large egg

½ cup milk

APPLES

2-3 large Yakima Fresh* Gala apples, peeled and sliced

¼ cup sugar

CREAM CHEESE FILLING

1 8-ounce package cream cheese, softened

½ cup sugar

3 tablespoons apple juice

TOPPING

1 tablespoon sugar

½ teaspoon ground cinnamon

Preheat oven to 350°F. Butter a 9-inch pie pan.

In a large mixer bowl, combine flour, baking powder, salt, pudding mix, butter, egg and milk. Beat for 2 minutes at medium speed. Pour into the prepared pan.

To prepare the apples, combine apples and sugar. Spread over the batter.

To prepare the cream cheese filling, combine cream cheese, sugar and apple juice in a small mixer bowl. Beat for 2 minutes at medium speed. Spoon over the apples to within 1 inch of the edges.

To prepare the topping, combine sugar and cinnamon. Sprinkle over the cream cheese filling.

Bake for 30-35 minutes, or until the filling is puffy. Let cool, then refrigerate for 2-3 hours, or until chilled. Makes 8 servings.

Tip: This can also be made with pitted Yakima Fresh cherries or other fresh seasonal fruit.

* Brands may vary by region; substitute a similar product.

Vanilla Cheesecake Bites with Madeleine Pecan Crust

Sugar Bowl Bakery

CRUST

⅓ cup packed light brown sugar

3 tablespoons pecan pieces

8 ounces Sugar Bowl Bakery* Madeleines

2 tablespoons butter, melted

FILLING

1 pound cream cheese, at room temperature

⅓ cup sour cream

¾ cup sugar

3 large eggs

1 egg yolk

1 teaspoon vanilla extract

2 tablespoons cornstarch

Preheat oven to 325°F.

To prepare the crust, combine brown sugar, pecans and Madeleines in a food processor. Add butter and blend until the mixture comes together.

To prepare the filling, using a paddle attachment, blend cream cheese, sour cream and sugar until fully combined, scraping down the sides of the bowl several times to make sure there are no lumps. Add eggs and yolk one at a time and mix until combined. Blend in vanilla and cornstarch.

To assemble, use a muffin pan with 2-inch-diameter cups. Press 1 teaspoon of the crust mixture into the bottom of each muffin cup, then top with 1 ounce (2 tablespoons) of cheesecake filling. Bake for 10 minutes, or until set. Let cool completely before unmolding. Makes 24 servings.

* Brands may vary by region; substitute a similar product.

Mini Carrot Cheesecakes

Grimmway Farms

CRUST

½ cup graham
cracker crumbs

3 tablespoons butter,
melted

1½ tablespoons sugar

2 tablespoons finely
grated Grimmway
Farms* carrots

FILLING

½ cup sugar

1 8-ounce package
cream cheese, softened

1 large egg

¼ teaspoon ground ginger

½ teaspoon vanilla extract

½ cup shredded Grimmway
Farms* carrots

Preheat oven to 350°F. Grease 24 mini cupcake cups.

To prepare the crust, combine all ingredients in a bowl and mix together with a fork. Spoon about a teaspoonful of the mixture into each cupcake cup, distributing evenly. Press with your fingers to create a crust.

To prepare the filling, combine sugar, cream cheese, egg, ginger and vanilla in a large bowl. Blend with an electric hand mixer until well combined and creamy. Fold in carrots. Spoon the mixture evenly over the crusts in the cupcake cups.

Bake for 15 minutes, or until a toothpick inserted in the center comes out clean. Let cool slightly and then refrigerate in the pan for at least 2 hours or up to 8 hours.

To serve, remove the cheesecakes from the pan with a small offset spatula. Makes 24 servings.

* Brands may vary by region; substitute a similar product.

Ginger Snap Fruit Tart

Unifrutti of America

1½ cups finely ground
ginger snaps

¼ teaspoon salt

7 tablespoons sugar,
divided

6 tablespoons butter,
melted

2 8-ounce packages cream
cheese, softened

1 teaspoon vanilla extract

1 cup whipping cream

1 tablespoon grated
orange zest

1 tablespoon chopped
crystallized ginger

3 ripe Grecian* kiwifruit

3 South African* oranges

10 red Californian*
grapes, halved

Preheat oven to 325°F. Coat a 9-inch springform pan with cooking spray.

Blend ginger snaps, salt and 1 tablespoon sugar. Stir in butter. Press onto the bottom of the pan. Bake on the center oven rack until golden, about 10 minutes. Let cool.

Beat together cream cheese, 2 tablespoons sugar and vanilla with a mixer at medium-high speed until smooth, 4-5 minutes. Set aside.

In a separate bowl, whip cream and 4 tablespoons sugar until soft peaks form. Stir in zest. Fold into the cream cheese mixture. Spread in the crust. Sprinkle with ginger. Chill for 2 hours.

Peel kiwis, cut into thin slices, and cut slices in half. Overlap kiwi slices around the perimeter of the tart. Peel and cut oranges in thin slices; place in a circle inside the kiwi slices. Arrange grapes cut-side down in the center. Chill for 2 hours. Makes 6-8 servings.

* Brands may vary by region; substitute a similar product.

The Great Pumpkin Pie

Splenda

½ 15-ounce package
   refrigerated piecrust

1 15-ounce can pumpkin

¾ cup Splenda No Calorie
   Sweetener, granulated

⅓ cup packed light
   brown sugar

2 teaspoons
   ground cinnamon

2 teaspoons ground ginger

½ teaspoon salt

⅛ teaspoon ground cloves

¾ cup half-and-half

3 large eggs, lightly
   beaten

1 teaspoon vanilla extract

Preheat oven to 375°F.

Unfold 1 piecrust; press out the fold lines. Fit the piecrust into a 9-inch pie pan according to package directions; fold the edges under and crimp.

In a bowl, stir together pumpkin and the next 7 ingredients until blended. Add eggs and vanilla, stirring until well blended. Pour the filling into the piecrust.

Bake for 50-60 minutes, or until set in the center. Let cool completely on a wire rack. Makes 8 servings.

Orange Cream Meringue Pie

Kings River Packing

5-6 Kings River*
   navel oranges

1½ cups sugar, divided

5 tablespoons cornstarch

1 packet (.25 ounce)
   unflavored gelatin

⅛ teaspoon salt

2 tablespoons grated
   orange zest, divided

4 large eggs, separated

1 cup heavy cream

1 teaspoon orange extract

1 prepared 9-inch
   deep-dish, single-pie
   crust, baked

1 Kings River* navel
   orange, peeled,
   segments cut away
   from membrane

Preheat oven to 350°F.

Zest and juice oranges to obtain 1½ cups juice.

In a medium saucepan, mix 1 cup sugar with cornstarch, gelatin and salt. Whisk in orange juice and 1 tablespoon zest. Cook over medium-high heat, stirring frequently, until it comes to a boil.

In a bowl, whisk together egg yolks and cream. Whisk in ½ cup of cooked juice mixture, then whisk all of egg/cream mixture into the saucepan. Bring to a boil and cook, stirring constantly, until thick. Remove from heat, stir in orange extract, and pour into the crust.

In a large metal bowl, whip egg whites until foamy. Gradually whip in ½ cup sugar until stiff peaks form. Spread over pie filling, sealing to the crust edges. Bake on the lower oven rack until golden brown, 10-15 minutes.

Cool completely on a rack. Sprinkle with remaining zest and top with a pinwheel of orange slices. Makes 6-8 servings.

Note: Feel free to try other orange varieties in this recipe, including Cara Cara.

Recipe developed by Christine W. Jackson, food stylist.

* Brands may vary by region; substitute a similar product.

Apple Mini Cakes

Farms Co S.A.

CARAMEL
1 cup sugar
½ cup water

APPLES
2 Richard Delicious* apples
¼ cup sugar
3½ tablespoons unsalted butter

BATTER
⅓ cup sugar
3 tablespoons unsalted butter, softened
½ teaspoon ground cinnamon
2 eggs
½ teaspoon vanilla-infused sugar
⅓ cup pastry flour
3½ ounces pistachios, chopped

Preheat oven to 350°F. To prepare the caramel, combine sugar and water in a heavy medium saucepan over medium heat. Cook, moving the saucepan gently from side to side, until the sugar has completely dissolved and the mixture is a nice golden caramel. Pour the caramel into 4 individual round cake molds (2.3 by 2.3 inches, 4 ounces).

To prepare the apples, peel 1 apple and thinly slice. Place the apple slices over the caramel and up the sides of the molds. Peel the other apple and finely dice. In a heavy medium saucepan, sauté the diced apple with the sugar and the butter over medium heat for about 5 minutes. Set aside and let cool.

To prepare the batter, combine sugar, butter and cinnamon in a bowl and whisk until a soft mixture forms. Add eggs and vanilla sugar; mix well. Stir in flour, sautéed apples and pistachios. Divide the mixture among the 4 molds. Bake for approximately 25 minutes, or until golden brown. Let cool and then chill in the fridge. Unmold and serve immediately. Makes 4 servings.

Tip: This can also be served warm with vanilla or pistachio ice cream, whipped cream or crème anglaise.

* Brands may vary by region; substitute a similar product.

FruitStand
Farms Co S.A.

Berry Good Cake with Sauce
Sun Belle

8 tablespoons
   unsalted butter

1 cup sugar

1 teaspoon vanilla extract

3 large eggs

1 cup sour cream

Grated zest of
   1 small lemon

2 cups flour

1 teaspoon baking powder

½ teaspoon baking soda

¼ teaspoon salt

2 cups (12 ounces)
   Sun Belle* blueberries,
   divided

SAUCE

¼ cup packed dark
   brown sugar

1 cup orange juice

Juice of 1 small lemon

1 teaspoon vanilla extract

3 tablespoons
   unsalted butter

3 cups (18 ounces)
   Sun Belle* blackberries

1 tablespoon cornstarch
   dissolved in 2 table-
   spoons water

Preheat oven to 350°F.

In a bowl, cream butter with sugar. Blend in vanilla, eggs, sour cream and zest.

In another bowl, sift flour, baking powder, baking soda and salt. Stir into the wet ingredients. Evenly fold in all but a handful of blueberries.

Spread batter in a greased 9-by-5-inch bread pan. Press in remaining blueberries. Bake for 1 hour, or until a toothpick comes out clean. Let cool in the pan.

To prepare the sauce, in a saucepan combine sugar, orange and lemon juice, vanilla and butter. Cook over medium heat until sugar has dissolved. Add blackberries and bring to a boil. Stir in cornstarch and simmer for 6-8 minutes, until thickened.

Spoon sauce over slices of cake. Makes 12-15 servings.

* Brands may vary by region; substitute a similar product.

Pound Cake with Fresh Fruit Compote
Ready Pac

½ cinnamon stick

½ teaspoon allspice
   berries, cracked

2 sprigs fresh thyme

Cheesecloth

2 cups fresh orange juice

1 tablespoon grated
   orange zest

½ cup sugar

1 teaspoon vanilla extract

2 tablespoons fresh
   lemon juice

1 64-ounce package Ready
   Pac* Fresh Mixed Fruit

1 Kirkland Signature
   pound cake

Place cinnamon stick, allspice and thyme in a double layer of cheesecloth. Roll into a small bundle and tie to secure. Place in a small saucepan.

Add orange juice, orange zest and sugar to the saucepan. Bring to a boil, then reduce the heat to low, cover, and simmer for 10-15 minutes, stirring occasionally. Remove from the heat and stir in vanilla and lemon juice. Let cool to room temperature. Remove the cheesecloth packet.

Meanwhile, place fruit in a large bowl. Pour the orange syrup over the fruit. Chill, covered, until cold. The compote can be made up to 4 hours in advance.

Serve slices of cake topped with chilled fruit compote and syrup. Makes 8-10 servings.

* Brands may vary by region; substitute a similar product.

Apple and Cherry Upside-Down Cake

Stemilt Growers

¾ cup unsalted butter, divided

⅓ cup packed light brown sugar

1 teaspoon fresh lemon juice

2 Stemilt* Fuji apples, peeled, cored, quartered and cut into slices

15-20 Stemilt* dark sweet cherries, pitted and halved

1 cup all-purpose unbleached flour

¾ teaspoon baking powder

¼ teaspoon baking soda

¼ teaspoon kosher salt

⅔ cup granulated sugar

1 large egg

½ teaspoon pure vanilla extract

⅔ cup plain yogurt

¼ cup milk (2%)

Preheat oven to 350°F.

In a large nonstick skillet over medium heat, melt 4 tablespoons (½ stick) butter and brown sugar. Add lemon juice and apples, tossing to coat; cook for 1 minute. Add cherries and cook for another minute. Remove from the heat.

Beginning with the apples, arrange the fruit in the bottom of a 9-inch round nonstick baking pan. Lay the apple slices in a slightly overlapping pattern around the outermost edge of the pan interior, creating a ring of apples and leaving a circular space in the center. Spoon the cherries into the center of the pan, pressing down slightly to fill the space. Pour the remaining pan syrup (⅓ cup maximum) over the fruit. Set aside.

In a medium bowl, combine flour, baking powder, baking soda and salt. Set aside.

In a separate bowl, beat remaining butter (1 stick) and granulated sugar. Add egg, vanilla, yogurt and milk; mix well. Gradually add the flour mixture, beating until well incorporated.

Pour the batter over the fruit, gently spreading to the edges of the pan, being careful not to disturb the fruit.

Bake for 45-50 minutes, or until a wooden toothpick inserted in the center comes out clean. Let cool in the pan for at least 1 hour. Invert the cake pan onto a platter and let rest for 5-10 minutes before removing the pan.

Cut the cake into wedges. Serve warm or at room temperature. Makes 8 servings.

Brands may vary by region; substitute a similar product.

Spanish Orange and Almond Cake

AMC Direct

1 orange

1 cinnamon stick

2 whole star anise

4 whole cloves

3 large eggs

9 ounces superfine sugar (scant 1¼ cups)

2 ounces (¼ cup) fine cornmeal or rice flour

1 teaspoon baking powder

7 ounces ground almonds

Confectioners' sugar, for dusting

Toasted sliced almonds and orange slices, for garnish

Whipped cream, for serving

Preheat oven to 350°F. Grease and line an 8-inch round cake pan with parchment paper.

Put orange (unpeeled) in a saucepan and add enough water to just cover. Add cinnamon stick, star anise and cloves. Bring to a boil, lower the heat, and simmer, uncovered, for 1 hour, adding more water if necessary. Let the orange cool in the pan, then cut in half, remove any pips, and puree in a food processor.

In a large bowl, beat eggs and sugar until creamy and thick. Fold in cornmeal, baking powder, ground almonds and the orange puree.

Pour into the prepared pan. Bake for 1 hour, or until a skewer inserted in the center comes out clean. Remove from the pan and let cool on a rack.

Dust with confectioners' sugar. Serve with sliced almonds, orange slices and whipped cream. Makes 8-10 servings.

PART OF THE AMC GROUP

Fruit and Ice Cream Red Velvet Cake

Kirkland Signature

Kirkland Signature red velvet cake with cream cheese icing

18 blueberries

8 blackberries

1½-ounce scoop of vanilla ice cream

Sprig of mint

Cut a 2-by-5-inch wedge from the cake.

Sprinkle blueberries and blackberries over the top of the cake.

Place a scoop of ice cream beside the cake.

Top with a sprig of mint. Makes 1 serving.

Crispy Chocolate Ice Cream Mud Pie

The Hershey Company

½ cup Hershey's Syrup, plus more for serving

⅓ cup Hershey's Special Dark Chocolate Chips or Hershey's Semi-Sweet Chocolate Chips

2 cups crisp rice cereal

4 cups (1 quart) vanilla ice cream, divided

4 cups (1 quart) chocolate ice cream, divided

Butter a 9-inch pie plate.

Place ½ cup chocolate syrup and chocolate chips in a medium microwave-safe bowl. Microwave at medium (50%) for 45 seconds, or until hot; stir until smooth. Reserve ¼ cup of the chocolate syrup mixture; set aside. Add cereal to the remaining chocolate syrup mixture, stirring until well coated; let cool slightly.

Place the cereal mixture in the prepared pie plate and press evenly, using the back of a spoon, onto the bottom and sides to form a crust. Place in the freezer for 15-20 minutes, or until firm.

Spread half of the vanilla ice cream in the crust. Spoon the reserved ¼ cup chocolate syrup mixture over the layer. Spread half of the chocolate ice cream over the sauce.

Top with alternating scoops of vanilla and chocolate ice cream. Cover and return to the freezer until serving time. Drizzle with additional syrup just before serving. Makes 8 servings.

Toffee Cream Cheese Bars

Raskas

2 cups graham cracker crumbs

4 tablespoons unsalted butter, melted

11 ounces Heath Bits'O Brickle toffee bits

1 14-ounce can sweetened
  condensed milk

1½ pounds Raskas* cream cheese, softened

¾ cup sour cream

½ cup sugar

1 teaspoon vanilla extract

5 large eggs

Preheat oven to 300°F. In a medium bowl, combine graham cracker crumbs with melted butter. Transfer to a 13-by-9-inch pan and pat evenly onto the bottom.

Combine toffee bits and sweetened condensed milk in the top of a double boiler and heat over simmering water until melted. Remove from the heat and let cool for about 5 minutes.

In a stand mixer, combine cream cheese, sour cream, sugar and vanilla. Beat until well blended and smooth. Add the toffee/condensed milk mixture and beat until blended. Add eggs one at a time, beating until fully incorporated. Pour the mixture over the crust.

Set the pan in a larger pan and add enough hot water to reach halfway up the sides. Bake for 1 hour, or until fully set to the touch. Let cool completely before slicing into bars. Makes 8-10 servings.

* Brands may vary by region; substitute a similar product.

SCHREIBER™

Holiday Plum Cake
Vie de France

Nonstick cooking spray
7 Vie de France butter croissants
3 15-ounce cans plums, divided
1½ cups sugar
2 teaspoons ground cinnamon
2 cups golden raisins, divided
½ cup butter, melted, divided
7 large eggs
16 ounces heavy cream

Coat a standard-size Bundt pan with cooking spray. Slice each croissant into 3 horizontal pieces.

Drain, then halve plums and remove pits.

In a small bowl, combine sugar and cinnamon.

Place the 7 croissant tops in the pan, cut side up and overlapping slightly.

Layer ⅓ of the plums, ⅓ of the raisins and ⅓ of the cinnamon sugar over the croissants. Drizzle with ⅓ of the melted butter. Top with a layer of croissant middles.

Add 2 more layers of plums, raisins, cinnamon sugar and melted butter. Top with a layer of croissant bottoms, cut side down.

Place the pan on a sheet pan. In a medium bowl, beat eggs and cream. Pour over the cake. Let stand for 30 minutes to absorb the liquid.

Preheat oven to 300°F.

Cover the pan with foil and bake for 90 minutes, or until a knife inserted in the center comes out clean. Let cool slightly, then remove the cake from the pan. Makes 7 servings.

Fruit and Nut Granola Bars
Kirkland Signature

2 cups old-fashioned oatmeal
1 cup shredded sweetened coconut, loosely packed
½ cup toasted wheat germ
3 tablespoons unsalted butter
⅔ cup honey
¼ cup packed light brown sugar
1½ teaspoons pure vanilla extract
¼ teaspoon kosher salt
3 cups (half of 30-ounce pouch) Kirkland Signature Wholesome Fruit & Nuts

Preheat oven to 350°F. Butter a 12-by-8-inch baking dish and line with parchment paper.

Mix oatmeal and coconut together on a sheet pan and bake for 10-15 minutes, stirring every 5 minutes, until lightly browned. Transfer to a large mixing bowl and stir in wheat germ.

Reduce oven temperature to 300°F.

In a small saucepan, combine butter, honey, brown sugar, vanilla and salt; bring to a boil over medium heat. Cook, stirring, for 1 minute, then pour over the toasted oatmeal mixture. Add fruit and nut mix. Stir until blended.

Pour into the prepared pan, lightly pressing into an even layer. Bake for 25-30 minutes, or until light golden brown.

Let cool completely (about 3 hours). Cut into 2-inch squares or 1-inch bites. Serve at room temperature. Makes 24 squares or 48 bites.

Tip: Store in an airtight container for up to a week.

Coffee Popcorn Balls
Starbucks Coffee

¼ cup butter
⅓ cup honey
⅔ cup maple syrup
1 teaspoon salt
3 packets Starbucks VIA Ready Brew
8 cups freshly popped popcorn, still warm

In a saucepan, combine butter, honey, maple syrup and salt. Bring to a boil, then reduce the heat and simmer for 3 minutes.

Dissolve VIA with a spoonful or two of hot water. Add to the saucepan carefully, as the mixture is very hot.

Pour the mixture over the popcorn, stirring with a wooden spoon. When the popcorn is evenly coated, turn out onto a sheet pan. Using an ice cream scoop, form popcorn balls. Makes about 12 servings.

Coffee Toffee with Milk Chocolate and Pretzels
Starbucks Coffee

2 cups sugar
½ cup water
⅛ cup (2 tablespoons) corn syrup
8 ounces unsalted butter
½ teaspoon salt
1 cup almond slivers, untoasted
1 cup chopped pretzels, divided
2 packets Starbucks VIA Ready Brew
½ teaspoon vanilla extract
¼ cup finely chopped milk chocolate

Grease a 13-by-9-by-2-inch pan.

Combine sugar, water and corn syrup in a saucepan and bring to a boil. When the temperature reaches 280°F, stir in butter.

When the temperature reaches 315°F, stir in salt, almonds and half of the pretzels.

Cook until it reaches 320°F. Remove from the heat and stir in VIA and vanilla. Immediately pour the toffee into the prepared pan.

Let cool for 15 minutes, then sprinkle with chocolate and spread to evenly cover the surface. Sprinkle with the remaining pretzels, gently pressing into the chocolate.

When the chocolate has hardened, break the toffee into squares. Store in an airtight container for up to 2 weeks at room temperature. Makes 8 servings.

Dessert Panini with Creamy Pistachio Chocolate Filling

Kirkland Signature/Setton Pistachio/Setton Farms

1 cup Kirkland Signature roasted, salted California pistachio nuts, shelled

¼ cup maple syrup or agave syrup

2 tablespoons unsweetened cocoa powder

1 teaspoon vanilla extract

¼ cup soy or coconut milk creamer

2 tablespoons organic safflower oil (or other neutral-tasting oil)

8 slices whole wheat bread

1 banana, sliced (optional)

2 tablespoons shelled pistachios, finely chopped

Place pistachios in a food processor and pulse until finely chopped. Add syrup, cocoa powder, vanilla, creamer and oil; blend until smooth.

Heat a panini press to medium. Spread each slice of bread with 1 tablespoon of the filling. Place banana slices on 4 bread slices and press 2 slices together to make sandwiches.

Grill the sandwiches until the bread is well toasted and grill marks appear, about 1 minute. Top with chopped pistachios. Makes 4 servings.

Recipe courtesy of www.sporkfoods.com, 2011.

Oatmeal Dream Dates

Tropicana/Quaker Oats

1¼ pounds pitted dates, coarsely chopped

2 cups Tropicana Pure Premium* orange juice

2½ cups all-purpose flour

1½ cups firmly packed dark brown sugar

½ teaspoon salt (optional)

¾ pound (3 sticks) margarine or butter, chilled and cut into pieces

2 cups Quaker Oats (quick or old fashioned, uncooked)

1½ cups shredded coconut, divided

1 cup chopped nuts

Preheat oven to 350°F.

In a medium saucepan, combine dates and orange juice; bring to a boil. Reduce heat and simmer for 15-20 minutes, or until thickened, stirring occasionally. Remove from the heat and let cool slightly.

In a large bowl, combine flour, sugar and salt. Cut in margarine with a pastry blender or 2 knives until crumbly. Stir in oats, 1 cup coconut and nuts.

Reserve 4 cups of the oat mixture for topping. Press the remaining oat mixture evenly onto the bottom of an ungreased 13-by-18-inch baking pan. Spread the date mixture evenly over the crust to within ¼ inch of the edges. Sprinkle with the reserved oat mixture. Sprinkle with ½ cup coconut, patting gently.

Bake for 35-40 minutes, or until light golden brown. Cool completely in the pan on a wire rack. Cut into bars. Store tightly covered. Makes 36 bars.

* Brands may vary by region; substitute a similar product.

Toffee Apple Coffee-Time Bars

The J.M. Smucker Co.

CRUST

2 cups Pillsbury Best All Purpose Flour

½ cup confectioners' sugar

1 cup butter, cut in pieces

FILLING

1 14-ounce can Eagle Brand Sweetened Condensed Milk

1 teaspoon vanilla extract

½ teaspoon ground cinnamon

1 large egg

1 cup peeled, chopped apple

1 cup chopped pecans

1 cup toffee baking bits

GLAZE

1 cup confectioners' sugar

2-3 tablespoons strong brewed Folgers* Classic Roast Coffee, cooled to room temperature

Preheat oven to 350°F.

To prepare the crust, combine flour and sugar in a medium bowl. Cut in butter with a pastry blender or fork until the mixture resembles coarse crumbs. Press into the bottom of an ungreased 13-by-9-inch pan. Bake for 15 minutes, or until set.

To prepare the filling, combine condensed milk, vanilla, cinnamon and egg in a large bowl and blend well. Stir in the remaining ingredients. Pour over the partially baked crust.

Bake for 35-40 minutes, or until the filling is set and the top is golden brown. Let cool for 10 minutes. Run a knife around the sides of the pan to loosen. Cool for 1 hour, or until completely cooled.

Combine the glaze ingredients, adding enough coffee for desired drizzling consistency. Blend until smooth. Drizzle over the bars. Let stand for 10 minutes, or until the glaze is set.

Cut into bars. Store in a loosely covered container. Makes 24 bars.

* Brands may vary by region; substitute a similar product.

Folgers

Dark Chocolate Super Fruit Crispy Squares

Brookside

3 tablespoons butter or margarine

1 10-ounce package regular marshmallows (about 40), or 4 cups miniature marshmallows

6 cups crispy rice cereal

1 cup Brookside* Dark Chocolate Açai with Blueberry (or Dark Chocolate Pomegranate)

In a large saucepan, melt butter over low heat. Add marshmallows and stir until melted. Remove from the heat.

To do this in the microwave, combine butter and marshmallows in a microwave-safe bowl and heat on high for 3 minutes, stirring after 2 minutes. Stir until smooth.

Add cereal and Dark Chocolate Açai to the melted marshmallows. Stir until well coated.

Using a buttered spatula, press the mixture evenly into a greased 13-by-9-by-2-inch pan.

Let cool. Cut into squares. Makes 12 servings.

Tips: Diet, reduced-calorie or tub margarine is not recommended. Store for no more than 2 days at room temperature in an airtight container. To freeze, place in layers separated by waxed paper in an airtight container; let stand at room temperature for 15 minutes before serving.

* Brands may vary by region; substitute a similar product.

Date Oatmeal Chocolate Chunk Cookies

SunDate

2 cubes (½ pound) butter, at room temperature

1½ cups firmly packed light brown sugar

2 large eggs, beaten

1 tablespoon vanilla extract

1½ cups flour

½ teaspoon salt

1 teaspoon baking soda

1½ teaspoons ground cinnamon

1½ cups chopped SunDate* Medjool dates

1 12-ounce package semi-sweet chocolate chunks

3 cups rolled oats

Preheat oven to 350°F. Line 2 baking sheets with parchment paper to prevent overbrowning the cookie bottoms.

In a large bowl, cream together butter and sugar until smooth and fluffy. Add eggs and vanilla, mixing until well incorporated.

In a separate bowl, mix flour, salt, baking soda and cinnamon. Add to the butter mixture and stir until blended.

Stir in dates and chocolate chunks. Stir in oats.

Spoon the dough by ¼-cup scoops or large spoonfuls onto the baking sheets, leaving at least 2 inches between cookies.

Bake until the edges are golden brown, about 14 minutes. Let cool for 5 minutes on the baking sheets, then move the cookies to a wire rack. Makes about 2 dozen large cookies.

* Brands may vary by region; substitute a similar product.

Chocolate Chunk Raisin Oatmeal Cookies
Sun-Maid Growers

¾ cup butter or margarine, softened

1 cup packed light brown sugar

½ cup granulated sugar

¼ cup milk

1 large egg

1 teaspoon vanilla extract

1 cup all-purpose flour

1 teaspoon ground cinnamon

½ teaspoon baking soda

¼ teaspoon salt

3 cups quick or old-fashioned oats

1 cup Sun-Maid Natural Raisins

1 cup coarsely chopped semisweet chocolate or chocolate chips

Preheat oven to 350°F.

In a large bowl, beat butter, sugars, milk, egg and vanilla until light and fluffy.

In a separate bowl, combine flour, cinnamon, baking soda and salt. Add to the butter mixture and mix well.

Stir in oats, raisins and chocolate.

Drop by tablespoonfuls 2 inches apart onto ungreased cookie sheets. Bake for 12-15 minutes, or until the cookies are golden brown. Remove to wire racks to cool. Makes 3 dozen cookies.

Variation: Omit the chocolate from the dough. Heat 1 cup semisweet or white chocolate chips with 1 teaspoon vegetable oil in the microwave on medium power (50%) for about 2 minutes. Stir until melted. Dip cookies halfway into the chocolate. Set on waxed paper to cool or refrigerate for 15 minutes.

Pumpkin Spice Cookies
Krusteaz

1 pouch Krusteaz Pumpkin Spice Quick Bread Mix

½ cup (1 stick) butter, softened

1 large egg

MAPLE FROSTING

4 ounces cream cheese, softened

3 tablespoons butter, softened

1 cup confectioners' sugar

3 tablespoons maple syrup

Preheat oven to 350°F. Lightly grease a cookie sheet.

In a medium bowl, stir together quick bread mix, butter and egg until a dough forms.

Drop the dough by heaping teaspoonfuls, 2 inches apart, on the prepared cookie sheet.

Bake for 8-10 minutes, or until the edges are light brown and the centers are set. Remove the cookies to a rack to cool.

To prepare the frosting, place cream cheese and butter in a mixing bowl. Using an electric beater, mix on medium speed until fluffy. Add the remaining ingredients. Mix on low speed until smooth.

Frost the cooled cookies. Makes 24 cookies.

KRUSTEAZ

Turbinado Cane-Sugar Cookies

Sugar In The Raw

⅓ cup plus 1 tablespoon Sugar In The Raw* turbinado sugar (see note), plus more for coating

1¼ cups unsalted butter, cold

2½ cups all-purpose flour

¼ cup fruit preserves (pineapple, mango, raspberry)

Preheat oven to 275°F. Place racks in the upper and lower third of the oven.

Place sugar in a bowl. Cut in butter until the mixture resembles coarse meal. Add flour and mix until moist, crumbly pieces form and no dry particles remain. Press the dough together in a plastic bag, then set on a sheet of plastic wrap. Use the plastic wrap to knead the dough until it holds together. Wrap tightly and freeze for 30 minutes or refrigerate until firm.

Measure 2 teaspoonfuls of dough, roll into 1-inch balls, and roll in sugar. Place on ungreased baking sheets 1 inch apart. Flatten slightly and make a round indentation in each. Bake for 45 minutes, rotating pans from top to bottom and front to back halfway through baking, until pale golden in color. Cool on a rack.

Fill a resealable plastic bag with fruit preserves; remove the air and seal the bag. Snip off a ¼-inch triangle from one corner. Squeeze about ½ teaspoon preserves on each cookie. Makes 4 dozen cookies.

Note: Turbinado is a natural, unrefined sugar made from sugar cane. To make it, juice is extracted from the sugar cane, then crystallized through evaporation.

* Brands may vary by region; substitute a similar product.

Peanut Butter and Jelly Cookies

The J.M. Smucker Co.

1 cup sugar, plus extra for coating dough

1 cup firmly packed light brown sugar

1 cup Crisco Butter Flavor Shortening

1 cup Jif* Creamy Peanut Butter

2 large eggs

¼ cup milk

2 teaspoons vanilla extract

3½ cups Pillsbury* Best All Purpose Flour

2 teaspoons baking soda

1 teaspoon salt

¾ cup Smucker's* Strawberry Jelly, or any Smucker's* jam, jelly or preserves

Preheat oven to 375°F.

In a large mixing bowl, combine sugar, brown sugar, shortening and peanut butter. Beat with an electric mixer until creamy. Beat in eggs, milk and vanilla.

In a separate bowl, stir together flour, baking soda and salt. Add to the peanut butter mixture and beat until blended.

Shape the dough into 1-inch balls. Roll in sugar. Place 2 inches apart on an ungreased cookie sheet.

Bake for 7 minutes. Remove from the oven. Using the back of a teaspoon, make a rounded indentation in the top of each cookie. Fill each with about ½ teaspoon jelly. Bake an additional 2 minutes. Remove to a wire rack to cool. Makes 5 dozen cookies.

* Brands may vary by region; substitute a similar product.

Easy Brandied Cherries
Delta Packing Company

Delta Fresh* cherries
Sugar
Brandy

TOOLS
Kitchen shears
Cherry pitter or stoner
  (optional, see note)
Pint jars, rings and
  new lids (see note)
A deep pot

Trim cherry stems to about ½ inch. Wash all cherries in cold water.

Fill jars with cherries, leaving ¼ inch of headspace below the top of the jar.

Add 1 tablespoon of sugar to each pint, then fill with brandy to the same ¼-inch headspace.

In a small pot of water, heat the lids to just below the boiling point to soften the rubber seal.

Place the lids on the jars and adjust the rings to fit snugly.

Place the jars in the deep pot and cover with water. Process in boiling water for 10 minutes.

For best results, wait about 3 months before enjoying.

Notes: Pitted cherries will not be as crisp. Always use new lids when canning—only the rings and jars are reusable.

* Brands may vary by region; substitute a similar product.

Bunny's Black Velvet Apricot Fruit Leather
Kingsburg Orchards

10 cups Kingsburg Orchards*
  Black Velvet apricots
½ cup sugar
Cheesecloth

Wash, pit, peel, and cut up apricots. Place the apricots in a blender and blend until smooth.

In a saucepan, heat the pureed fruit with sugar until syrupy, keeping the heat just below boiling. Remove from the heat and let the fruit cool.

Cover 2 baking sheets (with rimmed edges) with plastic wrap. Pour the cooled fruit onto the baking sheets to within ½ inch of the edges. Cover the baking sheets with cheesecloth, not allowing cheesecloth to touch the fruit.

Set the baking sheets in a 140°F oven for 8-12 hours, until the fruit leather peels away easily from the plastic wrap.

Let the fruit leather cool and dry. Then roll up the fruit leather with the plastic wrap still attached and cut into desired fruit roll-up lengths. Makes about 20 servings.

Tip: You can also dry the fruit by using the "dehydrate" setting in a convection oven.

* Brands may vary by region; substitute a similar product.

Grape Gumdrops
Kirkland Signature/Newman's Own

Vegetable oil
1 cup light corn syrup
1 cup sugar, plus more for coating
¾ cup Kirkland Signature/ Newman's Own grape juice
1 1¾-ounce package powdered fruit pectin
½ teaspoon baking soda
2 drops blue food color (optional)

Line a 9-by-5-by-3-inch loaf pan with aluminum foil. Brush with oil.

Combine corn syrup and sugar in a 1½-quart saucepan. Cook over medium-high heat, stirring constantly, until the sugar is dissolved. Then cook without stirring until a candy thermometer registers 300°F, or a small amount dropped into very cold water separates into hard but *not* brittle threads.

Meanwhile, combine grape juice, pectin and baking soda in a 2-quart saucepan. Cook over high heat, stirring constantly, until it boils (it will be foamy). Reduce heat and slowly add the hot sugar mixture in a thin stream, stirring constantly (1-2 minutes); remove from the heat. Stir in food color.

Pour into the prepared pan. Let stand for 2 minutes, then skim off foam. Let stand uncovered at room temperature for 24 hours. Lift from the pan and remove foil. Cut into ¾-inch pieces, dipping the knife or melon baller in sugar to prevent sticking. Roll the pieces in sugar. Let stand uncovered at room temperature for 1 hour. Store in an airtight container. Makes about 72 gumdrops, 28 calories each.

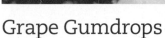

Alphabet Meringues
Kirkland Signature/Jelly Belly

Parchment paper
6 large egg whites
Pinch of salt
1½ teaspoons cream of tartar
½ teaspoon almond extract
1½ cups sugar
Pastry bag with a large flower tip
4-6 ounces assorted Kirkland Signature/ Jelly Belly jelly beans

Preheat oven to 170°F. Line a baking sheet with parchment paper. On the parchment, trace the outline of 10-12 uppercase letters of the alphabet about 4 inches high. Set aside.

In a clean, dry mixing bowl, beat egg whites, salt and cream of tartar with an electric beater until soft peaks form. With the beater running, add almond extract and then gradually add sugar. Beat until stiff and glossy.

Spoon the meringue mixture into the pastry bag. Pipe meringue onto the letter patterns on the parchment-lined baking sheet, using the tracing lines as a guide.

Select a variety of colors of jelly beans, or a single color theme, such as blue or red. Gently press the jelly beans into the sides of the meringues. Bake for 2½ hours, or until hard.

The meringues can be made up to 2 days ahead and stored in an airtight container. Makes 10-12 letters.

Index

Supplier Listing

Supplier Listing

Index Fresh, 143
www.avoterra.com
909-877-1577

International Seafood Ventures, LLC, 127
www.beringfisheries.com
310-475-6768

J & J Snack Foods Corp., 198
www.jjsnack.com
800-486-7622

Jacobs, Malcolm & Burtt, 73
415-285-0400

JBS/Swift, 108, 109
www.jbssa.com
800-555-2588

Jif, 226
www.jif.com
800-283-8915

Jimmy Dean, 19
www.jimmydean.com
800-925-3326

Katama Company, The, 167, 172
www.katamaco.com
425-657-2250

Kellogg Company, The, 23
www.kelloggs.com
800-962-1413

Kings River Packing, Inc., 213
www.kingorange.com
559-787-2056

Kingsburg Orchards, 67, 209, 227
www.kingsburgorchards.com
559-897-5132

Kirkland Signature Albacore, 85
800-800-8572

Kirkland Signature/Cott Corp., 49
www.cott.com
800-774-2678

Kirkland Signature/Jelly Belly Candy Company, 228
www.jellybelly.com
800-522-3267

Kirkland Signature/Kerry Inc., 57
800-235-3383

Kirkland Signature/Michael Foods, Inc., 25
www.michaelfoods.com
800-328-5474

Kirkland Signature/Olde Thompson, 39, 168
www.oldethompson.com
800-827-1565

Kirkland Signature/Orleans International, 186, 187
www.orleansintl.com
248-855-5556

Kirkland Signature/Palermo Villa, 190
www.palermospizza.com
888-571-7181

Kirkland Signature/Puratos Corporation, 115, 116, 117
www.puratos.us
856-428-4300

Kirkland Signature/Rader Farms, Inc., 187
www.raderfarms.com
360-354-6574 x13

Kirkland Signature/Regal Springs Tilapia Group, 132, 133
www.regalsprings.com
941-747-9161

Kirkland Signature/Rich Products, 218
www.richs.com
800-822-7555

Kirkland Signature/Snak King, 37
www.snakking.com
626-363-7711

Kirkland Signature/Sunsweet Growers, 15, 153
www.sunsweet.com
800-417-2253

Kirschenman Enterprises Inc., 66
559-741-7030

Kraft Foods, 126
www.kraftfoods.com

Krusteaz, 11, 225
www.krusteaz.com
800-457-7744

La Brea Bakery, 20, 182
www.labreabakery.com
866-876-5969

Lamb Co-Operative Inc., The, 112, 113, 114
www.australianlamb.com
800-865-2112

Legend Produce, 124
www.legendproduce.com
623-298-3782

M&R Company, 201
209-369-2725

Marine Harvest, 144, 145
www.marineharvest.com
800-780-3474

Market Source, 44
www.marketsource.com
414-906-8808

MAS Melons & Grapes LLC, 74
www.mas-fourstar.com
520-37-2372

Mastronardi Produce/SUNSET, 48, 55
www.sunsetproduce.com
519-326-1491

Mazola, 166
www.mazola.com
866-462-9652

Mazzetta Company, LLC, 100, 101, 102
www.mazzetta.com
847-433-1150

MCC of Wenatchee, 56
www.welovethepressure.com
800-843-5149

McCormick & Co., Inc., 156, 171
www.mccormick.com
800-632-5847

McDaniel Fruit Co., Inc., 143
www.mcdanielavocado.com
760-728-8438

Meduri Farms, Inc., 181
www.medurifarms.com
503-623-0308

Mission Produce, 143
www.missionpro.com
805-981-3650

Moark LLC, 24
www.moark.com
951-332-3300

Monterey Gourmet Foods, 15, 173
www.montereygourmetfoods.com
714-578-1464

Monterey Mushrooms, Inc., 40
www.montmush.com
800-333-MUSH

Morada Produce Company, 200
www.moradaproduce.com
209-546-1816

Morey's Seafood International LLC, 22
www.moreys.com

Mountain View Fruit Sales/IM Ripe, 30, 31
www.summerripe.com
559-637-9933

MountainKing Potatoes, 63
www.mtnking.com
800-395-2004

Mulholland Citrus, 74
www.mulhollandcitrus.com
559-528-2525

Multiexport Foods, 146
www.multiexportfoods.com
888-624-9773

National Beef Packing Co., LLC, 183
www.nationalbeef.com
800-449-2333

Nature's Partner, 195
www.naturespartner.com
213-627-2900

Supplier Listing